Daniel Halévy and His Times

A GENTLEMAN-COMMONER
IN THE THIRD REPUBLIC

Daniel Halévy in his late eighties (courtesy of Mme Louis Joxe)

Daniel Halévy
AND HIS TIMES

A GENTLEMAN-COMMONER
IN THE THIRD REPUBLIC

BY

ALAIN SILVERA

CORNELL UNIVERSITY PRESS

ITHACA, NEW YORK

Copyright © 1966 by Cornell University

CORNELL UNIVERSITY PRESS

First published 1966

Library of Congress Catalog Card Number: 66–20130

Printed in the United States of America
By Kingsport Press, Inc.

To the memory of my father

Preface

❧❧

"YOUR task, Halévy, is to respect everything," a friend remarked in 1900. Ten years later the same writer reminded him that he had passed his prime and already belonged to the lost generation—to "the party of the men of forty." Thus Charles Péguy, with his usual penetration, had discerned both the virtues and the limitations of his Dreyfusard companion.

Neither a man of action nor an original thinker in his own right, Daniel Halévy seemed destined to be a guide and interpreter, acting as a prism to his times and epitomizing in his own life and work the hopes and illusions of his contemporaries. But he also belonged to the generation that lived through the transition from the nineteenth century to our own, and it is as the chronicler of the transitional years from the Dreyfus Affair through the Moroccan crisis to the outbreak of the First World War that he has earned a place in the ranks of the *politiques et moralistes*.

With the advent of what Péguy called "the modern world," Halévy's value as a critic and observer becomes less important. His reflections on the course of events after the twenties remain sound and instructive, but they are mostly variations on old themes, frequently lapsing into polemics and lacking the depth and understanding of his earlier works. Overtaken by what he called, in an arresting phrase, the acceleration of history, he gives the impression of being out of tune with the new rhythm of a less familiar world; no longer a protagonist, his experience ceases to serve as a *témoignage*. The pattern of his life and thought, however, was firmly established before 1914. This study, therefore, is chiefly concerned with the earlier and more significant phase of Halévy's career. Moreover, by concentrating on the crucial reshuffling of ideas that followed in the wake of the Dreyfus Affair, I have also tried to trace the origins of a certain strand in conservative thinking that contributed to the downfall of the Third Republic. Here again, Halévy's role during the years that witnessed the stagnation and ultimate collapse of parliamentary democracy in France was, I think, overshadowed by his more direct involvement in the period marking the turn of the century. Blessed as he was with a longevity that enabled him to survive almost all his contemporaries, he remained rooted to the past, and it is as a living witness of that past, of a past immediately preceding our own, that he is treated in this biography.

Halévy's versatility imposes even more drastic limitations on anyone attempting to present an account of his life and times. Although himself a figure of the second rank, his intimacy with the great and the near great placed him in the forefront of his generation; at the same time, the remarkable range of his interests led him to explore a vast area of the history of his country and his times. In tracing his career I have naturally found it necessary to touch upon a wide variety of subjects which drew his attention, but I must in all fairness disclaim any pretence to match his, or other authorities', competence in all these different matters. Nor have I found it possible to do full justice to such persons as Sorel and Péguy, whose lives and achievements really lie beyond the scope of this book. My line of approach has been strictly biographical, and although Halévy's importance depends to a large extent on his relation to these other and more notable figures, I have sought, as much as possible, to keep this study within reasonable limits by focusing on Halévy throughout.

PREFACE

For whatever merit my book may have I am much in the debt of Daniel Halévy himself, who graciously consented to give me free access to his unpublished journals and correspondence. More important, he furnished me by his chats and reminiscences with the kind of information that no amount of delving in the printed sources could possibly have yielded. A note of appreciation is also due MM. André Spire, Jean Guéhenno, Henri Massis, Pierre Andreu, Henri Clouard, Robert Garric, and Jean Meuvret, whose conversation enriched my understanding of my subject. I owe thanks, too, to the following friends and colleagues for their help and encouragement: Professors Edward W. Fox of Cornell University, David H. Pinkney of the University of Missouri, Caroline Robbins of Bryn Mawr College, and Geoffrey Bruun, formerly of New York University. To the staff of Cornell University Press I am indebted for scrupulous editorial suggestions. I am particularly grateful to my wife for her unfailing assistance. My deepest gratitude is reserved for Professor H. Stuart Hughes, under whose direction this book was begun as a doctoral dissertation at Harvard. His guidance has been a constant inspiration from start to finish.

This study did not seem to call for a formal bibliography. Some indication of the range of primary and secondary sources on which I have relied will be found in the footnotes. Standard bibliographies, such as those compiled by Hugo P. Thieme or Hector Talvart and Joseph Place, contain a comprehensive list of Halévy's published works.

All quotations from the French sources are my own translation, except where otherwise stated.

A. S.

Bryn Mawr, Pennsylvania
February 1966

ix

Contents

❧❧

CHAPTER I

The Family

THE chronicle of the Halévy family is an admirable illustration of the effects of cultural adaptation. In less than three generations its members had succeeded in rising above their ghetto past to become completely identified with their new environment. That Daniel Halévy, proud descendant of a line of humble Jewish immigrants, should have commanded universal respect in his time as one of the worthiest exponents of the French national tradition is surely a tribute both to himself and to the seductive genius of his adopted country.[1]

I

Halévy's first French ancestor, his great-grandfather, had emigrated from Würzburg in his native Germany to Paris at the end of the eighteenth century, in the wake of the great Revolution which to him and to many like himself pointed the way to a new era of hope and fulfillment. Known at first under the name of Elie Halphen Lévy (which he later abbreviated to Halévy), he earned a modest living as a choirmaster, ultimately becoming cantor of the principal Jewish synagogue on Rue de la Victoire.[2] He also distinguished himself as a composer of religious music, but it was not until a Hebrew hymn that he wrote to commemorate

[1] Henri Clouard, *Histoire de la littérature française du symbolisme à nos jours* (Paris, 1949), II, 131; cf. Daniel Halévy, *Pays parisiens* (1st ed.; Paris, 1929), 127.

[2] Moshé Katan, "La Famille Halévy," *Evidences* (Mar., 1955), 7.

1

the Peace of Lunéville was greeted by much publicity, that his fame spread beyond the small Jewish community.[3] Widely performed in churches and temples in a French and a German version, this somewhat fulsome composition sang the praises of revolutionary France, "the most beautiful nation, splendor of creation," and predicted the dawn of a new age not only for the Jews of the Diaspora, but for all the disinherited of the world who had finally found a refuge in the homeland of liberty.[4]

Combining his musical talents with a taste for Talmudic scholarship that he had inherited from his father, a rabbi, Halévy soon turned his energies to championing the emancipation of his coreligionists. Realizing that the new liberties guaranteed by the Napoleonic codes called for a total reevaluation of traditional Judaism, he associated himself with other Jews recently settled in France who were also seeking to modify an obsolete religious orthodoxy no longer adapted to the conditions of modern society. Elected permanent secretary of the expanding Jewish community in Paris in 1808, he used his position to promote changes which anticipated some of the features of Reformed Judaism, and ten years later, he launched a journal whose title *L'Israélite français* reveals clearly enough the direction of his thinking.[5] His contributions to this publication, marred by a rather jejune enthusiasm in the redeeming virtues of assimilation, also show what appears to be a genuine desire to reconcile the progressive elements of an antiquated faith with the great hopes raised by the French Revolution. The same sentiment pervades his other strictly Jewish writings: the first manual of a Jewish catechism ever published in France, and *Limude Dat U-musar*, a compendium of moral maxims,

---

[3] Léon Halévy, *François Fromental Halévy: Sa vie et ses oeuvres* (Paris, 1862), 3–5; cf. Frank E. Manuel, *The New World of Henri Saint-Simon* (Cambridge, Mass., 1959), 420, n. 8.

[4] Katan, *op. cit.*, 8.   [5] Manuel, *loc. cit.*

which drew heavily on illustrations from French and classical literature in order to demonstrate the moral identity underlying Judaism and the French heritage.[6] The desire to recast an archaic dogmatism along more secular lines also marked the character of the Alliance Israélite, a movement that he founded at the height of the religious revival ushered in by the Restoration. The motto of this association, "Tiens au pays, conserve ta foi," neatly epitomized the nature of his progressive ideas.[7]

Elie Halévy married a Jewess belonging to a family long established in Nancy, and the couple lived on the Rue Montholon where their neighbors were Olinde Rodrigues, the sephardi banker from Bordeaux, and Hippolyte Lebas, the architect of Notre-Dame de Lorette. Lebas, a Protestant, encouraged Halévy to persevere in his good work of closing the gap between Gentile and Jew. He not only introduced him to Parisian literary circles, but also stimulated his inquisitive mind by initiating him into the finer aspects of French culture, and by teaching him Greek and Latin, rounded off his education. Elie Halévy's published works included a critical translation of Aesop's fables and fragments of a French-Hebrew dictionary which was the first of its kind. Halévy's younger son Léon completed the dictionary after his father's death.[8]

It was in such an environment, where traditional beliefs were gradually crumbling, that Elie's two sons were brought up. The elder, Jacques François Fromental, best known as the composer of La Juive, was also the founder of a new musical genre which his two most celebrated students at the Paris Conservatory, Bizet and Gounod, forged into a form of composition that was to dominate the French musical scene until almost the end of the century. The younger, Léon,

[6] Elie Halévy, *Limude dat U-Musar* (Metz, 1820), xii.
[7] Manuel, *op. cit.*, 345.   [8] Katan, *op. cit.*, 9.

displayed a more literary bent, but although he tried his hand at prose and verse, history, drama, and vaudeville, without ever succeeding in any of his pursuits, he is chiefly remembered today as one of Saint-Simon's most dedicated disciples.

Fromental preceded his brother at the Lycée Charlemagne, after which he studied at the Conservatory under Cherubini. In 1819 his cantata *Herminie* earned him the coveted Grand Prix de Rome and launched him into a distinguished musical career. With the appearance of *La Juive*, first performed in 1835, he was hailed as Meyerbeer's equal. In the following year he was appointed to the chair in composition at the Paris Conservatory, which under his guiding genius became the center of an immensely popular romantic school of music. In 1837 he became the first Jew ever to be elected to the Académie des Beaux-Arts, soon rising to the position of honorary secretary of that august body, a sinecure which brought with it a generous stipend together with luxurious living quarters on the Quai Conti.[9] His marriage with one of the daughters of Isaac Rodrigues-Henriques, a scion of those Jewish banking dynasties who were to be so closely associated with the financial ventures of the Second Empire, was a match which considerably enhanced his social position. The younger of his two daughters, Geneviève, later became the wife of Georges Bizet.[10]

Sainte-Beuve, who had been Fromental's schoolmate and who was to remain his lifelong friend, has left us a sympathetic portrait of the musician in his *Nouveaux Lundis*. Comparing him with La Bruyère's *honnête homme*, he praises his integrity and wide-ranging interests.

A judicious man, he could chat . . . with you throughout a dinner lasting the whole evening without saying a single word about music, or even introducing his own special subject. . . .

[9] *Ibid*, 10.
[10] Mina Curtiss, *Bizet and His World* (New York, 1958), 236.

He was like a bee, who, having found himself not wholly at home in the hive, was in search of some place outside where he could make his honey. . . . Everything interested, attracted, inspired him with the desire, or rather the regret that he had not made the subject in question his life's work.[11]

This attractive disposition which endeared Fromental to all those who knew him also marked the character of his younger brother Léon, Daniel Halévy's grandfather. But the versatility and inquisitiveness which were the dominant virtues of Fromental were to prove to be Léon's undoing. Endowed with an even livelier curiosity than Fromental's, he was temperamentally incapable of concentrating on any single pursuit. Unable to discipline his quite remarkable talents, he frittered away his genius, never settled on any career, and ended his life as a dismal failure—subject to fits of neurasthenia and depression.

His beginning, however, gave every sign of promise. An outstanding record at the Lycée Charlemagne, where he won highest honors at the *concours général*, seemed to destine him for the academic profession. But unwilling to conform with the religious tests required for admission to the Ecole Normale Supérieure, he decided to prepare for the bar instead. While still in his twenties he had already gained a minor reputation with a translation of Horace, a notable achievement for a young man with no formal classical training.[12] He combined further literary pursuits with the position of professor of rhetoric in a Parisian *lycée*, and in 1831 he was appointed to the chair of literature at the Ecole Polytechnique. Three years later, however, he unexpectedly resigned, and after what was to prove his first serious bout with a chronic nervous disorder he was induced by his family

[11] Charles-Augustin Sainte-Beuve, *Nouveaux Lundis* (Paris, 1883), 227, 240–243; cited by Curtiss, *op. cit.*, 24. See also Sainte-Beuve, *Nouveaux Lundis* (Calmann-Lévy ed.; Paris, 1875), I, 395–399; II, 227 ff.; IV, 322.

[12] Manuel, *op. cit.*, 346.

to abandon teaching for a modest clerical post in the Ministry of Public Instruction. It was at this time that he married the daughter of Hippolyte Lebas, who, having been appointed curator of the Institut, moved his entire family including his shiftless son-in-law to the spacious quarters that he occupied in that sumptuous palace. Lebas ultimately induced Léon to withdraw from the Ministry, and by securing his appointment as assistant librarian of the Institut provided him the opportunity of reading to his heart's delight.[13]

Léon was a prolific if erratic writer, not without talent, and with a particular penchant for translating the classics into the graceful French prose of the time. He also published several poems and fables of more than passing value, and a vast number of plays and light comedies. His more serious works include the masterly *Résumé de l'histoire des Juifs anciens*. This was followed by a history of the modern Jews and his two-volume *Histoire résumée de la littérature française*, which served as a standard text for successive generations of students at Polytechnique.

His chief title to fame, however, lies in his association with Saint-Simon, being one of the first to be drawn to the new gospel of socialism and remaining loyal to its exponent until the new religion fell into disrepute. What drew him to Saint-Simon was a yearning for some moral absolute: a yearning which he shared with many other young Jews of his age, who, denied the opportunity of participating in the intellectual life of their time, found a suitable outlet for their frustrations as well as a fitting substitute for their traditional beliefs in the New Christianity propounded by Saint-Simon. Debarred from established society, despairing of the faith of their elders, these restless intellectuals were inevitably drawn to one of the most challenging ideas in the air. That the first

[13] Pierre Guiral, *Prévost-Paradol, 1829–1870: Pensée et action d'un libéral sous le Second Empire* (Paris, 1955), 22 ff.

6

band of disciples who gathered around the master of the utopian crusade was made up almost entirely of Jews, mostly sons of partly-assimilated and well-to-do banking families, is hardly surprising.

Chief among these was Benjamin Olinde Rodrigues, a cousin by marriage of the Halévys, who in 1820 introduced the impressionable young author to Saint-Simon in the garden of the Palais-Royal. The conversion was immediate, the impact far-reaching. The socialist ideal was to transform the lethargic man of letters into a champion of a new faith to which he himself recruited other men of talent. Among these were the Pereire brothers, and a few years later he won over Gustave d'Eichthal, whose correspondence with John Stuart Mill illustrates the type of generous optimism that inspired all these earnest young liberals.[14]

Saint-Simonism gained in Halévy not only one of its staunchest advocates, but also its most persuasive propagandist. His editorial labors improved Saint-Simon's haphazard *Opinions littéraires, philosophiques et industrielles*, and his clear and graceful expository style (greatly prized by the master) earned him the position of editor of the group's official journal, *Le Producteur*, which he founded in 1825, shortly after Saint-Simon's death. It was largely thanks to Halévy's perseverance that a movement that was to mold the minds of an entire generation preserved some semblance of unity for almost a decade after its founder's death. Halévy succeeded in keeping *Le Producteur* alive for seven arduous years until the inevitable rupture with the movement's less reasonable followers forced him at last to acknowledge the futility of his efforts. Contrary to Saint-Simon's express desire that Rodrigues should be his heir, the latter-day adherents of *Le Producteur* had by the 1830's rallied around

[14] Manuel, *op. cit.*, 344. See also Robert F. Byrnes, *Antisemitism in Modern France*, Vol. I, *The Prologue to the Dreyfus Affair* (New Brunswick, N.J., 1950), 118.

the visionary Enfantin, whose grotesque deviations appealed to an entirely different sort of temper and threatened to discredit the good cause.

Léon Halévy's *Ode to Saint-Simon* which appeared in 1831 was the manifesto of the old guard against Enfantin's extravagant distortions. Denouncing the dangers of transforming the master's teachings into a mystical cult, Halévy's ode asserted that Saint-Simon had no intention of being worshipped as a prophet after his death. By breaking away from the visionaries who had perverted the essentially sane features of Saint-Simon's teachings, Halévy demonstrated that sober judgment which seems to have usually prevailed over his other eccentricities. But his defection also displayed a refreshing sense of dedication—a dedication that had originally drawn him to the socialist ideal and that he had managed to preserve throughout his fitful association with its motley group of disciples.

In his recollections Léon Halévy has left us a vivid portrait of Saint-Simon himself, and the general tone of his exegesis indicates the true bent of his own ideas. But it is in his *Ode* that we find the most penetrating insight into Saint-Simon's personality. By stressing the rational elements in his doctrine, Halévy applied a useful corrective to some of the more extravagant accretions with which the later converts had distorted the true meaning of Saint-Simon's socialist philosophy. He was one of the three members of the original band of disciples whom Saint-Simon summoned to his deathbed, and it was he who was chosen to deliver the funeral oration in which he paid tribute to the one who, as he put it, "fell asleep in a dream of public happiness." [15]

Turning away from the mystical absurdities which marked the deterioration of the Saint-Simonian cult into yet one more romantic fantasy, Léon Halévy emerged from this experience with a renewed faith in the principles of the

[15] Cited in Manuel, *op. cit.*, 423.

Enlightenment, which he had always associated with the master's socialism; Daniel Halévy was to recall how in his youth it was from his grandfather that he received his first inkling of the meaning of the words "humanity" and "naturalism." To the young Daniel the bracing prospect revealed by these words produced, as he put it, "un éblouissement," marking the first step in the direction of an abiding loyalty to that skeptical humanism which he shared with his grandfather.[16]

There was another dominant feature in Halévy's personality which can also be traced to such a hereditary source. Not only did he inherit a profound respect for the ideas of clarity and balance which had marked Léon's commitment to what was primarily a rationalist, reforming movement, but also a fine sense for appreciating pioneering trends of thought, responding to them with the same relish as had his Saint-Simonian grandfather. Their reactions to thought-provoking ideas were virtually identical, resting on the sheer delight produced by personal contact, especially in the gratifying enchantment resulting from conversation. Moreover, both of them sought their destiny by identifying themselves with a stronger, more assertive individual whose unorthodox ideas challenged accepted opinion. This craving for identification was undoubtedly the result of some sense of inferiority, an unconscious, perhaps hereditary awareness of not having altogether achieved assimilation. But it can also be traced to a quite genuine diffidence. Whatever its cause, this singular disposition took the form of an acute desire to yield to an external authority. The object of their affections was invariably that rare person who combined force of character with provocative ideas. With Léon Halévy, it was Saint-Simon; with his grandson Daniel, it was Péguy and Sorel.

[16] Daniel Halévy, *Note concernant deux passages du "Journal des années noires" par Jean Guéhenno* (Paris, n.d.), 10.

This distinctive family trait, which also recurred, as we shall see, in Léon's son Ludovic, had the advantage of distilling through a process of identification the peculiar temper of a particular generation. It is precisely this capacity for evoking some of the undercurrents of their times which invests the record of the Halévy family over a period of three generations with the quality of a *témoignage*.[17] Moreover, this receptivity was expressed essentially in human terms, the abstract idea being translated into the more tangible form of character and personality. The same perseverance with which the grandfather had sought the company of Saint-Simon was, in turn, displayed by the grandson when he attached himself to Péguy and Sorel. The following remark, taken from Léon Halévy's diary where he sets down his impression of Saint-Simon after their first encounter, foreshadowed the same turn of mind that was to draw Daniel Halévy almost a century later to the *boutique* of the *Cahiers de la Quinzaine*: "I had no sooner spoken to Saint-Simon than I was struck by his thought-provoking ideas, by those lively and incisive insights which upset all traditional opinion."[18]

II

Besides his two children, Valentine and Ludovic, Léon Halévy was also the father of a second son, Prévost-Paradol, whose kinship to the Halévy family has at last been unequivocally established by his latest biographer.[19] Léon had discreetly adopted his illegitimate child at an early age,

[17] Cf. Daniel Halévy's revealing comments in "Sur la Naissance de la Troisième République," *Bulletin de l'Union pour la Verité*, Apr. 24, 1937, 9 ff.; André Rousseaux in *Candide*, Apr. 17, 1930.

[18] Cited by Maxime Leroy, *La Vie littéraire du Comte Henri de Saint-Simon*, "Cahiers Verts," ed. Daniel Halévy, no. 54 (Paris, 1925), 291; see also pp. 6, 275. See Léon Halévy, *Ode à Saint-Simon* (Paris, n.d.), 5–6.

[19] Guiral, *op. cit.*, 30–33. But see Edmond and Jules Goncourt, *Journal des Goncourt: Mémoires de la vie littéraire* (Paris, 1887–1888), I, 183–184.

alleging that Paradol was an orphan of unknown parentage; and his wife, who might perhaps have suspected the truth, treated the precocious lad as one of her own. Paradol returned his father's devotion with a truly touching filial piety. It was indeed a source of pride for the melancholic would-be scholar to follow his son's spectacular career, beginning with Paradol's admission to the Rue d'Ulm which had been barred to him because of his name. It was with the same satisfaction that Léon watched his son climb the rungs of an academic profession to which he himself had aspired. Paradol tried repeatedly but without success to sponsor Léon's election to the French Academy which had elected him as its youngest member. And by furnishing his father with an entree into the exclusive *Journal des Débats,* the official organ of liberal thinking that counted Paradol as one of its most valued collaborators, he was largely responsible for raising the Halévy family into the charmed circle of the great Parisian *notables.*

It is at this point that Orleanism first filtered into the texture of the Halévy family, coming in, as it were, through the back door; and it is ironical that the instrument of this transformation of the Halévys into a dynasty of *notables* should have been the one member of the family who, although never concealing his connection with it, did not bear its name. Paradol's career is a remarkable example of a deliberate effort to adapt to the dominant group in French society. Despite his humble, even obscure origins, he succeeded by sheer personal charm and intellect not only to force his way into the great liberal bourgeoisie, but to become its most esteemed and talented champion. His *La France nouvelle,* for example, one of the most significant political treatises published under the Second Empire, became the classic manifesto of Orleanism, repeatedly invoked by succeeding generations of liberals as the final word on their political principles. It was through him that something of that elusive Orleanist spirit was communicated to his half-brother Ludovic, and which in turn shaped the political sympathies of Daniel Halévy.

Ludovic and Paradol, raised together as brothers, were united by a particularly warm bond of comradeship, enhanced no doubt by some guilty awareness of a blood relationship that was kept a secret from all but the most intimate friends of the family. Five years older than Ludovic, Paradol, already a full-fledged *normalien*, took in hand his younger brother's education. It was mainly as a result of his guidance, carried on intermittently over the years, that a good deal of his Orleanist ideas rubbed off on the particularly receptive mind of Ludovic.[20]

Paradol belonged to the most celebrated graduating class of the Ecole Normale, which included such outstanding figures as Taine, Edmond About, Challemel-Lacour, Jean-Jacques Weiss, and Francisque Sarcey, all of whom embodied during the last days of the Empire and the early Republic the distinct flavor of the Orleanist critical tradition —both in politics and letters—epitomized by Paradol's *La France nouvelle*.[21] If this tradition could not exactly be claimed by Daniel Halévy as his birthright, there is no doubt that his uncle's ideas decisively molded his early thinking. He tells us himself how his own beliefs emerged naturally from a sympathetic appreciation of Paradol's prolific writings; his uncle's extensive correspondence with Ludovic, piously preserved in the family archives, constituted a manual of liberal maxims from which the young Daniel was to derive his own Orleanist principles.[22] The bulky size of the correspondence can be attributed to Paradol's prolonged absences from the capital, which his brother, a Parisian to

[20] Guiral, *op. cit.*, 33, 98.

[21] For a study of its impact on French liberal thought, see Guiral, *op. cit.*, 489–580, and also Albert Thibaudet, *Histoire de la littérature française de 1789 à nos jours* (Paris, 1936), 452.

[22] Personal communication: Daniel Halévy.

the core, could never be induced to leave. His tenure of various academic posts in the provinces, his frequent journeys abroad and finally to Washington—where Napoleon III, in an effort to kill one of his severest critics with kindness, had appointed him minister—assured Ludovic of a constant flow of letters that provided him with a source of political edification. The close identity of their views was proudly acknowledged by Ludovic who expressed his indebtedness to his more gifted brother when he pithily remarked: "Paradol says what I think and I think what Paradol says."[23]

When we recall that it was the great Guizot who greeted Paradol to the French Academy, that his roommate at the Ecole Normale and lifelong companion was Hippolyte Taine, and that he was acknowledged in his time as the foremost spokesman of liberal Orleanism, which through more than twenty years of regular contributions to *Le Journal des Débats* he forged into a positive political doctrine, the Halévys' strong Orleanist bias becomes more clearly understandable. Yet this orientation, it must be remembered, was less a matter of doctrine than an elusive sympathy for a certain temper reflected in a certain style of life and thought. It can only be evoked in terms of a particularly rarefied social and political ambiance where polite conversation and graceful manners set the tone for a cluster of ideas which defies precise definition. It was in such a society, elegant, urbane, and almost exclusively literary, imbued with a deep sense of confidence in the superior merits of the *notable* virtues and the inherent wisdom which seemed to predestine that class to a position of political supremacy, that the young Daniel was brought up.[24]

[23] Ludovic Halévy, *Carnets* (Paris, 1935), II, 8.

[24] Cf. Jean-Ernest Charles in *La Grande Revue*, June, 1935, 667; Henri Clouard in *Nouvelles Littéraires*, Sept. 27, 1930; Jacques Emile Blanche, *Mes Modèles: Barrès, Proust, James, Moore* (Paris, 1928), 77. See also René Rémond, *La Droite en France* (2d ed.; Paris, 1963), 90–92, 112–115.

Like his father, and also his brother, Paradol showed traces of a nervous disorder never clearly diagnosed, and which culminated in his suicide in 1871 while ambassador in Washington. His children, who were brought up by the Halévy family, were also destined to equally sinister or unhappy ends: his son Hjalmar took his own life at eighteen, and his daughters either went mad or became nuns.[25]

III

Ludovic Halévy's name is chiefly associated with the stage, but he also displayed a talent for writing novels and essays which established his reputation in his own time and on which his claim as a critic and chronicler of his age ultimately rests.

Some of these certainly deserve to be rescued from oblivion. His recollections, in particular, only brief extracts of which have been published by his son, constitute an invaluable source on the society of the Second Empire of which he was in so many ways a typical representative.[26] It is not only the frivolity of the salons or the backstage gossip of the Opéra that are brought to life in his memoirs; these also contain vivid accounts of the world of finance and banking, of the Legislative Assembly with which he was closely associated, and of the immediate entourage of such contrasting political celebrities as Gambetta and the Duc de Morny. His journalistic efforts, particularly his *Récits de guerre* and *La Débâcle*, are superb examples of war reporting. Among his works of fiction, *La Famille Cardinal* can still be read with pleasure, and *Criquette* and *L'Abbé Constantin*—a kind of nineteenth-century French version of *The Vicar of Wakefield*—demonstrate even more persua-

[25] Jacques Emile Blanche, *La Pêche aux souvenirs* (Paris, 1949), 110; Guiral, *op. cit.*, 728–729.
[26] See Adrien Dansette, *Le Boulangisme, 1886–1890* (Paris, 1938), iv.

sively his gift for storytelling.[27] His curiosity was insatiable, his judgments on contemporaries, acute; his chronicle of Parisian society is marked by a sure command of historical trends. It is these dominant virtues of the social historian that he bequeathed to his son Daniel.

After a relatively undistinguished record at the *lycée*, Ludovic joined the civil service at the early age of eighteen. Still a junior official in the newly-established Ministry of Algerian Affairs, he was soon to try his hand at vaudeville, writing at first under a pseudonym so as not to offend the susceptibilities of his family. His first notable success in that genre came in 1855 with a prologue that he wrote to celebrate the inauguration of Offenbach's Théâtre des Champs-Elysées. An amalgam between the *normalien canulard* and German buffoonery, this first composition set the tone for a whole string of musical productions which have traditionally been associated with the gay life of Paris under the Second Empire. After another dramatic triumph, *Orpheus in Hades*, for which he wrote the libretto with Hector Crémieux, the next twenty years were marked by a collaboration with Offenbach and Henri Meilhac, with whom he produced an endless stream of light musical comedies. These achieved immense popularity with the Parisian public and confirmed his reputation as the most successful librettist of his day.

The frivolity of these works communicates admirably the spirit of an epoch which was itself notoriously frivolous, yet Halévy's librettos, for all their facility and deliberate pandering to the taste of a rather undiscriminating audience, are not entirely devoid of merit.[28] Written in a disarmingly comic vein, but with a firm grasp of the frailties of human

[27] See the article on Ludovic Halévy in *La Grande Encyclopédie*, XIX, 756–757.
[28] Cf. Albert Thibaudet, *Histoire de la littérature française*, 394–395.

nature, Halévy's plots often conceal an undercurrent of social criticism. Combined with Meilhac's theatrical effects and Offenbach's captivating tunes, they invest the operettas with considerable value as social documents. Halévy was sometimes capable of applying his talents to more ambitious themes. By subordinating his virtuosity to greater subjects he showed that he could also rise above mere brilliance. Bizet's *Carmen,* for which he wrote the libretto at short notice, indicates that he was not incapable of composing dramatic works of an entirely different order.

Until 1866 Halévy combined his nights at the Opéra with the duties of general secretary of the Corps Législatif, a position which for several years entailed the task of drafting the authorized version of the parliamentary debates. It was the Duc de Morny, president of the Legislature, who had secured this post for Halévy after the dissolution of the Algerian Ministry had robbed his friend of a comfortable sinecure, partly in gratitude for the librettist's assistance in revising an opera which he had himself composed.[29] Favorably impressed by Halévy's engaging style and anxious to win over the discriminating Orleanist opposition, Morny sought in this way to divert criticism by providing the readers of *Le Moniteur* with literary entertainment if not political edification. Halévy followed Morny's wishes to the letter: his adroit reporting not only increased the popularity of *Le Moniteur* but also contributed to carrying out the regime's policy of elevating political debate to a polite but largely innocuous level. Halévy himself had no illusions about the effectiveness of such tactics. His familiarity with the affairs of the Legislature inspired him with a lasting distrust for politicians. Immediately after the death of his patron he resigned his post, noting in his diary:

[29] Ludovic Halévy, *Carnets,* I, 38–40. The opera, M. *Choufleury restera chez lui,* was ultimately performed in 1865.

From the seven years that I have just passed in the midst of the representatives of my country, I have formed the profoundest political indifference. As for convictions, there are none, absolutely none, on the Right as well as the Left. These . . . people amount to precious little and aspire to become something. That is all.

This same aversion also recurs in Daniel Halévy, who recalled his father's advice to his two sons on the threshold of life that they could embark on any career that they pleased save politics.[30]

The natural complement of Ludovic's antipathy for the market place of politics was an equally strong affinity for Orleanism, splendidly remote from partisan interests and which, to his mind, could alone confer on political life a respectable dignity. His deference to such precious sentiments had been communicated by Prévost-Paradol; it was now further enhanced by his friendship with that consummate statesman Morny, a Bonapartist only by birth and expediency, but in fact an Orleanist in all but name.[31] A frequent guest at Morny's country estate in Nades, Ludovic Halévy was initiated into the exclusive circle of the great *notable* dynasties and introduced to the Orleanist princes themselves under whose auspices Morny had made his political debut. From such exponents of the great liberal tradition as the younger Broglie and the Duc Decazes, from Lord Granville and the other Whig magnates who gravitated around Nades, Halévy learned to associate political wisdom with the refinement of men of good breeding whom he could scarcely resist from contrasting with "our horrible little politicians, parvenus and pretentious." [32]

There was much in Halévy's sympathies which denotes the snobbishness of the social climber. Himself a parvenu,

---

[30] *Carnets*, I, 64; cf. Jacques Bainville, *Lectures* (Paris, n.d.), 59.
[31] *Carnets*, I, 41 ff., 178 ff.   [32] *Ibid.*, I, 43.

lionized by Parisian society because of his celebrity, he sought to overcome his modest origins by an almost too sedulous attachment to the values of the higher set. Yet he was by no means blind to the political limitations of the great liberal patricians. Observing them from afar, aping their manners, even secretly aspiring to be counted as one of them, he preserved enough detachment from the gatherings at Nades to invest his accounts with the quality of a valuable *témoignage* on both the virtues and the shortcomings of the European elites. Despite its incontrovertible predilections for the vanishing breed of Orleanists, his diary also shows that he clearly realized that the *notables* would be incapable of leading the country in the years ahead, and he predicted that to carry out the inevitable transition to a more democratic society new men would be needed. He was highly impressed, for instance, with the outstanding qualities displayed by the young Gambetta. Meeting him through the Rothschilds', he was one of the first to hail the fiery radical as the worthy spokesman of the *nouvelles couches*, of that popular wave of the future which, he felt, would undoubtedly sweep away the frivolity of the Empire.[33] For the task of steering the country through the radical transformations that he anticipated, Halévy had few illusions about the competence of his Orleanist friends, sensing that such capable opportunists as Gambetta, less wedded to the past, would be better suited to preside over the destinies of the new France. Yet his journal also betrays the fond hope that an alliance between Broglie and Gambetta—which he contemplated as a political possibility as early as 1869—might also carry into the new regime something of the old liberal values.

Daniel Halévy's historical reconstruction of this era re-

[33] Ludovic Halévy, *Trois Dîners avec Gambetta*, ed. Daniel Halévy (Paris, 1936), 15 ff.

flects the same hopes—or the same illusions—only partly
mitigated by experience. It is indeed remarkable that the
father's deference to character transcending party loyalties
should foreshadow the same regard for the qualities of
personal leadership that his son was to stress in *La Fin des
notables*. The difference was merely one of time, not of
temperament. If Daniel Halévy was later to deplore the
political eclipse of the Broglie dynasty, whose shortcomings
he never really denied, it was only because the turn of events
had clearly demonstrated that even Gambetta had proved
incapable of checking the partisan interests of his followers.
Yet in his history of this period, Daniel, like his father, did
not fail to give Gambetta his due, acknowledging his
superior talents and regretting only that these had not been
subordinated to the higher interests of a truly liberal Republic. Just as Daniel deplored the elimination of both
Gambetta and Broglie from the high councils of state, his
father had also accorded them both an equal sympathy on
the grounds that they alone could have guided the authoritarian Empire into a progressive, yet conservative, Republic.

A good deal of Ludovic Halévy's wistful regret for the
fading charm of a decadent yet graceful age stemmed from
his desire to invest political affairs with dignity. His premonitions of the perils inherent in mass democracy dominated
by electoral politics and cheap demagoguery flowed from
the same source. To conserve an ethic of quality he naturally believed that some form of elitist organization of government would be necessary. If he maintained an abiding
loyalty to the principles of Orleanism even after its political
decline, it was largely because he identified these principles
with a form of political liberty that the Opportunist rulers of
the Third Republic had failed to preserve. And if Daniel, in
his turn, shared his father's loyalty with an even stronger,
more nostalgic conviction, it was because he also regarded

the Orleanist tradition not as an anachronism, but as the most valuable ingredient in his country's liberal heritage.[34]

The Orleanist flavor with which the father had so deliberately impregnated the family atmosphere became an almost natural attribute to the succeeding generations of the Halévys. Daniel Halévy could stake a claim to Orleanism almost as a birthright. Born and bred in a milieu which had come to call itself Orleanist, the son of the first librettist ever to be elected to the French Academy represented the first generation of a family of Jewish emigrees who could unequivocally affirm their identity with the great liberal bourgeoisie of Paris. Yet he too attached a particular significance to this elusive loyalty. Interpreting it in the broadest sense by giving it an additional dimension, he could proclaim to all those who might reproach him for his inconsistency that "the France which haunts my mind is the France of Louis Philippe, the France of Lafayette and Proudhon, Delacroix and Guizot." [35]

Such an assertion points to yet another trait that father and son had in common. Both Halévys shared the same curiosity for what they called the "inner life" of the laboring poor, and the father's concern for the social problem in his own day foreshadowed the son's more earnest devotion to the cause of socialism at the turn of the century. The published extracts from Ludovic Halévy's diary reveal only partially the extent to which the popular librettist's curiosity was absorbed by other matters. To be sure, his remarks on fashionable society, the Academy, and the world of politics illustrate a remarkable talent for observation which recurs only in a subdued form in the rest of his works. But these

[34] Ludovic Halévy, *Carnets*, I, 173–178. Charles Péguy, "De la Situation faite au parti intellectuel," *Cahiers de la Quinzaine* (lᵉ cahier de da 9ᵉᵐᵉ série, Oct. 6, 1907), 69.

[35] Daniel Halévy, *Note concernant deux passages*, 13; cf. *La Fin des notables* (Paris, 1930), 70.

entries are also interspersed with reflections on the inevitable rise of the working class to a position of political importance. Such passages are notable for the glimpses that they offer us into the manners and customs of the capital's working class accompanied by copious records of their conversations. Some of Halévy's verbatim reports of casual chats with commoners bring to mind Restif de la Bretonne's portrait of an earlier Paris. Less crude yet equally lively, Halévy's reporting is distinguished by the librettist's eye for character and his gift for dialogue. There is little moralizing here, only a genuine curiosity about people from all walks of life. Ludovic Halévy's accounts of his encounters with the stage crew at the Opéra, with cab drivers and shop owners, with the artisans of the expanding *faubourgs* which he would visit on his daily constitutional, illustrate an awareness of the "social question" quite unusual for his times. And the manner of Daniel Halévy's investigation of those peasants of the Centre whom he visited with faithful regularity for over half a century is reminiscent of his father's own journeys to the Paris *faubourgs* in search of the same itinerant workmen whose development over the years he observed with persistent curiosity.

Ludovic's records show little trace of the patronizing air which one might have expected from a person in his position. Instead, he merely displayed a disarming desire to inform himself, and the fact that his inquisitiveness seems to have seldom aroused resentment indicates that he, like his son, possessed a rare capacity for breaking through class barriers. His accounts invariably reflect an engaging bonhomie which endeared him to all those who met him. Georges Sorel, who knew him only at the end of his life when fits of melancholia had already impaired his nimble wit and what had once been a brilliant gift for conversation, was favorably impressed not only by his zest for life but also by his unusual concern for the lot of the laboring classes.

Rarely given to unnecessary flattery, Sorel was undoubtedly sincere when he confided to Jean Variot: "It will be a long time before French literature can produce a writer of Ludovic Halévy's caliber." Perceiving the uncanny similarity between father and son which all friends of the family have observed, he added, perhaps with some exaggeration: "Obviously, Daniel Halévy was born with superior gifts. . . . He is the son of a man who was one of the most eminent psychologists of the nineteenth century." [36]

What Sorel found particularly significant in Halévy's plays and novels was that under the disarming innocence of the comic mood, his literary efforts show an uncommon grasp of the contradictions of a decadent bourgeois society, engrossed with material gain and the superficial allurements of parliamentary democracy. The apparent frivolity of the musical genre which he used to such effect should not detract, insisted Sorel, from the very real merits of his social criticism. Sorel believed that such works as the immensely popular *La Belle Hélène*, despite its fanciful drollery and gratuitous levity, went further than Voltaire in posing the problem of religious hypocrisy through the ages, and he regarded Halévy's novels, especially the two-volume saga of *La Famille Cardinal*, as far more valuable documents than the didactic *Nana*. This chronicle of Parisian *moeurs* depicts with devastating realism the plight of the lower orders of the capital's middle class, exposing the prevalent cant of a society which refused to acknowledge that prostitution frequently afforded a poor girl the only means of rising above her rank. Writing in a disarmingly unpretentious vein and fully exploiting the comic spirit, Halévy was capable of telling us more about the shifting class structure of the Second Empire than other contemporary novelists. With none of Zola's deliberate moralizing, his social studies were

[36] Cited by Jean Variot, *Propos de Georges Sorel* (Paris, 1935), 165. See also Abel Hermant, *La Vie littéraire* (Paris, n.d.), II, 75.

hailed by Sorel as "simply magnificent," while their plea for human understanding serves as a useful corrective to the depths of human degradation portrayed in Zola's more naturalistic novels.[37]

The decade of the sixties during which Halévy reached his prime should not be too rashly dismissed as a mere orgy of *Offenbachiade*—a frivolous chapter in French arts and letters utterly devoid of serious purpose. The seductive charm of its dramatic productions rarely failed to captivate even the most fastidious tastes, providing Wagner no less than Nietzsche with something more than ordinary entertainment. If the banalities of the Goncourts dominated for a while the Parisian literary scene, the age also produced its Sainte-Beuve, while Baudelaire's discernment of *le spleen de Paris* buried underneath the surface merriment betrays the nuances of a society more complex than its surface levity. The climate of taste and sensibility associated with the era of "gaslight and shadow" [38] was expressed not only in Grévin and the contemporary vogue for Japanese prints, but also in Degas. And when we remember that a critic of Taine's stature did not regard it as in the least degrading to be known as a regular contributor to Marcellin's *La Vie Parisienne*, we realize after all, that to the elite of the day the glittering stage lights of Hortense Schneider and Desclée formed an integral part of a general culture indiscriminately shared by all.[39] To Ludovic's generation, the ponderous speculations of a Renan or a Taine were not necessarily at variance with the trifling joviality of Offenbach's enchanting melodies.

The elite of the French capital was bound not only by intimate social ties, but also by an underlying identity of

[37] Variot, *op. cit.*, 164.

[38] The title of Roger L. Williams' book published in New York, 1957.

[39] *Le Siècle d'Offenbach* (Paris, 1959), 15–16. See also J. E. C. Bodley, *France* (London, 1907), 520.

sentiment which contributed to creating a common culture, making the transition from one set of authors and artists to another almost imperceptible. Parisian society under the Empire was drawn together in the great salons which not only set the tone of the age but also gathered the most diverse talents into one extensive social coterie. Moreover, this elite, for all its distinction, seemed to share a common enthusiasm for a certain form of entertainment to which Halévy had devoted his talents and in which admirers like Baudelaire occasionally discovered a "gravité dans le frivole."

Yet Ludovic's contributions to this society went further. He was not only the creator of a new dramatic genre which furnished many of his contemporaries with an inexhaustible source of delight; he also contributed to broadening the basis of this common culture by playing the role of a go-between, serving as a link between the various segments of society and communicating through his mediating talents with some of the dominant currents of the time. His virtues as a mediator are demonstrated by the ease with which he seemed capable of crossing all social barriers. He was as much at home in the company of the ballet dancers at the Opéra, of the demi-mondaines, and of Dumas *fils*, as he was in the salon of Mme de Loynes or in the more solemn entourage of Renan or Taine, his colleagues at the Academy. From all these corners of society he not only culled gems of gossip, *beaux mots* and the like, but also formed invaluable impressions which, dutifully committed to his diary, offer us a magnificent commentary on Parisian society under the Empire and the early Republic.

The astounding scope of Halévy's interests is revealed in the fifty-five bulky volumes of his "Carnets," which cover the years from 1862 to 1899. These constitute a veritable gold mine of information. With an insatiable curiosity, reading widely and voraciously, cataloguing and clipping, Halévy assembled a unique assortment of impressions and anecdotes on his times—a compendious chronicle of more than three decades of French social history. His record of the vicissitudes of Mme de Loynes's salon, for instance, is surely of as much value to the historian of the first decades of the Republic as are the more familiar accounts of Mme Juliette Adam's. Emerging from the obscure world of Second Empire cocottes where Halévy had first met her as Mme de Tourbet, Mme de Loynes achieved a modest celebrity under her second name, and as the mistress of Jules Lemaître presided over a salon which became the center of the antirevisionist camp during the Dreyfus Affair. It was Mme de Loynes who was responsible for launching Boulanger into politics, while her drawing room also served as Rochefort's political headquarters. But Halévy placed it all in proper perspective by reminding us that she attained her greatest triumph when she succeeded in inducing Renan to spend an intimate evening with Mlle Dumay, the most celebrated café-concert singer of the day.[40]

Halévy was not merely a habitué of salons and a contributor to *La Vie Parisienne*; he was also a political observer. As early as 1866 he predicted that the Empire would collapse not through internal dissension as most Orleanists believed, but as a result of its ambiguous policy on the Rhine. In August he prophesied in his diary that the Emperor's vacillation would not only provoke war but also pave the way for a violent upheaval at home.[41] He deplored Napoleon III's personal intervention in foreign affairs as a national calamity that threatened to jeopardize the constructive reforms so patiently accomplished during his reign. In 1870 on the eve of the Ems telegram, he correctly gauged public reaction to rumors of war, noting in his "Carnets"

[40] Ludovic Halévy, *Carnets*, I, 9 ff.   [41] *Ibid.*, I, 138; II, 125.

that if the Government proved incapable of resisting Prussian provocations, it would not only seal the future of the Empire but also open the floodgates to revolution and anarchy.[42]

During the Franco-Prussian War, the versatile Halévy displayed yet one more of his talents by becoming a newspaper correspondent. *La Débâcle*, which dates from this period, is one of the earliest examples of French war reporting, containing a vivid account of the distress of the civilian population of Paris during the siege, and his *L'Invasion*, first published in 1871, covers the tragic events of the Commune, which he witnessed with his usual flair for the dramatic. It seems that Daniel Halévy deliberately sought to match his father's journalistic style, sententious and succinct; the form of the vignette, and the character sketches interspersed with dialogue, which abound in his own travel books, are plainly modelled on his father's earlier narratives.

Many years later, André Siegfried was to pay tribute to Ludovic Halévy's "sensitive evocation of people and things" and to praise his "lucid and acute meditations on the course of events." [43] This judgment would fit the son no less than the father. Awarded the coveted Grand Prix de la Ville de Paris because he epitomized the particular flavor of his native city, Daniel was indeed the worthy son of the man who declared that the most beautiful landscape in the world was a Parisian wall covered with posters.[44] The "Parisian type," as Ludovic has been called, "that universally curious and inquisitive mind, that charming man of a charming era," [45] certainly shaped his son's personality to an unusual

[42] *Ibid.*, II, 178.

[43] André Siegfried in *Elie Halévy: 1870–1937* (Paris, 1937), 18; see also Daniel Halévy, "Notes de famille," *La Revue de France*, July 15, 1929, 740.

[44] Cited by Siegfried Kracauer, *Jacques Offenbach ou le secret du Second Empire* (Paris, 1937), 13. Cf. Ludovic Halévy, *Carnets*, I, 21.

[45] Siegfried, *op. cit.*, 11; see also Jules Clarétie, *La Vie à Paris* (Paris, n.d.), XXI, 181.

extent. Neither Ludovic nor his son ever became original thinkers. But they seemed admirably suited to translate some of the thought-provoking ideas of their more imaginative contemporaries. Although both chose to call themselves Orleanists, that ambiguous label does not quite convey the precise nature of their loyalties, for they exhibited to the same degree an originality of their own, which drew their interests in a direction far removed from the conventional preoccupations of the circles to which they belonged. They both combined a reverence for the past with more than a merely speculative curiosity in progressive trends that threatened to undermine the supremacy of their class. It was this concern for the "social problem," coupled with an equally genuine loyalty to liberalism in its traditional form, which lends to their judgment a unique flavor, setting them apart from others.[46]

Unlike his brother Elie, whose attitude was entirely that of a scholar, betraying scarcely any trace of parental influence, Daniel's entire disposition was marked by a deliberate effort to emulate his father. Ludovic's copious recollections, his thumbnail sketches of contemporaries, and his vast collection of newspaper clippings provided his son not only with the source material but also with the inspiration for *La Fin des notables*. As a historian, Daniel Halévy proudly acknowledged his filial debt: "I believe that my ideas on history can not be understood unless one goes back to the life and thought of my father. When I wrote my two books on history, I had the feeling that my hand was guided by his commitment to syndicalism could also be traced to that

[46] Cf. Robert Dreyfus, "Ludovic Halévy," *Pages Libres*, May 16, 1908, 554.

[47] MS letter from Daniel Halévy to author. The reference is to the two volumes of *La Fin des notables*. Some of Elie Halévy's friends regarded his mother's influence as decisive, cf. Léon Brunschwicg, "Elie Halévy," *Revue de Métaphysique et de Morale*, July, 1937, 679–680.

predilection for social reform and moral improvement communicated by his father. "When I devoted my attention to social questions, I was drawn by the same curiosity that had stimulated my father. . . . The man to whom I am chiefly indebted for my interest in syndicalism is my father." [48]

Resemblances of this order, defying any neat formula, can only be explained in terms of affinities of character. It was essentially a matter of temper, of style, which the younger Halévy seemed to have both inherited and learned from his father, a temper which one of their acquaintances has defined as a recurrent Halévy trait, "un certain goût de la liberté"—a pronounced liberal disposition which runs right through the family. [49] This taste for liberty in its broadest sense was the product of a remarkably tolerant and flexible pluralism, which took the form of a reverence for character and a genuine solicitude for the laboring classes. Yet it would be only partly true to say that the Halévys' concern for the people was merely the result of an almost too self-conscious awareness of the family's rapid rise to a position of social eminence. It was also part and parcel of a general thirst for experience, another trait which both men shared to the same degree.

Analogies between father and son rush to one's attention with uncanny frequency. Their diaries, for instance, are written in an almost identical vein, revealing the same avidity for questioning people and books. In their way of life, their personal deportment, even their physical appearance, the resemblance was no less striking. [50] They both displayed a leisurely delight in the seductions of Paris, appreciating the polite conversation and the wit of the salons, the Opéra, or

[48] Cited by René Johannet, "Les Enchantements de Daniel Halévy," *La Minerve française*, Apr. 15, 1920, 170.

[49] Jean-Ernest Charles, "Les *Carnets* de Ludovic Halévy," *La Grande Revue*, June, 1935, 667.

[50] The physical likeness is brought out in the family portraits by Degas and Jacques Emile Blanche, now the property of M. and Mme Louis Joxe.

the Institut with the same relish with which they reacted to the robust humor and good sense of the workmen of the *faubourgs*. And just as the father seemed quite capable of combining on the same Sunday a visit to Mme de Loynes's with an afternoon outing in the company of his bookbinder in Montrouge, his son would spend endless hours at his aunt's or with the Comtesse de Noailles, while at the same time pursuing his crusading zeal in the popular district of the Porte de la Chapelle.

Like his father's, Daniel Halévy's roots were entirely Parisian. Both were products of the capital; by their marriages and the traditions they thus acquired, they gradually moved away from their ancestral Judaism and came to identify themselves with the local dynasties of the higher bourgeoisie. Through family connections with the Berthelots and the Bréguets, the Vaudoyers, the Hachettes and others, they not only gained a vested interest in the dominant class but also reflected in their persons the features of the Parisian *notable par excellence* whose ties with the rest of France went no further than the possession of a summer estate in the country—preferably not too far from the capital.[51] Their attachment to Paris was genuine and profound, as much the result of breeding and upbringing as an acquired taste. And the son of the librettist of *La Vie Parisienne* could think of no more suitable title for his autobiography than *Pays parisiens*.

Yet the very success of their adjustment produced in both an identical sense of having fallen short of the French ideal; for Paris, they both knew, was but a distorted version of a broader national experience, which neither of them could ever presume to fathom. *Pays parisiens* by its very title reveals the author's sense of inferiority before the "real"

---

[51] Ludovic's country home in Sucy-en-Brie was inherited by Elie; Daniel's was in Jouy-en-Josase. For the comments of a country neighbor, see J. E. C. Bodley, *France*, 14–15, 44.

Frenchman who would always preserve a sentimental attachment to his province of birth and tradition, his native *pays*.[52] The Halévys were conscious of being Parisian and nothing else; they felt that they lacked a secure footing in the national tradition, that they had no roots in the real France. And this very real awareness acted both as a limitation to their national consciousness and as a fresh incentive to assert their nationalism with even greater emphasis.

More important, this nagging consciousness of an incompleteness in their national identity helps to explain the inordinate zeal with which father and son sought to discover that other France which an exclusively Parisian upbringing, for all its rewards, was quite incapable of revealing. We shall see later how this sense of deficiency, of falling just short of a total integration with the national psyche, prompted Daniel to seek in Charles Péguy a kind of alter ego admirably suited to fill this gap and to provide him, through a process of vicarious experience, with a richer sense of national identity. For under the flimsy carapace of his *normalien* rhetoric, the son of the illiterate chairmender of Orléans remained to the core a crude peasant of the Beauce who stoutly incarnated that other France which his friend yearned to discover. Péguy was a living symbol of a real native tradition, a tradition that the descendant of German-Jewish immigrants, now a scion of the high Parisian bourgeoisie, regarded as the natural complement of his Orleanist heritage.

One of the most intriguing aspects of Daniel Halévy's character was the persistence with which he forged for himself (and nurtured throughout his life) a cult of Péguy, for only through Péguy could he penetrate that archaic France to which he himself could never aspire to belong. Here again, this need for identification with some more permanent strain in the national character bore a singular

[52] Cf. Halévy, *Pays parisiens* (rev. ed.; Paris, 1932), 6–12; Ludovic Halévy, *Carnets*, I, 21.

resemblance to the way that Ludovic had subordinated his own personality to that of Prévost-Paradol. Like his father, Daniel also attempted to fill a certain void by yielding to a person who represented to the highest degree that side of the national legacy that was lacking in his own experience. Paradol was to Ludovic the model of the Orleanist *notable*; and for Daniel, Péguy incarnated the very essence of a popular tradition which Daniel, by now himself a second generation *notable*, sought to unravel and annex to his own cultural heritage. This cumulative process of identification covering two generations is a remarkable example of cultural assimilation. It is a tribute to the elder Halévy's perseverance in achieving in his own lifetime the status of a full-fledged *notable* that his son never questioned the basis of his own acquired footing, and was acknowledged by all his contemporaries as a living symbol of the Orleanist tradition.[53]

Daniel Halévy's attachment to his father was profound. As with so many Jewish families, the Halévys were united by unusually intimate ties, and just as Ludovic Halévy cherished the memory of Léon, Daniel in his turn showed an exceptional devotion to his father, an almost abnormal devotion which went far beyond mere filial piety. If so much of the deportment of the *notable* rubbed off on the son's personality, this can no doubt be explained by the very conditions of his upbringing: sheer physical proximity with his father and his father's circle, during the formative years of his life and beyond, accounts for the astonishing resemblance in their characters. Father and son always lived under the same roof. Even after he married and acquired a family of his own, Daniel remained in the same house as his parents; he was already thirty-six when his father died in 1908.

[53] Cf. *inter alia*, Charles Péguy, *Victor-Marie, Comte Hugo* (Gallimard ed.; Paris, 1934), 18; and Blanche, *La Pêche aux souvenirs*, 110.

Daniel's mother survived her husband by more than twenty years. Nee Louise Bréguet, Mme Halévy was of Protestant Swiss stock. Abraham Bréguet, the first member of the family to settle in France, was an enterprising Calvinist clockmaker from Neuchâtel who emigrated to Paris in 1772. It was in his workshop on the Quai de l'Horloge that he perfected the modern watch as well as other mechanical devices such as the podoscaphe, an ingenious instrument designed for counting one's steps on long walks. The succeeding generations of the family carried on the ancestor's inventive genius, and Louis Bréguet, Daniel's cousin, became a pioneer in the French airplane industry. Like the Lebas, the Bréguets and their offshoots belonged to the Parisian *haute société protestante,* an inbred group which, over the years, developed a hereditary tie with the worlds of the Institut and of high finance that survived France's successive changes of regime.[54] Ludovic Halévy married Louise Bréguet in 1867; their first son, Elie, was born in 1870 in Etretat, the Bréguet estate in Normandy, and Daniel was born two years later on the 13th of December, in Paris.[55]

IV

Raised in such a milieu, the two brothers received an upbringing determined as much by their formal schooling as by an environment dominated by a family that in its ramifications represented the elite of the first decades of the Republic. Daniel spent a blissful youth in the family home at 22, Rue de Douai that was situated on the slopes of Montmartre; at a time when Pigalle was no more than a suburban park, Montmartre itself resembled today's residential Passy.

[54] Cf. Emmanuel Beau de Loménie, *Les Responsabilités des dynasties bourgeoises* (3 vols.; Paris, 1943–1954), *passim.*
[55] Paul Guth, "Daniel Halévy," *La Revue de Paris,* Jan. 15, 1954, 139 ff.

The *hôtel particulier* where Daniel was brought up was a veritable museum. The portrait painter Jacques Emile Blanche, familiar with the most exclusive Parisian residences, called it a historical gem: "None of the houses that I have ever visited can compare with the Halévys', which recalled the Paris of the eighteenth century." [56] All the celebrities of the neighborhood seemed to revolve around the Halévys', attracted to their drawing room by the delights of good conversation and the hospitality of their hosts. In the same house lived Georges Bizet, the husband of Daniel's cousin, Geneviève. Farther down the Rue de Douai lived one of her less fortunate suitors, Maupassant, and an older but still fervent admirer, Gounod. The painters of the *quartier*—still traditionally associated with artists—were Degas, Manet, Gustave Doré, and Puvis de Chavannes, and within a short radius of the Halévy residence lived a whole galaxy of critics from *Le Journal des Débats* and *La Revue des Deux Mondes*—Edmond About, John Lemoinne, Francisque Sarcey, and others. Renan and Taine, Ludovic's colleagues at the Academy, were regular dinner guests, but a more frequent visitor and Halévy's favorite walking companion was his cousin Marcelin Berthelot the chemist.[57]

A precocious lad, Daniel seems to have taken full advantage of the intellectual opportunities provided by this choice environment. Surrounded by such overwhelming talent, it was inevitable that the impressionable adolescent should develop an inordinate deference for character, a deference already manifested in the very first entries of a diary which he faithfully kept from the age of sixteen until shortly before his death in 1962. The essentially derivative quality of Halévy's ideas can be traced to a youth almost too generously endowed with varied stimulation. It was as

---

[56] Blanche, *La Pêche aux souvenirs*, 108; see also Blanche, *Mes Modèles*, 100.

[57] Curtiss, *op. cit.*, 263, 253.

though the growth of his own creative genius was stunted by an excessive exposure to that of others. Intimidated by the sheer impossibility of emulating the talented men who revolved around the family circle, he inevitably succumbed to a certain diffidence combined with a characteristic bent for yielding to forceful personalities. Moreover, the very versatility of this ambiance fostered a propensity for a discursive intellect and a desultory curiosity, which despite its obvious advantages was to prove a decisive hindrance in Halévy's career. As a boy, he already showed a marked predilection for observation, for remaining ever alert to the unique delights afforded by his surroundings, rather than for setting out on an independent course of his own. And as an old man, looking back on the fond hopes and lost opportunities of his youth, dimly aware that he had somehow spent his life more as a spectator than as a participant, he wistfully remarked: "Well then, what about life—my own life, which has never lived up to those magnificently stirring and tender examples of my youth." [58]

Halévy's taste for an ethic of quality, and an unhurried, almost leisurely attitude, as distinct from mere dilettantism, were determined by the very conditions of his upbringing. Even within his own circle he always sought out those who displayed the more enduring qualities of heart and mind. When he later attempted to evoke the *genius loci* of the *Pays parisiens* of his gilded adolescence, he eschewed the more obvious celebrities to focus on those less prominent individuals who because of their personal integrity had left their mark on his memory. With more than a suggestion of self-vindication, a half avowal of personal failure, he justified his interest in the obscure by dismissing as unwarranted, the sanction of fame that often neglects less conspicuous qualities: "There are public virtues, which confer celebrity on

[58] Daniel Halévy, *Degas parle* . . . (Paris, 1960), 152.

some persons, even the most mediocre. . . . But there are
still other virtues, virtues of an intimate and private nature,
which are far more significant." [59]

It is not altogether futile to dwell on some of these now
forgotten family acquaintances who presided over the young
Halévy's early years, particularly since he himself later
attached a paramount importance to their lasting influence
on his character. Nor are they, for that matter, devoid of a
certain intrinsic charm of their own. Among those rescued
from oblivion in his autobiography was Mrs. Howland, who
had of the Anglo-Saxon nothing but her name, for she had
rashly married an American who, unable to endure the
tedium of Paris, promptly returned to his country, "thus
proving both his good sense and his good taste." [60] There was
also that intriguing idler Cavé whose sole claim to fame—
apart from the fact that he was Degas's closest friend—was
that, as Halévy tells us, ". . . his whole career had been
devoted to idleness. He had done nothing with his life;
nothing—absolutely nothing." [61] Cavé's mother had
achieved the rare feat of being the mistress of both Delacroix
and Ingres, and though her indolent son had acquired a
natural taste for art, the only position he ever held was that
of official stage censor, a sinecure requiring regular attend-
ance at all theater performances. Although certainly not an
exacting task, even this pleasant occupation did not suit for
long that "Ariel of inactivity." [62]

Then there was Mme Duclaux, nee Robinson, a gifted
English lady who was on intimate terms with Henry James,
George Moore, Browning, Pater, and others. First married to
James Darmesteter the Orientalist, she settled in Paris, and
after her husband's death married Emile Duclaux, the
founder of the Pasteur Institute. She was also noted for her

[59] Daniel Halévy, *Pays parisiens* (1929 ed.), 57; see also Daniel Halévy,
Agricol Perdiguier: Mémoires d'un compagnon (Moulins, 1914), 60.
[60] Halévy, *Pays*, 58.   [61] *Ibid.*, 63.   [62] *Ibid.*, 72.

salon where Halévy learned at an early age the art of polite conversation and graceful manners from such guests as Renan and Taine, Bourget and Barrès. For over half a century, she served as the reviewer of French literature for the *Times Literary Supplement*; as the exponent of English arts and letters in her adopted country, she played an important part as a cultural intermediary.[63]

But beyond doubt the single person who left the most permanent impression on the young Halévy during these formative years was the painter Degas. Precisely the same age as Daniel's father, Degas had been Ludovic's schoolmate at the Lycée Louis-le-Grand and had remained his constant friend and companion in the backstage of the Opéra, where their respective pursuits drew them every day.[64] An ingrained misanthrope, bitter, irascible, and austere, this solitary bachelor was virtually adopted by the Halévys. Degas seems to have found in the young Daniel the only outlet for his dried-up affections, treating him as a son and taking in hand his education.[65] But the impact that he made on the adolescent's mind went deeper than he knew. Through him, Daniel was to learn how to combine a decent respect for tradition with a proper regard for innovation. At a time when Impressionism was attempting to translate a broader image of man and nature, Degas's technique, striving to evoke the precise gesture and movement set within the limits of a tangible reality, seemed to stand for a more indigenous and concrete tradition in the visual arts.[66] He stoutly defended the old school of Ingres and Delacroix, who were rapidly passing out of fashion, while at the same time he

[63] *Times Literary Supplement* (London), Apr. 1, 1960, 207; Halévy paid her a posthumous tribute in *Les Trois Mary* (Paris, 1959), which includes extracts from her correspondence with Barrès.

[64] Halévy, *Degas parle*, 8.

[65] Daniel Halévy, "Carnets," entries for Aug., Sept., 1911.

[66] François Fosca, *Degas et Bonnard* (Paris, 1924), 13 ff.; *La Revue de Genève*, Feb., 1924, 253–257.

championed younger painters like Gauguin, continuing for his part to pursue a course of his own which opened new vistas in aesthetic sensibility.[67]

But although Degas doubtless contributed to shaping Halévy's taste, his impact was still more profound: it was essentially his strong personality which made the greatest impression on the younger man. With a highly independent viewpoint on all subjects, a lively wit, and a trenchant judgment, Degas had a rare talent for exposing all that was false and tawdry. By denouncing the cant and hypocrisy of current bourgeois morality, he undoubtedly paved the way for his young admirer's subsequent appreciation of Sorel's more systematic social criticism. For Degas, surprisingly enough, resembled Sorel in many ways, perhaps most strikingly in the peremptory character of his conversation and in his remarkably assertive personality. Like Sorel, he had a sharp tongue and an infinite capacity for devastating sarcasm, and his incisive observations, couched in telling epigrams and adorned with the appropriate tale and anecdote, left an indelible impression on all those who heard him talk.[68] Halévy's diary abounds in admiring comments on Degas's dazzling wit and provocative statements. As a lad of sixteen, he wrote: "Today M. Degas is coming for lunch. And to dine with Degas is to partake of the most superb banquet I can imagine. . . . To my mind, Degas is the very incarnation of intelligence." At twenty-three, after a visit to his nearby studio, he remarked: "Degas, what a man! Is it possible to listen to a more delightful speaker?" And in 1898 at the height of the Dreyfus Affair, which permanently severed his family's ties with the anti-Semitic painter,

[67] Halévy, Degas parle, 160.
[68] Cf. Joseph Hone, The Life of George Moore (London, 1936), 159; S. N. Behrman, Portrait of Max (New York, 1960), 133. On Sorel, see Pierre Andreu, Notre Maître, M. Sorel (Paris, 1953), 286–287; Georges Goriely, Le Pluralisme dramatique de Georges Sorel (Paris, 1962), 28.

Halévy, despite his militant Dreyfusism, insisted that he still identified Degas with his fondest memories. "There go," he exclaimed in despair, "the most splendid recollections of my youth. . . . This is civil war." [69]

To Halévy, Degas stood for that rare combination of a native popular tradition grafted on Orleanist values, the embodiment of a robust national temperament hewn out of native oak yet varnished with a fine finish. Degas was lionized by a society which he really despised; yet, although at odds with the beau monde, he reluctantly remained an integral part of it.[70] Le Journal des Débats was his daily newspaper and Proudhon his favorite author. In this Degas foreshadowed Halévy's ability to commit himself to the socialist cause while preserving his niche within the Establishment, which he, like Degas, despised and admired at the same time. Degas's disdain for politicians, his preoccupation with the moral essence of the popular soul, his sympathy for the simple folk of the Paris faubourgs and country hamlets that he regularly visited with the Halévys on their traditional excursions—all these sentiments, illogically combined with a firm and obstinate attachment to those liberal values somehow embodied in the polite conversation and good manners of upper class society, constituted the main elements in his character. They also became the most enduring forces shaping his protégé's sympathies. Halévy deliberately attached himself to Degas, and here again, by permanently identifying his most cherished beliefs with a strong, assertive personality, he demonstrated a need to express himself in a derivative manner. He not only ascribed to Degas many of the loyalties which he later acquired independently; he

---

[69] "Carnets," entries for Oct. 26, 1888; Nov. 4, 1895; Jan. 21, 1898.

[70] Daniel Halévy (ed.), Lettres de Degas, "Cahiers Verts," no. 9 (Paris, 1931), 53.

actually insisted on tracing these to the impact which, he contended, Degas had made on his early years.[71]

In this sense, if Degas occupied a unique position in Halévy's affections, it was largely because he fulfilled the young man's compulsive desire for identification. Halévy's cult of Degas was the first in a lifelong series of attachments to others: to Proudhon and Nietzsche among the figures of the past; to Sorel and Péguy, above all, among the living; but also, though to a lesser extent, to some of the more forceful writers whom he attracted to his "Cahiers Verts" in the thirties—Drieu la Rochelle and Arnaud Dandieu, for instance, and Robert Garric, and Jean Guéhenno. Yet it was the memory of Degas which held the choicest place in Halévy's heart, and none of the other objects of his hero-worship ever aroused quite the same devotion that he always preserved for the dead painter.

The importance of Degas in shaping Halévy's development can scarcely be exaggerated. Degas set a living example of the noble life, but his views on politics, art, and society also determined the direction of Halévy's beliefs. In particular, his contempt for mass democracy and electoral demagoguery and his intuitive perception of the simple grandeur of the common people were to become abiding articles of faith in Halévy's own outlook. It is significant that when in old age Halévy turned his thoughts to writing an autobiography, he was impelled to express his own life in terms of the man who had most decisively molded his youth and whose memory was so inextricably intertwined with his own reminiscences that the final product of his labors was, in effect, an impressionistic biography of Degas. It is no less significant that this volume *Degas parle . . .* , his last published work, should be written in the form of a dialogue. By

[71] "Carnets," entries for Sept. 3, 1921; Dec. 8, 1924.

gracefully blending retrospection with verbatim transcripts of Degas's conversation (drawn from a diary where, with faithful piety, he had committed not only his hero's very words but even his tone and gesture), Halévy succeeded in communicating the particular flavor of the man to whom, as he confessed: "I owe all that is finest in me." [72]

[72] Pp. 156–157.

CHAPTER II

The Early Years

❧

WITH Degas as his mentor, his parents and grandparents to watch over his education, and an older brother whose exceptional brilliance could only serve as a further incentive to excel, the young Daniel started life under the most auspicious circumstances. The cosy intimacy of his immediate surroundings and the cordial domestic ties that bound him to some of the most prominent families of his time also contributed to shaping a particularly urbane and leisurely mode of existence. "The dominant features of my life," he tells us, "have been delight and enchantment . . . , my private life has provided me with nothing but the purest joys."[1]

I

It was a sign of the Halévys' rising fortunes that Ludovic could now afford to send his two sons to Condorcet, the most distinguished right bank *lycée*, which counted such notable figures as Darlu and Mallarmé among its teachers. The gentle discipline that governed the school, the unusual intimacy that bound students and masters, and the quite remarkable caliber of the teaching staff had earned for Condorcet the reputation of being a particularly exciting place to study. Unlike other schools, Condorcet was not closed to the world outside, and because it was so receptive

---

[1] Cited by René Johannet, "Les Enchantements de Daniel Halévy," *La Minerve française*, Apr. 15, 1920, 170.

to current literary trends (Symbolism was at its height in the eighties), it was regarded as the most suitable stepping stone into the career of letters.

Elie Halévy had entered this charmed circle two years before Daniel,[2] paving the way for his brother's initiation to that vital stimulus to French *lycée* youth, the *professeur de philo*. At Condorcet, that venerable position was held by M. Darlu, under whose guidance Elie, together with two of his former schoolmates, Xavier Léon and Léon Bruncschvicg, founded the *Revue de Métaphysique et de Morale* in January 1893. Darlu's influence on Daniel, although less direct, was nonetheless important and perhaps even, as with his classmate Proust, more far-reaching than in his brother's case. Darlu's inspired teaching fired his imagination, but from his class of rhetoric he also learned the value of a dialectical discipline that served to keep in check his rambling curiosity.[3]

From the outset, Daniel displayed a predilection for literary pursuits rather than for scholarship in the stricter sense, and he was soon acknowledged as leader of a literary coterie among his fellow pupils, the most talented of whom was Proust. The other members of the circle were his cousin Jacques Bizet; Fernand Gregh the poet; Robert Dreyfus, critic and historian; the playwrights Louis de la Salle, Robert de Flers, and Gaston de Caillavet who was the son of Anatole France's mistress. From outside Condorcet, the

[2] Daniel's relationship with his brother, although always affectionate, was never really intimate, and in their later years their political opinions drew them apart. See Alain [Emile Chartier], *Correspondence avec Elie et Florence Halévy* (Paris, 1958), 13. The two are frequently mistaken for each other, as for instance in Luis Diez del Corral's *The Rape of Europe*, trans. by H. V. Livermore (London, 1959), 50.

[3] Daniel Halévy, "Carnets," entries for Mar. and Nov., 1889. Cf. Henri Massis, *D'André Gide à Marcel Proust* (Lyon, 1949), 34 ff. Darlu must be ranked with Alain and Bergson, who were also Paris *lycée* professors for many years, as among those teachers of the *classe de philo* who exerted a very real influence on their pupils.

group was joined by Gabriel Trarieux, Henri Barbusse, Léon Blum, and the musician Henri Rabaud. Guided by Mallarmé, their English teacher, these budding aspirants to literary fame took their first steps in letters soon after graduation by launching a magazine called *Le Banquet*, whose title, evoking Plato's *Symposium*, was meant as a tribute to both Mallarmé and M. Darlu.[4]

Le Banquet was in line with earlier college reviews, mostly handwritten and passed around among the students and to some of their parents and relatives. Among those which Halévy had edited before his final year were *La Revue Lilas*, *La Revue Verte* (a title, incidentally, which recurred in the twenties when he founded the "Cahiers Verts," a cross between Péguy's *Cahiers de la Quinzaine* and this earlier school magazine), and *La Revue de Seconde*. All these literary efforts, now valuable collectors' items, afforded their authors a chance to pour forth their creative energies and experiment in literary adventures. Though somewhat mannered and abounding in the inevitable pastiches of Baudelaire and the later Symbolists, the reviews also contain literary manifestos of one sort or another, as revolutionary as they were ephemeral. Thus, Halévy started his *Revue de Seconde* as a protest against the decadent prose of the day and announced the creation of a new school called Subtilism of which he was the self-proclaimed founder and leader. Yet for all their preciosity, many of the contributions to the

[4] The title was Halévy's idea. Cf. Laurent Lesage, *Marcel Proust and His Literary Friends* (Urbana, Ill., 1958), 45. See also André Ferré, *Les Années de collège de Marcel Proust* (Paris, 1960), who evokes the redoubtable M. Darlu and also reprints extracts from *Le Banquet*. Cf. Louis de Robert, *Comment Débuta Marcel Proust* (Paris, 1926); Jacques Emile Blanche, *Mes Modèles: Barrès, Proust, James, Moore* (Paris, 1928), 100 ff.; Jeanne-Marie Pouquet, *Le Salon de Mme Arman de Caillavet* (Paris, 1926), 194 ff., and Marcel Proust, *Lettres à Bibesco* (Lausanne, 1949), 90. On Condorcet, see especially George D. Painter, *Proust: The Early Years* (Boston and Toronto, 1959), 74 ff., but for a critical estimate see Julien Benda, *La Jeunesse d'un clerc* (Paris, 1936), 118.

reviews are not entirely devoid of merit. Proust, for one, always prized *Le Banquet* as having more than an anti-quarian value. In reply to Halévy's wry suggestion that their literary experiments be preserved for the sake of posterity, Proust summarized their chief virtue as lying, as he fancifully put it, in "the fleeting reflections of the mobility of imaginations at play." [5] This was certainly the case with his own contributions, *Les Plaisirs et les jours*, a collection of miscel-laneous essays, stories and poems, scattered here and there in *Le Banquet* and the earlier reviews, and containing many of the themes which recur in *A la Recherche du temps perdu.*[6]

Halévy's contributions were more modest, including frag-ments of a translation of Ibsen, an ambitious but unfinished tragedy in verse, and, in the second number, a pioneering study of Nietzsche. But it was largely thanks to his editorial perseverance that eight complete issues of *Le Banquet* were turned out between 1892 and 1893.[7] His father's assistance and the benevolence of Mme Straus also assured the little band of authors of early literary success. It was Mme Straus, for instance, who persuaded a reluctant Anatole France to write a preface for Proust's *Les Plaisirs et les jours,* and through the generosity of his father's friend Louis Ganderax, editor of *La Revue de Paris,* Daniel secured per-mission to use that review's printing press, thus giving a wider circulation to the literary efforts of his companions.[8] Through a series of luncheon parties at his home he also sought to promote his more talented friends' desire to achieve mutual recognition by bringing together his school-mates from Condorcet with Gide and Valéry, the young contributors to *La Conque,* rival journal of the Lycée Henri

---

[5] Painter, *Proust: The Early Years*, 76.

[6] Martin Turnell, *The Novel in France* (New York, 1958), 338, 340–342; Painter, *Proust: The Early Years*, 141–143; Lesage, *Proust*, 45.

[7] Fernand Gregh, *L'Age d'or* (Paris, 1947), 71 ff.

[8] Gregh, *L'Age d'or,* 160 ff.

IV. After these short-lived reviews had died a natural death, he used his family connections to help his friends in need, securing for Gregh an editorial post with Calmann-Lévy, his father's publisher, while *tante* Geneviève (as Halévy always called his cousin, Mme Straus), was persuaded to provide Robert Dreyfus with the position of legal counsel to the Rothschilds.[9] More important in advancing their careers was Halévy's role in introducing them to established literary circles. It was largely as a result of his initiative that many of his companions were furnished with an entrée into *La Revue Blanche*, whose editors virtually recruited their contributors in Mme Straus's salon. Gregh, Robert de Flers, and Henri Barbusse were particularly fortunate in this respect. Thus, it was under the shadow of Verlaine and Mallarmé, but also as the protégés of Mme Straus that Halévy and his friends made their literary debut.[10]

His aunt's salon, one of the most celebrated in Paris, was frequented by the leading personalities of the Third Republic, but it was not exclusively literary, nor—until the Dreyfus Affair split it asunder—was it ever merely political. The celebrities who came every Thursday to the Boulevard Haussmann were really attracted by the sheer charm and wit of its hostess, whose drawing room Proust once described as being in "the Meilhac and Halévy style." The only daughter of Fromental Halévy and the widow of Georges Bizet, she had remarried the leading attorney of the Rothschild family, but her social ascent was never marred by any trace of snobbishness or vanity. Mme Straus was a woman of unusual grace and beauty. Her famous portrait by Delaunay, which now hangs in the Louvre, had created a sensation at the 1878 salon. Proust had paid her the compliment of compar-

[9] Gregh, *Mon Amitié avec Marcel Proust* (Paris, 1958), 43.
[10] Gregh, *L'Age d'or*, 187 ff.; Léon Blum, *Souvenirs sur l'Affaire* (Paris, 1935), 27; Richard L. Stokes, *Léon Blum* (New York, 1937), 29–33.

ing her to the Mona Lisa, and Degas had implored Daniel's mother to be allowed the special favor of watching her comb her hair. She presided over the most famous artists, authors, and statesmen of her time: Forain and Degas, Paul Bourget, Anatole France, Jules Renard, Hervieu and Porto-Riche were honored to be her guests. From the Faubourg Saint-Germain came the aristocracy, the Comte Othenin d'Haussonville, proud descendant of Mme de Staël and a living symbol of Orleanism, the Princesse Mathilde for the Bonapartists, and Louis de Turenne representing the Legitimist nobility. She also received the diplomatic corps, Lord Lytton, the British ambassador, being one of the more frequent guests—and of course, Charles Haas, the first Jew ever to be admitted to the Jockey Club.[11]

In this ambiance the young Halévy naturally breathed the air of a society just one rung below the Faubourg Saint-Germain, a society where the great Parisian bourgeoisie and the aristocracy converged to set the tone of current taste and opinion. It was inevitable that such surroundings should increase his sympathies for the great *notables*, whose merits seemed enhanced in contrast to the ostentation which he associated with the gatherings at Mme Juliette Adam's and the other Opportunist salons. He preserved from his visits to Mme Straus a feeling that this was perhaps the last remaining link with that urbane set which Prévost-Paradol had frequented, and he tells us himself that listening to the nostalgic evocations of the vanished age of the Broglies and the Decazes, he was suddenly inspired with the ambition to write the story of "la fin des notables."[12]

Halévy's "Carnets" contains the most thorough chronicle of Mme Straus's salon until the Dreyfus Affair brought about its collapse. Like a Saint-Simon to the manner born,

---

[11] Painter, *Proust: The Early Years*, 112–115.

[12] Daniel Halévy, "Carnets," entry for May 17, 1897: "Je me mets à rêver à cette histoire de la Troisième. . . . C'est mon grand rêve."

he draws a charming portrait of his aunt presiding over her court. The galaxy of worthies who were drawn by her charm are evoked in lively sketches, but his diary also fixes such ephemeral details as the precise gesture, the tone of voice, even the exact seating arrangements around his aunt's dinner table. It was from this setting that Halévy derived his quest for a brilliance that was to give his books and essays the peculiar sparkle of good conversation. His graceful prose, mellow but also incisive, flowed from the fundamental salon postulate which demanded that intelligent people should always strive to shine, and which condemned inarticulateness as an unpardonable sin. In this sense, his aunt's salon made for ease of writing: Halévy's essays could never be dull, though perhaps for the same reason they could never be really profound.[13]

His own evocation of this society has, of course, been overshadowed by Proust's more imaginative reconstruction of *The Guermantes' Way,* for it was by sitting at Mme Straus's feet that Halévy's friend found the inspiration for *A la Recherche du temps perdu.*[14] It was Daniel's aunt who opened for him the way to the Faubourg Saint-Germain and all the rich delights that its titled denizens held for the aspiring author. Proust met many of the real characters who served as the models for the literary creations of his great novel at the salon on the Boulevard Haussmann. Charles Haas and Emile Straus were amalgamated into Swann, Anatole France was transformed into Bergotte (also inspired in part by Henri Bergson), and Mme Straus herself was recast as the Duchesse de Guermantes.[15]

[13] Cf. Julien Benda, *Les Cahiers d'un clerc: 1936–1949* (Paris, 1949), 274–275.
[14] Gabriel Marcel, review of the second edition of Halévy's *Pays parisiens* in *Europe Nouvelle,* Aug. 14, 1932, 978; Marcel Proust, *Correspondence générale* (Paris, 1930–1936), VI, 232–233.
[15] Gregh, *Mon Amitié,* 43; Blanche, *Mes Modèles,* 103–111. On Haas, see Painter, *Proust: The Early Years,* 115–119.

Halévy deserves some of the credit for encouraging the young Proust's literary endeavors. The latter has immortalized him in *Jean Santeuil*, where Halévy can be identified as the hero's tormentor who cruelly bullied the delicate and extremely vulnerable child that the hero was. Halévy recalled that "there was something about him which we found unpleasant. His kindness and tender attentions seemed mere mannerisms and poses, and we took occasion to tell him so to his face. Poor unhappy boy, we were beastly to him." [16] Yet Halévy could never bring himself to deprive his friend of the kind of encouragement for which he yearned; and although his first premonitions of Proust's homosexuality came to him in the form of embarrassing advances, he spared no effort to further his career. Proust, for his part, always dreaded his friend's sarcasm, surpassed only by Elie's.[17] Nor could he as a social climber, hankering for the amenities of Mme Straus's salon, conceal his envy for his more favored companion who accepted such pleasures as a matter of course.

These somewhat fatuous pursuits foreshadow some of the dominant traits that were to mark the character of a Halévy grown to manhood. It was during these years that he gradually discovered that he was best suited to act as a mediator, promoting the advancement of those who were more gifted than himself. And what was still a somewhat uncertain critical judgment matured over the years to make him one of the foremost critics of his generation, whose name became associated with the most celebrated publishing venture of the inter-war years. Placed in charge of the "Cahiers Verts" by Bernard Grasset in the twenties, Halévy cast his net with such discrimination that scarcely any of the

[16] *Pays parisiens* (rev. ed.; Paris, 1932), 19; cited by Painter, *Proust: The Early Years*, 77.

[17] Painter, *Proust: The Early Years*, 78, 216; Proust, *Correspondence*, IV, 175.

outstanding postwar crop of writers escaped his attention.[18] Yet the very success of this endeavor provided him with the modest satisfaction that by fostering his natural predilection to act as a foil to others, he had, in fact, conformed to the real bent of his talents. Looking back as a mature editor on what he regarded as a life well spent, championing worthy causes and lending his support to promising authors, he noted that his vocation for acting as a go-between could be traced to these early years at Condorcet:

The lives of others are constantly impinging on my own. This is a difficulty which I have always encountered. I have always sought and enjoyed the spectacle of intellect and character: Péguy, Proudhon, Sorel. . . . I have sketched portraits. . . . I was drawn to Degas. . . . And now, it is Garric, Guéhenno, Chamson, Jouve who arouse my curiosity—but this, after all, is the main thing: to keep in touch with these problems.

But there is more than a slight note of regret in his further reflection that such stubborn inquisitiveness, by absorbing all his energies, had also contributed to hindering his own self-fulfillment: "Well then, what about myself? My very curiosity deprives me of any personal ambition." [19]

II

For the *jeunesse dorée* of the Lycée Condorcet, the decade of the nineties was a time of great expectations. To those who, like Halévy, had been spared the worry of earning a living, literary ambition seemed to be the be-all and the end-all of existence. It is important to underline the literary orientation of these young men. Living in a circle totally divorced from politics, imbued with a consuming interest in arts and letters, they existed in a kind of vacuum where the latest *beau mot* of Forain or the dramatic review of *La*

[18] Jean Guéhenno, *La Foi difficile* (Paris, 1958), 92; Jean de Fabrègues, "Daniel Halévy," *La France Catholique*, Jan. 29, 1960.
[19] "Carnets," entry for Oct. 17, 1924.

Revue de Paris eclipsed electoral results, cabinet changes, or social reform.

The generation of 1870 was born in the shadow of Sedan and the Commune. The former had swept away the glittering splendor of the Empire, and the latter, by crushing the menace of a proletarian revolution, had at least temporarily seemed to lay the labor problem to rest. The establishment of the Republic had resulted almost by accident from the rivalries of the provincial gentry, the Opportunists and the electoral committees from the Midi. The great Parisian bourgeoisie had played a negligible role in the decisive political maneuvers at Versailles. Discredited by the growing sympathy it had shown for the fallen Empire, it was viewed with hostility by Opportunists, Radicals, and Legitimists alike. For their part, the Parisian *notables,* secretly hankering after their lost supremacy, anticipated the future with foreboding. Their salons' scorn for a National Assembly of rustics was surpassed only by their fear of the specter of the *nouvelles couches* evoked in Gambetta's fiery speeches. During the dark days of the Commune they had rallied behind Thiers, grudgingly acknowledged as the savior of the social order from the menace of the Paris insurrection. But with Jules Grévy at the Elysée and the *petites gens* coming into their own, the *fait accompli* of the Third Republic came to be regarded with haughty disdain.

Halévy's milieu cannot, of course, be called Legitimist, although it could hardly resist casting an envious eye in the direction of the titled nobility of the Faubourg Saint-Germain, aping its taste and manners while at the same time scarcely concealing its contempt for the political ineptitude of Chambord. Nor did it choose to call itself Bonapartist, an obviously discredited term which was to become associated with such adventurers as Déroulède and Boulanger, who drew their support from totally different middle-class elements. Although the political fortunes and social eminence of this milieu were indeed closely identified with the Second Empire, whose mode of life it had epitomized to some extent, it was in fact quite distinct both politically and socially from the defunct regime with which it has commonly been associated.

This society called itself "Orleanist"—but this was no more than a convenient label setting it apart from the Opportunists, the *nouveaux riches* and the provincial cliques who rose to power with the new order. Whether from sheer necessity or a quite genuine distaste for politics, these self-styled "Orleanists" deliberately adopted an attitude of political indifference. Yet if they dismissed affairs of state as beneath their dignity, they still held on to their dominant position in the realm of letters by claiming an exclusive right to set the tone for current taste and opinion. Having preserved a quasi monopoly of the Institut and the leading Parisian reviews, these Orleanists formed a set which survived the collapse of the Empire by maintaining its predominance in the republic of letters, thus succeeding in casting themselves in the role of an apolitical coterie of literati unlikely to disturb the new establishment. Until the Dreyfus revolution transformed French society along more egalitarian lines, their authority as the sole guardians of arts and letters was beyond dispute. Their social and cultural preeminence during the first decades of what was nominally a democratic and antielitist regime was the result of their own political prudence.

But if this political neutrality was itself a condition for survival, the Orleanists' preclusive claim to cultural distinction also invested them with a special attraction for the new rulers of France. The republic of letters over which the *notables* presided became an indispensable adjunct to the elevation of the republic of Opportunists. Once the Seize Mai had finally settled the legality of the regime, the Opportunist *arrivistes* inevitably succumbed to the attrac-

DANIEL HALÉVY AND HIS TIMES

tion of the salons which could alone give their Republic the
dignity that it lacked. The Orleanists, for their part, were not
averse to extending their favors to the politicians, and by the
eighties they had gradually come to terms with a Republic
which, for all its shortcomings, seemed assured of permanence. This fusion was not without its obvious advantages,
for although the Orleanists might protest that they had been
merely forced to make a virtue of necessity, they had little
cause to deplore what for them was a most profitable
bargain. No longer reproached for their past, and increasingly at odds with the die-hard monarchists, they were
welcomed into the political fold on their own terms: their
sons secured posts in the *grands corps d'état*, while their
supremacy in the world of letters remained virtually un-
challenged.[20]

Daniel Halévy's sympathies and antipathies were inevitably shaped by these external conditions into which he was
born. Raised during the very time when this *modus vivendi*
was being reached, he was predisposed almost from birth to
regard literary pursuits as the nearly exclusive domain of his
class. An almost inbred contempt for democratic politics can
also be traced to the same source, and he recalled, for
instance, that in his youth political discussion was proscribed
from a home pervaded with a stubborn attachment to the
Orleanist values of the past. But he made it clear that while
he shared the family nostalgia harking back to Orleanist
forbears, this ideal was less a matter of political allegiance
than a peculiar temper derived from Mme de Staël or
Benjamin Constant.[21]

Halévy's Orleanist presumptions were, of course, of dubi-

[20] Cf. Ludovic Halévy, *Trois Dîners avec Gambetta, passim*. See also
Daniel Halévy, "Remarques," *Société d'Histoire de la Troisième République*,
Dec. 16, 1938, 140–144; and René Rémond, *La Droite en France* (2d ed.;
Paris, 1963), 82–91.

[21] Frédéric Lefèvre, *Une Heure avec . . .* (Paris, 1924), 163; cf.
Charles Péguy, *Victor-Marie, Comte Hugo*, 162.

ous validity. Yet there can be no doubt that the conditions of his upbringing, reinforced by subsequent attachments, produced in him a very real sense of affinity with a tradition that he came to regard quite legitimately as his own. One of Halévy's more discerning biographers defined his "tender and meditative soul, refined, sober and graceful," in terms of an environment "which recalls that elusive atmosphere of the years 1825–1835." [22] It is more the rarefied liberalism of that bygone age, rather than any clear-cut political doctrine which distinguished it, that should be stressed. Indeed, Halévy's Orleanist loyalties can only be evoked in terms of such an elusive atmosphere, and this atmosphere itself can be directly ascribed—as he himself insisted—to those tangible domestic and parental influences to which he attached such paramount importance. In 1906 at the very height of his dedication to Sorel's theories of revolutionary syndicalism, he could frankly confide in his "Carnets": "I feel so strongly Orleanist—but in such an unorthodox manner!" And after a futile attempt to define the precise character of his fugitive Orleanism, he confessed that it could only be reduced to a certain atmosphere which prevailed in his home: "Molded by family and my education; a dweller in old homes, repositories of a long past—if I should forget this, I would be mutilated." [23]

This singular trait in Daniel Halévy's character was the chief source of delight to those who sought his company. All his friends have confirmed that the secret of his charm lay precisely in a certain evanescent quality which he himself, even in the intimacy of his diary, was incapable of expressing in writing. Despite the innumerable testimonies of friends and admirers, it is perhaps the reflections of one of his most persistent detractors (who shared with Péguy the dubious honor of having been challenged by Halévy to a duel) which

[22] Réne Johannet, *Itinéraires d'intellectuels* (Paris, 1920), 42.
[23] Entry for Aug. 8, 1906.

deserve to be noted. To this observer, Halévy's home and the memories that it enshrined seemed to be an integral part of his personality. M. Jean Guéhenno, the son of a socialist cobbler from Brittany, with something of the *normalien's* vanity, could scarcely conceal his envy as he was initiated into the marvels of his benefactor's home. His account of the *hôtel particulier* at 39, Quai de l'Horloge is a fitting commentary on the extract from Halévy's diary cited above.[24]

Overlooking the poplars of the Seine from the Ile de la Cité, it seemed to represent the quintessence of Daniel Halévy, "culture itself, what time alone can create." To the young revolutionary the stately mansion stood as a symbol of all that he loathed: "It was the very first house where I could see all those things which I had sworn to despise—tradition in all its power and all its majesty." Generations of artists and artisans had succeeded in transforming what had once been the Bréguet workshop into a residence distinguished for its "simple elegance":

The whole place was like a tranquil soul, a living memory inhabited by lovely pictures blended together by a *genius loci*. . . . As you opened a door, you never knew where you would step in . . . into which staircase or century. It could be Louis XVI or Louis Philippe or either of the two Napoleons. The house was like an historical puzzle. . . . It was a rare advantage to grow up in the midst of such splendid memories, to learn of the past from the very walls which surrounded you. All that you touched, all that caught your eye would inevitably shape your sensibility and set you on the path of good taste and genuine beauty.[25]

Moreover, an abhorrence for the Republic seemed to flow directly from such a setting, and M. Guéhenno correctly remarked: "Halévy was by birth and by family tradition, a conservative bourgeois who could hardly avoid despising *la*

[24] Guéhenno, *La Foi difficile*, 89–95.　　[25] *Ibid.*, 95.

Gueuse." [26] Robert Dreyfus, less favored in his pedigree, likewise envied his friend's good fortune. But he added that Halévy's heredity also shaped his lively imagination, fostering "a taste for novelty and an exceptionally keen receptivity to literary beauty." [27] René de Kérallain, a Breton noble who over the years constantly encouraged Halévy in his literary endeavors endorsed this view in a somewhat flamboyant letter: "You are endowed with the most remarkable literary virtues. . . . You are a master of poetry and prose. . . . You possess all the natural and acquired gifts of the literary profession. . . ." [28]

Scarcely insensitive to such encouragement, Halévy wasted no effort in grooming himself for the *métier littéraire* to which he seemed naturally destined. Like the rest of his generation of writers he was at first swept by the current literary movement which, rebelling against that intermediate phase of Symbolism that went under the name of Parnasse, provided a fertile field for experiment in the conveniently vague theory of "art for art's sake." His earlier contributions to *Le Banquet* had already conformed to this trend. After leaving school, but still under the aegis of Mallarmé, he published some verse and the traditional pastiches of *l'Après-midi d'un faune* in *La Revue Blanche*, the most *avant-garde* publication of the nineties. At the same time, his first prose efforts, mostly mannered accounts of Italian journeys and sketches of artists and authors he had encountered, easily found their way into *La Revue de Paris*.

Toward the Republic, Halévy's sentiments during these years can best be described as indifferent if not downright hostile. As a lad he had even gone as far as to cheer for the man on the black charger who, by challenging the prosaic regime, could not fail to arouse his enthusiasm for the

[26] *Ibid.,* 90.
[27] Robert Dreyfus, *De M. Thiers à Marcel Proust* (Paris, 1939), 66.
[28] René de Kérallain, *Correspondence* (Quimper, 1933–1935), III, 287.

sparkle of the epopee—but the Boulangist zeal of an adolescent cannot, of course, be taken too seriously.[29] His
disdain for the Republic was nonetheless sincere. Unlike
Julien Benda or even Péguy whose loyalty to the Republic
flowed from a genuine gratitude to a regime identified with
equality of opportunity and a career open to talent, Halévy
owed nothing to the Republic and could therefore afford to
ignore it, even denigrate it with a clear conscience.[30]

If he expressed any political opinions at all during the
years that immediately preceded the Dreyfus Affair, these
could most suitably be defined as anarchist. His literary
pretensions and would-be rebelliousness inclined him to view
with sympathy the intransigence of a group of older men,
themselves more artists than political agitators, who challenged the Republic in the name of a theory of absolute
individualism. Judging by the entries in his diary, Halévy
seemed to think that philosophical anarchism was the
natural counterpart of his literary principles. In keeping with
the spirit of La Revue Blanche, his own political reflections
took the form of defying all established authority, Republican or other.

Between 1891 and 1896, in the years that spanned his
graduation from Condorcet to the outbreak of the Dreyfus
Affair, his "Carnets" reveal a growing sympathy for anarchist
ideas, which were gaining ground in many Parisian circles.
He subscribed to La Révolte, the fiery journal that Jean
Grave was publishing from his garret on the Rue
Mouffetard, read Kropotkin, copying large extracts from his
work in his "Carnets," delighted in the verbal violence of
Octave Mirbeau and Sébastien Faure, and carried on a
spirited correspondence with Paul Adam, unreservedly sub-

[29] Extract from "Carnets," 1897; reprinted in Degas parle . . . (Paris,
1960), 121.
[30] Cf. Benda, La Jeunesse d'un clerc, 38; André Spire, Souvenirs à bâtons
rompus (Paris, 1959), 7.

scribing to his apology of crime. Undeterred by the anarchists' excesses culminating in Vaillant's notorious plot in 1893, he maintained a perplexing attachment for such disreputable principles until the sobering realities revealed by the Dreyfus Affair finally brought him to his senses.

There was, of course, much in the young Halévy's attitude which smacked of a dilettante's affectation. By styling himself an anarchist, even within the privacy of his diary, he was deliberately striking a pose, but he was also reacting to the restless spirit of a decade in which, as Barrès put it, "boredom yawned as it contemplated a faded positivist universe." [31] To Halévy, as to so many other of his well-to-do right bank companions, anarchism was more than a passing fancy, a convenient pretext for assuming heroic airs. It also pointed the way to the passionate upheaval precipitated by the Dreyfus Affair, which afforded the same young men with a more suitable opportunity to break free from the dead hand of positivism.

The prevalent philosophy of scientism had greatly contributed to discoloring life. By confining all intellectual endeavor within the rigid limits of naturalist laws it had dried up the sources of spontaneity and stifled the turbulent spirit of the rising generation. Admittedly, to those who displayed genuine talent, Symbolism opened up rich literary prospects. The pioneering poetics of Verlaine and Mallarmé provided many with the inducement to strike out on an independent course which would satisfy the instincts of rebellious youth. A poet like Gregh, a novelist like Gide, even a critic like Blum, are cases in point. But to Halévy, all too conscious of his inferior talents, such a course seemed hazardous, and it was by his choice of a career that he was to express his personal defiance. Immediately after his gradua-

[31] Maurice Barrès, *Taches d'encre*, cited in Agathon [Henri Massis and Alfred de Tarde], *Les Jeunes Gens d'aujourd'hui* (Paris, 1919), 233. For this period see James Joll, *The Anarchists* (London, 1964), 149–173.

tion, he startled family and friends by proclaiming his resolve to study Semitic languages. This was a most singular decision, for whereas a course of study at the Sorbonne, the law faculty, or even the Ecole des Sciences Politiques (where many of his friends such as Proust and Spire pursued their studies) was a natural stepping stone to a literary vocation, Oriental studies could have no possible relevance for a man of letters and required attending the obscure Ecole des Langues Orientales, isolated from the heart of Parisian literary activity.

Yet it was precisely from this that the young rebel seemed anxious to escape. Weary of the artificial restraints imposed by the literary coteries to which he had been introduced at an unusually early age, and increasingly convinced of his creative limitations, he was anxious to assert his own individuality in this highly unorthodox manner. His resolution to enter that school and to submit to the rigors of an austere discipline was also partly prompted by a desire to emulate his brother, who had been admitted first in his class to the Ecole Normale.[32] Already well versed in modern languages and the classics, he hoped, no doubt, that a strict training in philology would help to keep in check his desultory habits. Whatever his motives, he did well in his studies, mastering Arabic, Hebrew, and even Aramaic, and he graduated with a dissertation on the decline of the 'Umayyad Caliphate, a topic anticipating, in its theme of aristocratic decadence, his *La Fin des notables.*[33]

But what chiefly determined Halévy's choice of a career was the example of Renan, whose pioneering works on Semitic philology he was reading with juvenile avidity during these years. Since he never pursued his early academic interests, it was ultimately Renan's more general works, such

[32] "Carnets," entries for 1891, 1892, confirmed by personal communication: Daniel Halévy.

[33] Johannet in *Le Temps*, June 4, 1936.

as the *Dialogues et fragments philosophiques* and the other meditative essays, rather than his scholarly monographs, which made the more lasting impression; and he always maintained that the great sage's "speculations, doubts and literary rambles" never failed to provide him with constant delight.[34]

The persistence of Halévy's admiration for the man whom he always acknowledged as his undisputed master gives us a clue to the character of his own moral development. His abiding loyalty to moral skepticism, which was to fall into disrepute by the end of the nineties, serves only to underline his independent position, even among his own contemporaries. It is perhaps this uncommon capacity to remain in tune with an elusive philosophical mood which, more than anything else, sets him apart from others, and which in turn predisposed him to welcome with a discernment rare for his times the provocative ideas of Sorel, whose debt to Renan was equally great. The true measure of Halévy's originality as a critic is demonstrated by the fact that he stood almost alone in championing a moral tradition that ran counter to prevailing trends. Yet it should be noted that what had originally drawn him to the *Essais de morale et de critique* was that its author was his teacher of Semitic philology, and it was only later, largely under the influence of Sorel, that what had been a source of intellectual edification became also a moral guide.

It is difficult to conceive today the extent to which Renan —and only to a lesser degree Taine—held in thrall the generation who reached manhood during the nineties. It has become commonplace to regard these two eminent thinkers as the most authoritative exponents of a positivism reaching its apogee at the turn of the century, as the high priests of an

[34] Halévy, review of *Jugements* by Henri Massis, *La Revue de Genève*, Sept. 1923, 357; cf. Agathon, *L'Esprit de la nouvelle Sorbonne* (Paris, 1911), 13.

all-powerful school of philosophical determinism in which the late nineteenth century was steeped. Yet if each in his own way preserved something of that initial faith in science which they transmitted from their teacher Auguste Comte, they differed radically both in style and temperament from the naive scientism associated with Spencer or Littré. Neither Renan nor Taine can possibly be identified with the kind of optimism with which their English counterpart espoused Social Darwinism, and the egalitarian principles propounded by their compatriot Littré on the basis of crude Comtian postulates was rejected by both as incompatible with their own elitist views. To Halévy's contemporaries, it was Littré who was regarded as the real interpreter of positivism in France, as the official spokesman of a systematic social theory that was invoked as the final vindication for the creation of a republican form of government. Hostile to this radical version of Comte's ideas, Renan and Taine faced the future of their country with frank misgivings. Rising above their youthful faith in the inevitability of social progress, they stood out as the champions of a moral skepticism that ran counter to the high hopes raised by the establishment of the new Republic.

The conservative drift of their ideas did not, however, detract from the essence of Comte's legacy. As social critics, both Taine and Renan merely adapted those conservative elements already inherent in positivist thinking to the troubled conditions of their changing times. As disillusioned liberals of the generation of 1848, mellowed by age and experience, they leaned increasingly in the direction of a traditionalism that was completely at odds with the democratic principles of the Third Republic.[35] The humiliation of Sedan followed by the sobering spectacle of the Commune and the subsequent instability culminating in the fragile

---

[35] Halévy, *La Fin des notables* (Paris, 1930), 70–80.

compromise of the Third Republic hardly seemed in their view to conform with the optimistic tenor of the positivist doctrine. The intellectual temper of a France deeply split by irreconcilable political and social divisions was a far cry from the self-confidence which prevailed across the Channel. *La Réforme intellectuelle et morale de la France* and *Les Origines de la France contemporaine*, both of which appeared in the wake of the national disasters of the seventies, illustrate the particular twist that both Renan and Taine had given to positivist thought in France.

It was not until the Radical excesses following the Dreyfusard victory had reinforced his doubts on the validity of the principles of 1789 that Halévy returned with renewed eagerness to Taine's more austere condemnation of the French Revolution.[36] More immediately, it was Renan who made the greater appeal to his young mind. The source of this attraction lay essentially in Renan's greater refinement and literary grace. But more important, by evading the necessity of taking a firm political stand in the name of a delicate personal sensibility, Renan also provided Halévy with a convenient justification for his own ambiguous sentiments toward the Republic. Halévy's vicarious identification with Renan's varying and often contradictory shades of feeling on this crucial matter, no less than on others, had the unique advantage of not forcing him, in his turn, to declare himself for or against the Republic. Without necessarily proclaiming his hostility to democratic institutions Halévy could remain silent on their obvious shortcomings.[37]

It was Renan who had proclaimed that "truth lies in shades of meaning," and by conforming to this maxim in his

[36] Halévy, *Histoire d'une histoire* (Paris, 1939), 24 ff.; on Taine, see his "Notes sur Taine et *Les Origines de la France contemporaine*," in *Le Journal des Débats: Revue Hebdomadaire*, Jan., 1928, 7–30. Cf. Albert Thibaudet, "Au Centenaire de Taine," *Nouvelle Revue française*, July 15, 1928, 89–91.

[37] "Carnets," entries for Oct., 1898; May, 1912; Dec., 1927.

own works of erudition as well as in those of more topical concern, he not only enriched a French positivist tradition that, through his medium, verged on an almost total nihilism, but also gave to his ex cathedra pronouncements a convincing tone of sincerity and a certain inner coherence. Renan had an infinite capacity for indulging in paradox, excelling in the art of concealing his thought under layers of gracefully contrived prose. His genius consisted in winning over his reader by the sheer elegance of his style. From his youthful *L'Avenir de la science*—written in 1848, prudently discarded, and not published until 1890—up to the dark and foreboding *Dialogues et fragments philosophiques* of his final years, all his public utterances, evasive yet persuasive, could not fail to captivate an increasingly appreciative audience. His social theory, at least in its essentials, seemed to flow from the central postulate that science had irrevocably replaced orthodox religion. But his extreme caution impelled him to qualify this sweeping contention with such an elaborate array of conditions that his final judgment appeared to be a plain warning that the realm of certainty revealed by rational inquiry must necessarily be confined within very strict limits. His final verdict could, in fact, be interpreted as a repudiation of the naive optimism of the entire positivist approach, so that paradoxically, his main achievement could be legitimately regarded as having helped to undermine the very foundations of that moral rationalism which he was supposed to uphold.[38]

In particular, the upshot of his conveniently enigmatic pronouncements on the destiny of France and the Republic was that the author of *La Réforme intellectuelle et morale de la France*—which had in no uncertain terms advocated a royalist restoration and a hierarchical organization of society

[38] Albert L. Guérard, *French Prophets of Yesterday* (London, 1913), 227 ff.; Gabriel Monod, *Les Maîtres de l'histoire* (Paris, 1926), xiii; Georges Guy-Grand, "Frères ennemis," *La Grande Revue*, Apr., 1934, 594.

as the essential conditions for national survival—could with apparently equal conviction vindicate in his *Caliban* the advent of the common man, arguing that democracy in France was capable of infinite improvement. Such was the ambiguity of his position that it is not difficult to see how Renan could easily become all things to all men. By Charles Maurras and the Action Française he was regarded as a monarchist, and Louis Dimier placed him in a prominent position among his *Maîtres de la contre-révolution.*[39] By Barrès and the Opportunists alike he was considered a sound Republican, consecrated by officialdom as one of the founding fathers of the Republic. His *L'Avenir de la science* was invoked as the final authority for Ferry's educational reforms, yet he was accorded an official state funeral in his native clerical Brittany in the teeth of violent nationalist opposition. Whereas Drumont hailed him as the founder of scientific anti-Semitism, his own family always counted him among the Dreyfusards. The Church denounced this unfrocked priest, while at the same time his immensely popular *Life of Jesus* led many Catholics back to the fold and contributed in no small way to the religious revival which marked the end of the century.[40]

Perhaps the shrewdest estimate of Renan was made by Péguy, who dismissed this renegade Catholic as nothing more than a prolific "supplier of ideas." [41] Yet it was precisely for this reason that Péguy's dilettante companion had fallen under Renan's spell. Renan's vacillations, which Péguy rejected as fatuous or morally subversive, was welcomed by the young Halévy, who could never resist the

[39] Charlotte Muret, *French Royalist Doctrines in France since the Revolution* (New York, 1933), 239.
[40] H. W. Wardman, *Ernest Renan: A Critical Biography* (London, 1964), 208; Dora Bierer, "Renan and His interpreters," *Journal of Modern History*, December, 1953, 375.
[41] Cited in Jean and Jérôme Tharaud, *Notre Cher Péguy* (Paris, 1926), I, 39.

delight of intellectual stimulation. The exquisite diversity of his thought, which to other Frenchmen bound by traditional ties of race or religion might seem dangerously heretical or inconsistent, aroused the sympathy of Halévy, whose heredity spared him such inconvenient hindrances. Like his father or his Saint-Simonian grandfather, he could not fail to be enraptured by the sheer éclat of originality, and he succumbed to Renan's studied elegance with the same enchantment that marked all his other sympathies.

It is hardly surprising, however, that Renan had a totally different effect on others. The incredible suppleness of his reasoning, circumscribed by a maddening dialectic, soon deprived him of the support of many admirers no longer able to find a single shred of positive guidance in his rambling speculations. To those who, like Romain Rolland or the younger Henri Massis, sought from their elders some guiding principle of action, Renan's pervasive prudence inevitably proved intolerable, the initial delight produced by his subtle evasiveness ultimately yielding to doubt and confusion after the fascination of his intellectual magic had been dispelled. Where Halévy found an inexhaustible source of inspiration, others discovered no escape from the feeling that Renan had only contributed to stifling their moral convictions. From his "cloister" on the Rue d'Ulm, a sentimental romantic like Romain Rolland suffered untold agony under the yoke that Renan imposed on his free will, while the unrepentant Catholic Henri Massis, following in the steps of the reconverted Péguy, protested that his deepest religious beliefs had been irreparably warped by the "intellectual debauchery," as he put it, "of Renan's truths and half-truths." [42]

No less than Romain Rolland, Péguy or even Massis, Halévy could hardly escape from the prevailing *fin-de-siècle*

[42] Romain Rolland, *Le Cloître de la rue d'Ulm: Journal de Romain Rolland à l'Ecole Normale, 1886–1889* (Paris, 1952), 27, 200, 374; Massis, *Evocations*, Vol. I, *Souvenirs, 1905–1911* (Paris, 1931), 52, 224–227.

melancholy, from the repressive sentiment of feeling hemmed in by a rigorous scientism. But unlike the others, he did not trace the source of this malaise to Renan. Instead, the provocative thinker never failed to satisfy his almost voluptuous craving for an intellectual "experience" that stimulated his imagination long after the initial impression had passed. He tells us himself that it was Renan who constantly stirred his curiosity by unfolding before his marvelled gaze the most thrilling spectacle of man's progress through the ages, while at the same time placing him on his guard against the pitfalls of human frailty. Renan's example served both as a spur and a restraint, and if Halévy too never quite escaped from a certain nagging doubt about ultimate values, this in itself provided him with a mysterious gratification, a kind of intellectual masochism, which he seems to have secretly enjoyed. As late as the nineteen thirties, when Renan's memory no longer exercised the slightest influence, Halévy still preserved a boundless admiration for his *directeur de conscience*. It was Renan, he maintained, who had sustained his fancy by evoking both the grandeur and the fragility of man's creative endeavors, and who, above all, had taught him the supreme virtue of approaching all human problems from every possible angle.[43]

Renan's tactful restraint was admirably adapted to suit Halévy's needs, setting the pattern for his own eclectic approach and accounting to a large extent for the persistent ambiguities marking the whole course of his intellectual progress. By adopting Renan's method of approach, he could always conveniently rationalize the paradoxical attachments that were to beset his career. Justifying his own irresolution by invoking Renan's example, he could persuade himself of the essential validity of his own shifting loyalties, which

[43] Halévy, preface to Marcel-Henri Jaspar, *Ernest Renan et sa république* (Paris, 1934), x. Cf. Emile Faguet, *Politiques et moralistes du dix-neuvième siècle* (Paris, 1900), III, 376, 379.

plainly disturbed him far less than one might at first suppose. His conduct during the Dreyfus Affair, for instance, when he was carried away by a revolutionary zeal that he later deplored, could be easily redressed by invoking the necessity of broadening his "experience" in the name of a Renanien empiricism.[44] In the same way, after all the vagaries of his contradictory commitments to the *notables* and the salons on the one hand, and to revolutionary syndicalism and Péguy on the other, he could always fall back with a maddening equanimity on the serene detachment that constituted the very essence of the Renanien attitude.

Such an attitude not only helped to explain Halévy's quite remarkable nimbleness in reconciling contradictions; it also had the further advantage of furnishing him with a valid justification for gracefully retreating from imprudent loyalties. The "Apologie pour notre passé," the poignant repudiation of his recklessness during the Dreyfus Affair, is an example in point. This agonizing reappraisal of youthful folly, in which he sought to demonstrate by an exasperatingly subtle reasoning that his audacity was guided by an inner logic, illustrates the particular resilience of this special dispensation. In much the same way, Halévy invoked this same dispensation to explain all his subsequent sympathies, always resorting to some convenient corrective or qualification that absolved him from personal guilt and permitted him to resume the balance and poise of a *moraliste.*[45]

Yet like his master, Halévy could not altogether avoid participating in events. Torn between the impulse of "revolutionary hope," as he called it, and a very genuine reverence for tradition, his entire career is marked by this disquieting ambiguity. And if the prudent tone of the

[44] Halévy, *Luttes et problèmes* (Paris, 1911), 52.
[45] Cf. his own version of Renan's *Dialogues et fragments philosophiques,* "Entretien," *Les Lettres,* April, 1907, 203–210.

moraliste sometimes gives way to partisanship, this very ambivalence invests his judgment with a certain liveliness, which does not necessarily detract from the usual solemnity of the moral critic. For underlying his conflicting attachments we can discern a fundamental pessimism—a certain caution that pervades his writing, and which alone gives it some semblance of unity.

During the restless decade of the nineties, on the eve of his commitment to a revolutionary crusade, Halévy was impregnated with Renan's reflections on the heritage of the French Revolution. These reflections were calculated to dispel the allurements of intemperate action and place him on his guard against all forms of revolutionary enthusiasm that either directly or indirectly invoked the principles of '89. Renan, like Taine, had subjected these national myths to a rigorous scrutiny and had found them wanting. The moral plight of their country had led them to forge a critique of its revolutionary legacy.[46] They stoutly condemned the optimistic fervor of the eighteenth century, based on postulates of abstract reasoning, as having brought in its train a catastrophic upheaval from which French society had never recovered. It was this spirit of abstraction, they contended, that lay at the root of France's woes. Moral rationalism, which they identified with Jacobin ideology, had opened the floodgates to political instability, reducing politics to demagoguery and imperiling the national order. And this for the sake of an ideal that, tantamount to a religious gospel, had undoubtedly renovated the rest of Europe, but at the price of exhausting the country where it had been conceived. In Renan's words, pronounced on the centennial anniversary of the Revolution, and which Halévy was fond of quoting, "in

---

[46] André Bellessort, *Les Intellectuels et l'avènement de la Troisième République* (Paris, 1931), 247–249; A. Albert-Petit, "Du Rôle éminent des médiocres: A propos d'un essai de Daniel Halévy," *Le Journal des Débats*, May 25, 1934, 838.

politics, a principle, which in the course of a hundred years has merely succeeded in wearing out our country, cannot possibly be a sound principle." [47]

The effect of such a devastating critique of the main-springs of "revolutionary hope" was to have a decisive influence on Halévy's position toward the Third Republic, but it also determined the peculiar character of his radical sympathies. Although during these early years he inevitably succumbed to the conservative view that the Revolution had been a grievous error fraught with the direst consequences for his country's welfare, he resisted the forthright condemnation of Taine in favor of the more cautious Renan. Like his master, he reserved final judgment on this crucial issue. Not unlike the former seminarian who had rebelled against the religious dogmatism of Saint-Sulpice, he too was casting about in the nineties for some progressive crusade on which to fasten his hopes. Yet it was Renan himself who stood as a living symbol of the practical limits to any form of *engagement*. His example served to check Halévy's enthusiasm while simultaneously inciting him to strike out on a revolutionary course. What guidance could the hapless Halévy possibly find in such an equivocal precedent? Two things at least, he persuaded himself, were beyond dispute: Renan had taught that since all that pertained to the spirit was vague and uncertain, one could only have recourse to myths; and Taine had reinforced his conservative instincts by insisting that, since the realm of the social was so transitory and elusive, tradition alone could serve as a guide for action.[48] It would be no exaggeration to say that it was these two fundamental ideas that determined Halévy's conduct in the years ahead; timidly absorbed at the turn of the century, at times almost totally rejected, they nevertheless

[47] Cited in Halévy, *Luttes*, 55; and again in Halévy, *Histoire d'une histoire*, 24.
[48] Halévy, *Luttes*, 51, 101.

constituted the hard core of his credo. The entire course of his thinking, swayed this way and that by a host of contradictory impulses, ultimately rested on this conservative persuasion, for even his subsequent incursions into revolutionary ideas can be traced to his underlying premise that "revolutionary hope," as he conceived it, was an organic element in the French tradition.

The influence of Renan and Taine was to some extent offset by other circumstances on the eve of the Affair. To the young Halévy, the ideals of '89 were not only an integral part of his intellectual heritage, they were part and parcel of the environment into which he was born, indissolubly linked with the bourgeois values identified with his own family and class. Although not necessarily profound, his attachment to these principles was nonetheless rooted in emotion and habit, and to this extent at least served to counteract the strictly intellectual allurements of his conservative elders. His personal dilemma was foreshadowed by his teacher's own experience; here again the way in which the old master had resolved a similar conflict set a significant precedent. It was Renan who gave Halévy his cue by proclaiming a despair with bourgeois values, sounding the death knell of the great positivist dream, before the entire Academy: "We are living in the shadow of darkness, breathing the perfume from an empty vase; after us, people will live in the shadow of a shadow. I fear that all this is a trifle frivolous." [49] But against such professions of what Halévy admiringly called Renan's nihilism, "poli et masqué," [50] the wise skeptic seemed at the same time to urge his disciple to enjoy with a clear conscience the fruits of his social position. Turning to Halévy's father in Mme de Loynes's salon, he exclaimed with a resignation not unmixed with glee: "Let's admit that it is

[49] Cited by Georges Fonsegrive, *L'Evolution des idées dans la France contemporaine* (Paris, 1917), 13.
[50] Halévy, *La Fin des notables*, 72.

good to live in an age of decadence."[51] By Renan's first
censure, the whole basis of the fin-de-siècle middle-class
morality stood condemned, while the latter exclamation,
sanctioning the need for compromise, could easily be interpreted as an encouragement to persevere in a course of
purely aesthetic self-gratification. Justifying his egotistic dilettantism by invoking Renan's elusive message, Halévy could
safely follow Barrès and his culte du moi.

It is between these two poles of attraction, already implicit in his mentor's life and experience, that we can chart
Halévy's own moral development. Renan was not only
responsible for sharpening his sensibility and arousing his
social conscience; Renan's example also seemed to guide
Halévy's very actions in the years which lay immediately
ahead. It was also Renan who paved the way for the younger
man's more sympathetic understanding of Sorel's ideas, after
the turmoil of the Dreyfus Affair had afforded him the
chance of putting his "revolutionary hope" to the test.
Halévy's "Apologie pour notre passé," no less than his
dedication to Sorel's theories of revolutionary syndicalism,
can be traced to the formative influence of his first and
foremost "director of conscience."

III

Renan's reflections bordering on nihilism also prepared
Halévy for an equally decisive encounter. Even before the
outbreak of the Dreyfus Affair, more than dimly aware
of the fragility of his own society, he could hardly resist
some of the more explosive ideas that challenged the supremacy of his class. Sensing that he was part of a culture
which, for all the delights that it afforded him, was indubi-
tably on the verge of collapse, he was naturally drawn to

[51] Cited by Halévy in preface to Jaspar, Ernest Renan, xi; cf. Halévy, My
Friend Degas, trans. by Mina Curtiss (Middletown, Conn., 1964), 116, n.
2.

Nietzsche, who was making his first impact on a handful of solitary intellectuals in the early nineties. We find Halévy in the forefront of a small band of independent men of letters who—already stimulated by Renan and Taine, the undisputed *maîtres à penser* of the generation of 1870—were particularly susceptible to the charms of *Zarathustra*. Increasingly alarmed by the spectre of the revolt of the masses and the advent of an egalitarian civilization that threatened to destroy his cultural heritage—half-cherished and half-condemned—Halévy was inevitably bemused by a bold poetic philosophy, heroic and elitist, which promised to elevate man above materialism and mass mediocrity.[52]

The discovery of Nietzsche was to be Halévy's first great personal event, an event that not only coincided with the disintegration of his positivist illusions but also pointed the way to the future. The poignant life of the recluse of Sils-Maria was bound to arouse his romantic sympathies, and *Der Fall Wagner* and its condemnation of Bayreuth's scandalous pandering to middle-class taste echoed his personal disillusionment with the decadent Parisian salons. By unfolding the vast potentialities of a heroic sensibility, Nietzsche's bracing prophecies not only filled a personal void but also contributed to making Halévy all the more conscious of the spiritual hollowness of his life. That Halévy found in Nietzsche a deliverance from his own plight demonstrates, no doubt, the extent of the moral exhaustion that Renan had, after all, produced in his disciple. Halévy later confided to Jules Romains that through Nietzsche:

I discovered the abyss lying beneath a life which seemed so blissful . . . and I became aware of the necessity for a radical change. . . . I discovered that this wretched literary ambiance, Wagnerian and Tolstoian, in which I had been raised was

[52] Agathon, *op. cit.*, 274; Reino Virtanen, "Nietzsche and the Action Française," *Journal of Modern History*, Apr., 1950, 196.

nothing but a snare, a stage-effect destined to be swept away. . . .[53]

In a more general way, Halévy's enthusiasm for this new revelation also reflected the malaise of an entire generation, increasingly at odds with itself, weary of archaic ideas and hackneyed sentiments, and seeking to escape from the confinement of bourgeois values.[54]

Appropriately enough, his first translation of Nietzsche— the first recorded in France—was Le Cas Wagner, in which the romantic musician was arraigned by his quondam friend as the chief instrument of bourgeois decadence.[55] With exemplary fidelity, Halévy persisted in his devotion to Nietzsche throughout his life. His first articles and miscellaneous translations of fragments from Nietzsche's works date from 1892. In 1909 he gained a modest fame by publishing a biographical study of the German philosopher; after devoting a series of articles to various aspects of Nietzsche's life, he turned out a second, definitive biography in 1944.[56]

Many of these writings have been dismissed by academic critics as sentimental versions of the tragic destiny of Nietzsche the man—"an unfinished symphony," " a tale of his poignant martyrdom," "more pathetic than a novel,"— rather than as serious contributions to scholarship.[57] Yet it must be stressed that Halévy never made any claim to

[53] MS letter from Halévy to Jules Romains, dated Oct. 7, 1947.

[54] Cf. Halévy, "Michele Amari," La Revue de Paris, Mar., 1897, 69–86.

[55] Geneviève Bianquis, Nietzsche en France (Paris, 1929), 32 ff. His earliest translations of fragments from Nietzsche appeared in 1892 and 1894 in Le Banquet, L'Ermitage, and La Revue Blanche.

[56] Sorel brought Halévy's first Nietzsche to Croce's attention, cf. "Letteri di Georges Sorel a B. Croce," La Critica, XXVI (1928), 191–192, the original letter being dated Nov. 23, 1908.

[57] Joseph Chenu in La Nef, Feb., 1946, 136; Pierre Dournes, Nietzsche vivant (Paris, 1948), 7; Léon Daudet, Souvenirs (Paris, n.d.), 426. But see also Maurice Barrès, Mes Cahiers (Paris, 1929–1957), XIII, 53, and William James's opinion as recorded by Maurice Sachs, The Decade of Illusion: Paris 1918–1928 (New York, 1933), 133.

scholarly pretension; his avowed aim was to portray a philosopher whose influence, then as now, spread far beyond the universities. His biographical efforts should be judged on their own merits, in fact, more as chapters in Halévy's own autobiography than as a strictly philosophical endeavor.

His approach to Nietzsche was highly personal and some-times—if we are to believe his hostile critics—even cavalier. It was to a large extent a matter of self-gratification, and indeed, for the young Barrésien infatuated with the *culte du moi*, this could scarcely have been otherwise. His biographies seek to reflect the sense of communion that he succeeded in achieving with the tormented life of his hero, a communion that one admirer called an *amitié cérébrale* of comparable intensity with the *amitié vivante* that he demonstrated for Péguy.[58] The most lasting inspiration derived from Nietzsche was a taste for heroic vitalism, and this was an inspiration of the same order as those he later found in Péguy's *mystique* or Sorel's syndicalist myth. His approach to the problems raised by Nietzsche's reflections was determined by his personal quest, and although this quest, in turn, was partly shaped by the prevailing climate of sensibility both in Paris and elsewhere, his response to Nietzsche possessed a personal quality of its own.

Zarathustra, which he was engaged in translating at the height of the Dreyfus Affair, gave a recipe for overcoming the dangers of decadence. The seductive theories of the transvaluation of all values and of eternal recurrence pre-served Halévy from the allurements of Jacobin theory and acted as an antidote against the facile optimism that re-newed the Republican loyalties of so many of his Dreyfusard companions. By the same token, the moral superiority that Nietzsche associated with elites put Halévy in the proper frame of mind to appreciate the full significance of Sorel's

[58] Georges Loisy in a RTF (Radiodifusion Télévision Française) broadcast delivered in May, 1960. Unpublished typescript, II, 12.

myth of the general strike as the indispensable basis for a moral regeneration. For both these philosophers had stressed the idea that since conscience is always an individual thing, the greatest happiness can be identified only with the strongest, the most heroic, personality.[59]

From Nietzsche Halévy also learned to challenge the current dogma that democracy was an end in itself. And his endeavor to define it as an individual and collective ideal—an effort that was later to take the form of an ambitious scheme to enlighten the rising masses in his Université Populaire—can also be traced to the same source. Captivated by Nietzsche's provocative question, "Can man be ennobled?" he hailed the German prophet as the precursor of the truest form of socialism, of a moral code whose purpose should be not to flatter the masses with sentimental jargon or humiliate them with charity, but instead to reawaken in them a sense of the dignity of labor by stressing the integrity of craftsmanship and the sublime quality of syndicalist action.[60]

Nietzsche's stirring evocation of heroic deeds was translated by Halévy into a socialist program for his times—a program which, primarily concerned with raising the working classes to new heights of heroism, also marked a turning point in the development of a certain strand in French socialist theory. That this should have been perceived by Daniel Halévy demonstrates a sensibility to the moral aspects of the revolutionary movement rarely found among its champions in France. The same sensibility, as we shall see, led him to discern a socialist affinity which united

[59] Halévy, "Georg Brandès et la démocratie," Pages Libres, Mar. 15, 1902, 172; cf. Geneviève Bianquis, "Nietzsche, sa vie et sa pensée d'après Charles Andler," Revue de Synthèse historique, Jan., 1923, 122; Irving Louis Horowitz, Radicalism and the Revolt against Reason (London, 1961), 151-153.

[60] Hubert Lagardelle, "Nietzsche et son temps," Le Mouvement Socialiste, Oct. 1909, 194-205.

Proudhon, Sorel, and Péguy. In the same way, the admiration that he later displayed for the rugged individualism of the peasants of the Centre can also be traced to Zarathustra's admonition to his band of disciples to remain rooted to the soil and seek a principle of action in a philosophy of nature.[61]

It is no doubt significant that the two subjects of Halévy's biographical labors, to which he returned repeatedly in the course of a long writing career, should have been Nietzsche the aristocrat, and Proudhon the plebeian—two men of radically different temperaments who, when seen through Halévy's biographical prism, appear linked by striking similarities. Although his treatment of both was primarily biographical, situating their ideas within the context of their times, underlining their personal trials, their despair, and their solitude, it seems that he found in both certain common traits of character, which to him, at least, were of supreme significance.[62] Both thinkers, whom Halévy regarded as prophets or poets rather than as philosophers in the stricter sense, exalted power but not necessarily brute force. They stressed the notion of struggle, which they regarded as a liberating force that alone would rescue the individual from succumbing to the allurement of the Apollonian spirit or the mediocre refinements of a bourgeois ethic. Both glorified the redeeming virtues of labor, which they identified with an ideal of strife. Both were proud souls who rebelled against the conventions of their times, and who by sheer intuitive effort became, in Halévy's phrase, "créateurs de moeurs."[63] They differed in time and place, in their origins and class, and in the circumstances of their lives. But

---

[61] Halévy, "Le Travail de Zarathoustra," *Cahiers de la Quinzaine* (12ᵉᵐᵉ cahier de la 10ᵉᵐᵉ série, 1909), 21, 42 ff.; cf. Guy-Grand, *La Philosophie syndicaliste* (Paris, 1911), 213.

[62] Cf. Guy-Grand, *La Philosophie syndicaliste*, 194, 199–237.

[63] "Le Travail de Zarathoustra," 42.

to Halévy they seemed to pose a set of related questions which later formed the heart of his own *Luttes et problèmes* —the title of his most introspective book.

His own thoughts, which as a biographer he naturally expressed in the form of life studies of his two heroes, oscillated between the divergent sensibilities of the aristocrat and the commoner. Yet it appeared to Halévy that Nietzsche and Proudhon, swimming against the current of their day, raised essentially the same type of questions—how to reconcile traditional culture with moral progress, how to relate authority with democracy and a hierarchical order with individual liberties. And they both formulated a synthesis from the conflicting postulates of aristocratic order and proletarian emancipation in the form of an almost identical elitist ideal that would bind together superior men regardless of class into a community of heroes.

Inspired with the zeal of a Nietzschean convert, Halévy emerged from the turmoil of the Dreyfus Affair to discover in Péguy and Sorel, and through them, in their common ancestor Proudhon, the sequel, the perfect culmination of his own quest for heroic values in his time. It was Péguy in particular who was to fulfill his need for hero-worship, whereas the militant syndicalists whom he sought out seemed, to the Nietzschean enthusiast, to represent a remarkable breed of men foreshadowing the elite, the moral vanguard of the future.

In a more immediate sense, Nietzsche also contributed to arousing Halévy's taste for action and stirred his desire to verify within the limits of his own experience the validity of his rambling speculations. The outbreak of the Dreyfus Affair coincided with the precise moment when Halévy, hankering to escape from the confinement of his milieu and yearning for a chance to put his ideas to the test, was casting about for a revolutionary ideal which could resolve his inner contradictions and channel his restless energies. The exhilaration provoked by the Affair and the passions which it aroused provided him with an admirable opportunity to translate Nietzsche's lyrical fantasies into a principle of action. If he jumped into the fray with such alacrity, this was doubtless because he welcomed the chance of being absorbed in a good fight.

By the turn of the century, Halévy was not only disillusioned with the futility of his mode of existence; he also dreaded the dangers to which he and his generation were exposed by relying too exclusively on intellectual speculation divorced from experience. This prevailing habit of thinking in a void, he admitted later, fostered an unhealthy climate of despair.

We all craved for an ideal, but which ideal? We all yearned for some kind of hope, but which hope? We really had no masters to steer our thoughts, which remained feeble and vague, repeating monotonously, perhaps with ardor but certainly with little originality, the great human aspirations of a crumbling nineteenth century.[64]

The Dreyfus Affair was welcomed as a deliverance from all these doubts. It replaced a despair verging on nihilism with a new faith in a revolutionary creed. It forced him to reconcile his enviable social position, his strictly literary predilections, with the imperative demands of social reform and immediate action. And by affording him a chance of participating in a crusading movement, it permitted him to reconcile the socialist fervor released by "revolutionary hope" with the cherished principles of his humanist legacy.

IV

The years which spanned Halévy's graduation from the Ecole des Langues Orientales to the outbreak of the Dreyfus Affair were uneventful. His formal education was over; his

[64] Halévy, *Charles Péguy et "Les Cahiers de la Quinzaine"* (rev. ed.; Paris, 1918), 20; cf. Rolland, *Péguy* (Paris, 1944), I, 16.

literary career had scarcely begun. The rigors of an academic discipline had persuaded him that the true bent of his talent was clearly not scholarly; and after three years at the University, he drifted back to the world of letters from which he had vainly attempted to isolate himself. In October 1894, having successfully completed his thesis, he was awarded the *licence ès lettres* in Arabic. The following month, his translation of fragments from Nietzsche's aphorisms published in *La Revue Blanche* marked his return to the republic of letters.

Der Fall Wagner, which he had translated with the help of Robert Dreyfus in 1892, had already earned him a minor reputation, but it was not until 1897 that he wrote his first significant essays on the celebrated quarrel between Nietzsche and Wagner.[65] The character of Halévy's other publications during this phase of his life already revealed his wide-ranging interests and desultory curiosity, but the articles which found their way into *La Revue de Paris* also demonstrated a growing preoccupation with social problems. Thus, in addition to "Vénétie et Toscane" (1898)—an impressionistic and somewhat mannered account of an Italian voyage—and a few juvenile sketches such as "Michele Amari" (1892) and "H.-B. Stowe" (1898), his contributions to Louis Ganderax's review included two original studies on labor conditions, "Avant le Congrès socialiste" and "Les Maisons du peuple en Belgique." These social investigations, written in 1899 at the height of the Dreyfus Affair, foreshadowed Halévy's first major work, the more mature *Essais sur le mouvement ouvrier en France,* which was published under the auspices of Lucien Herr and Péguy in 1901.[66] Nietzsche, however, remained his principal con-

[65] "Nietzsche et Wagner," *La Revue de Paris,* Nov. and Dec., 1897, 302–327, 649–674; and *Le Cas Wagner* (Paris, 1892).

[66] *La Librairie Georges Bellais,* Péguy's first publishing venture. See Halévy, *Péguy,* 43–44.

cern during these early years, and it was his consuming interest in the life of the German philosopher which led him to combine the traditional grand tour of Italy with side trips to Basel and Bayreuth, Sils-Maria and even Turin. From the start, Halévy seemed quite capable of reconciling his vocation as a gentleman of leisure with more serious pursuits.

Until the end of the nineties, the pace of Halévy's life was as restless as that of his hero. He too wandered across Europe; while in Paris, he moved fitfully from salon to salon, or remained at the family estate at Sucy-en-Brie where he read voraciously and sought to master the writer's craft. He had embarked on his literary career with that characteristic diffidence which was to beset the whole course of his life, yet he looked back to this decade not only as his period of apprenticeship, but also as the time of his personal odyssey. Indeed, the "Carnets" make it clear that apart from his intellectual preoccupations, Halévy was also seeking the security that could come only with matrimony and a permanent resting place in his native city. "I was," he recalled in 1932, "a disoriented Parisian. What a sad plight! Where could I find my roots in this large, turbulent city?" By the end of 1898, even as the Dreyfus Affair rescued him from the speculations of a Nietzschean nihilist, so his marriage in his new home, which faced the Place Dauphine as well as the Quai de l'Horloge, resolved the crisis in his personal life. The quest for his Ithaca, as he fancifully called it, had come to an end.[67]

Unlike his brother who had broken away from the family circle to enter the Ecole Normale, Daniel had demonstrated exemplary filial devotion by remaining by the side of his ailing father, first in the Montmartre of his youth, and then briefly in an apartment near the Parc Monceau. He never seemed to have contemplated the possibility of living inde-

---

[67] Halévy, Pays, 148.

pendently, and it was not merely out of a sense of duty that in 1897 he accompanied his parents to join his cousins the Berthelots in the spacious Bréguet mansion where he was destined to spend the rest of his life.[68] In his new home overlooking the Seine from the Ile de la Cité, Halévy could at last face the future with greater equanimity. Here, in November of the following year, he married Marianne Vaudoyer, and here too, his son Léon, and his daughter Françoise (who in 1936 became Mme Louis Joxe) raised their own families in what remains one of the most graceful eighteenth-century *hôtels particuliers* on the Quai de l'Horloge.

[68] The Berthelots, who had formerly lived at the Institut, subsequently moved out of the Bréguet house. Cf. Halévy, *My Friend Degas*, trans. by Mina Curtiss, 86, n. 8.

CHAPTER III

The Affair

❧❦

THERE are unique events in the life of a nation whose repercussions leave an indelible mark not only on the fabric of state and society but also on all those who lived through them. Such, in the history of modern France, was the impact of the Dreyfus Affair.

I

Because of its sheer dramatic appeal, the Affair is still remembered as a *cause célèbre*, certainly the most memorable in recent French history, abounding in riddles and not infrequently resembling a melodramatic *roman-feuilleton*, as Sorel was tempted to call it in retrospect.[1] To others the plight of Dreyfus assumed the proportions of a tragedy culminating in his ultimate vindication and a just retribution for those guilty of perpetrating a miscarriage of justice. The crisis has commonly been interpreted in terms of its political and social consequences on the course of the Third Republic, and more recently, as a harbinger of the twentieth century that witnessed the unfolding of two of its principal elements, anti-Semitism and the assault on parliamentary democracy.[2] But the Affair would also repay study if it is seen

[1] Georges Sorel, *La Révolution dreyfusienne* (2d ed.; Paris, 1911), 7; cf. Henri Marcel, *Histoire et psychologie de l'Affaire Dreyfus* (Paris, 1954), 121.

[2] R. A. Winnacker, "The Influence of the Dreyfus Affair on the Political Development of France," *Papers of the Michigan Academy of Science, Arts and Letters*, XXI (1935), 465–478; Winnacker, "The Délégation des

through the experience of the generation of 1870, whose ideas and sentiments were decisively shaped by these eventful years. To Charles Péguy, the Affair possessed a mystical grandeur of enormous significance—and he died, unshaken in this conviction, on the eve of the Battle of the Marne. Albert Thibaudet could still write in 1930 that the Affair had been "the greatest battle in the history of our republic," and Daniel Halévy, who survived all of his contemporaries, maintained as recently as 1960 that the Affair had been "a moral crisis of unique intensity in our country's history." [3]

It is among such Frenchmen, still in their late twenties at the end of the century, that we may discern a link connecting the *crise de conscience* that they endured with the *crise de régime* traversed by their country. For Halévy and his generation, it was the Affair that aroused them to a self-awareness as citizens of the Republic, and determined the particular character of their loyalty to a regime that they had helped uphold. Moreover, a crisis during which the very word "intellectual" was coined for the first time set a precedent for intellectuals to intervene actively in political matters and established their position as a distinct element in French life.

These aspects of the Dreyfus Affair, inextricably intertwined, were epitomized in Daniel Halévy's personal conduct. The replacement of one ruling group by another was to become his principal concern as an observer of his times, while the decomposition of the initial Dreyfusard sentiment into the république des comités by way of the Combist *politique* constituted the heart of his meditations as a

Gauches," *Journal of Modern History*, Dec., 1937, 449–470; Hannah Arendt, *The Origins of Totalitarianism* (New York, 1951), 89–120. See also Ernst Nolte, *Three Faces of Fascism: Action Française, Italian Fascism, National Socialism*, trans. by Leila Vennewitz (New York, 1966), 54–58.

[3] Albert Thibaudet, "Reflexions," *Nouvelle Revue française*, Dec. 1, 1930, 871; Daniel Halévy, *Degas parle . . .* (Paris, 1960), 119.

chronicler of his generation. To the extent that Halévy was so intimately associated with these events and that he himself deliberately set out to be the spokesman of his Dreyfusard companions, it is necessary to examine first the external situation through which he lived. In the second place, we shall study the effect produced by the crisis on his own sentiments, showing how his participation in the Affair affected the development of his political and social beliefs.

II

Reduced to its simplest terms, the Dreyfus Affair proper was concerned with the culpability of an Alsatian-Jewish Army officer charged with espionage. The irregularities of his trial and the subsequent disclosure of irrefutable evidence that persuaded many that he had been wrongly condemned on the basis of forged testimony raised the issue of justice in the Republic. Moreover, revision of the trial entailed a challenge against the very existence of the national order, for revisionism would lead, through a chain of largely fortuitous circumstances, to the dislocation of the three conservative pillars of the state—the Army, the Church, and the Magistracy.

This was the second phase of the Affair. The third phase was a corollary of this national crisis. The disintegration of the old order ushered in a new ruling group, the Combist Radical and Socialist coalition. Resting their authority on a victory to which they had only partly contributed, these "new notables," as Halévy later called them, were able to exploit the disarray of the opposition to pursue their own ends and impose their will on vanquished opponents and former allies alike.

On November 1, 1894, *Le Figaro* disclosed that a French officer had been arrested on the charge of espionage. Two days later, Edouard Drumont's anti-Semitic *La Libre Parole* proclaimed in a banner headline: "High Treason. Arrest of

Jewish officer, Captain Dreyfus." On that same day, Daniel Halévy returned from Tuscany to his Parisian residence. He read the newspapers, noted in his diary that the culprit should be shot, then settled down to write an account of his Italian travels for *La Revue de Paris*.[4]

At the end of 1894, the future of France under the Republic seemed one of peaceful and gradual bourgeois development. The regime, now securely established, gave every sign of stability, and France appeared destined to enjoy a long period of religious peace and social harmony. Anarchist plots, which had reached their peak two years earlier when Auguste Vaillant had hurled his bomb into the Chamber, had declined in intensity and ceased to spread terror. Socialism had assumed a parliamentary guise, and an embryonic labor movement did not yet pose any serious threat to the propertied classes. Not without difficulty, the Republic had braved the storm of Boulangism which, by compromising many of the Radicals, had opened the way for a consolidation of the regime under the undisputed leadership of the Opportunists, whose moderation reflected the interests not only of the founding fathers of the Republic but also of the vast majority of Frenchmen.

The achievements of the Opportunists, the heirs of Gambetta, although hardly spectacular, possessed at least the advantage of winning over to the Republic those discontented elements that had almost assured the triumph of Boulangism. Their record, both at home and abroad, was one of appeasement. By adopting a policy calculated to rally the widest possible support for the precarious regime and to lay all controversial issues to rest, they largely succeeded in making the Republic almost universally acceptable, if not respectable. Well before Méline, they had already committed their party to a program of protectionism, and by

---

[4] Halévy, "Carnets," entries for Nov. 1894.

associating themselves with the interests of both the middle
class and the peasantry, they had contributed to reinforcing
the stability of the moderate Republic. Although in diplo-
macy their accomplishments were less notable, they had
helped to allay the nationalists' fear of isolation by laying the
groundwork for the Franco-Russian entente. Equally important was their policy of conciliation with the Catholics, a
policy that, Radical objections notwithstanding, was proclaimed in words if not yet in deeds by such professions of
good faith as Loubet's declaration in 1892 favoring religious
appeasement.

Loubet, however, fell in November of that year when he
rejected a parliamentary committee's request that the Chamber be authorized to investigate the legal dossier against
the Baron Jacques de Reinach. The mysterious suicide
of the financial agent of the Panama lobby spelled the doom
of the Opportunists as a party. Just as the Boulanger fiasco
had discredited the Radicals, the Panama scandal was to
eliminate their successors, replacing them by a new political
group. This group, under the name of Moderates or
Progressistes, now assumed the reins of power. Such minis-
tries of "Republican concentration" as Dupuy's or Ribot's
further set the tone to the new orientation of the moderate
Republic, while in the opposition, Goblet and Pelletan
joined hands with Millerand and the Socialists to form the
nucleus of a small and as yet insignificant Radical coalition.
The bourgeois Republic seemed to have triumphed over all
its opponents.[5]

What gave this political transformation some guarantee
of permanence was a profound change in public opinion
heralded by Pope Leo XIII's policy of the Ralliement. Two
pronouncements marked this turning point in the Vatican's

[5] François Goguel, *Les Partis politiques sous la Troisième République* (3d
ed.; Paris, n.d.), 72–79; D. W. Brogan, *The Development of Modern
France* (New York, 1944), 264–265.

attitude to the godless regime. Cardinal Lavigerie's famous toast in 1890 was endorsed two years later by a papal encyclical exhorting all the faithful to rally to the Republic, now acknowledged as France's legitimate government. *Inter Sollicitudiness* was accompanied by active papal pressure to force the intransigent monarchists, still hankering after a restoration of Throne and Altar, to comply with Rome's wishes. Despite some diehard opposition to the Pope's injunction, there were many moderate Catholics, like Jacques Piou and Albert de Mun, who were prepared to lead the conservative and devout bourgeoisie into a genuine reconciliation with the laic Republic. Their task was facilitated by the good will demonstrated by many Moderates who were not averse to welcoming the clericals into the Republican fold. Even Spuller, Gambetta's veteran ally, hailed the Vatican's new course in the name of the "esprit nouveau" of the Republic, anxious to meet the Catholics half way, while Jules Ferry greeted the papal encyclical by declaring that "our Republic is open to all,"—thus officially sanctioning both the "new spirit" and the Ralliement in the name of the dominant party in the Republic.[6]

These encouraging signs of a new era of good feelings were translated into political terms by the 1893 election, a decisive event, which seemed to confirm the more conciliatory tempers that prevailed on both sides. Since the abortive Seize Mai, France had been ruled by unstable coalitions in which the minority Radicals had been forced to subordinate their program of social reform to the more pressing task of defending republican institutions.[7] The 1893 election was the first in the Republic's history to be held in a general mood of *détente*. With the Right no longer threatening to overthrow the regime, now almost universally acknowledged as legitimate, the Moderates could at last repudiate their

[6] Robert David, *La Troisième République* (Paris, 1934), 183.
[7] Goguel, *ibid.*, 78.

marriage of convenience with the Radicals and join with the Catholic Right on a common program of social preservation. With the Ralliement acting as the catalyst, the election assured the triumph of this natural alliance, while the Radicals moved closer to the Socialists, thus merging into a new Left—a *parti du mouvement,* in M. Goguel's terminology.[8]

This Moderate-Catholic coalition formed the nucleus of a ruling elite of which Méline, whose stable ministry lasted for an unprecedented period of two years, was perhaps the most typical example. To this group, preparing to embark on a course of gradual economic and social consolidation, the Dreyfus Affair came as an unwelcome distraction. At the same time, the Socialists and the Radicals both recoiled from the Affair, dismissing it as a bourgeois family quarrel in which they saw no reason to intervene. In these circumstances, it is no wonder that the Affair was to be fought outside Parliament, in the press and by the intellectuals.[9]

To many of these, the politicians' reluctance to cope with the issues raised by the Affair served to underline the inadequacies of a form of government clearly incapable of maintaining the most elementary civil liberties. In the first stages of the crisis, however, most of these intellectuals had rallied to the Republic as the natural bulwark of their own principles of justice. But in the face of the government's incompetence, they emerged from the Affair thoroughly disillusioned with parliamentary democracy. This trend was reinforced by their revulsion against the Combist aftermath, many of the Dreyfusards finding in the abuses of the Radicals in power a recurrence of the same evils against

[8] *Ibid.,* 71.
[9] René Rémond, "Les Intellectuels et la politique," *Revue française de Science Politique,* Dec., 1959, 867; Pierre Miquel, *L'Affaire Dreyfus* (Paris, 1959), 8; Joseph Reinach, *Histoire de l'Affaire Dreyfus* (Paris, n.d.), V, 579.

which they had fought during the Affair itself. Moreover, the political shortcomings of the Republic had revealed to many its underlying social imperfections, and Sorel echoed the feelings of a growing segment of dissident Dreyfusards when he observed that "the result of the Dreyfus Affair was to hasten the collapse of a social structure which barely made it possible for a parliamentary regime to function." [10] On the other hand, one of the most important features of the Affair was that it brought writers and professors out of their studies, forcing them to confront public issues. Anatole France's M. Bergeret, diverted from his antiquarian researches to come to terms with political realities, illustrates Albert Thibaudet's judgment that "the Dreyfus Affair was not merely an intellectual affair, but the affair *of* the intellectuals." [11]

Since the abdication of responsibility by all the political leaders revealed a flaw in the parliamentary process, we must seek the real significance of the Affair not in party platforms or speeches delivered before the Chamber but rather in the thoughts and actions of intellectuals outside the political arena. [12] Men like Halévy or Péguy were pulled into the maelstrom by the sheer logic of events, joining in a battle charged with emotional significance only out of a sense of outraged conscience not to remain silent. These young men, the generation born around 1870, had no political axe to grind: their conduct during the Affair was dictated by purely abstract principles of right and wrong. It was no doubt for this reason that they jumped into the fray with less hesitation than the politicians who, with an eye on their con-

[10] Sorel, *La Révolution dreyfusienne*, 64.

[11] *Histoire de la littérature française de 1789 à nos jours* (Paris, 1934), 411; cf. Thibaudet, *La République des professeurs* (Paris, 1927), 105, and Alexandre Zévaès, *Le Cinquantennaire de "J'Accuse"* (Paris, 1948), 22.

[12] René Johannet, *Itinéraires d'intellectuels* (Paris, 1921), 43; Charles Péguy, "Echange de lettres avec Emile Boivin," *Feuillets de l'Amitié Charles Péguy*, no. 60, 11.

stituencies, simply could not afford to take any risks. Feeling betrayed by their elders and their deputies, the young elite stepped into the breach, constituting themselves the leaders of opinion. They were forced to rise to the occasion not only by Parliament's reluctance to redress a violation of justice, but also by the folly of the General Staff and the stubborn prejudice of the courts. That not a single general dared to protest against the blatant iniquity, that the 1898 Chamber counted no more than three outspoken revisionists—all of whom failed to be returned in the May elections—was a national disgrace.[13] In these circumstances, the obligation of upholding the nation's honor fell upon the intellectuals alone. Unwittingly, sometimes reluctantly, young men like Halévy found themselves engaged in a civil war they had not sought but which invested their actions with the gravest consequences. Their response to the national peril, less partial than that of the politicians, provides us with a juster appreciation of the peculiar character of the Affair.

III

On the eve of the Dreyfus Affair, Halévy professed no political allegiance, and to him, as to many others in his position, the Republic was an object of mild indifference. By forcing him to renounce his natural apathy the Affair became a baptism of fire. His commitment forced him to reconcile his vague sentiments with his responsibilities both as a citizen and as an intellectual and to define his political creed in terms of a broader social philosophy that was to determine his position on the subsequent vagaries of the Third Republic.

Why did Halévy become a Dreyfusard and what was the precise nature of his *engagement?* To answer these questions we must rely not only on the almost daily reflections provoked by the dramatic events, dutifully committed to his

[13] Sorel, *La Révolution dreyfusienne,* 39; David, *op. cit.,* 298.

diary as the plot unfolded in the crucial years from 1897 to 1901, but also on an agonizing self-appraisal, the "Apologie pour notre passé," to which he submitted both himself and his generation ten years after the Affair. The former—which remains unpublished—serves as a corrective to the latter, and the two documents taken together provide us with an invaluable insight into some of the more elusive forces which went into the Affair. Not the least merit of this evidence is that it contains a candid record of the unique impact that Dreyfus' plight made on a certain segment of French society. Halévy's personal impressions and his subsequent reconsiderations serve as a kind of prism through which we may discern the real sentiments and attitudes of other less articulate or more discreet members of his generation. The Dreyfus Affair, which was so largely a matter of feeling, can perhaps be best understood if we can trace its effects on the limited field of a single but not untypical personal experience.

In a letter to Halévy written in 1910, Romain Rolland, after explaining why already in 1898 he had opted to remain "above the fight," noted that "every great crisis has the effect of unraveling the unknown depths of one's secret being." [14] This remark was particularly relevant to Halévy, for the national emergency forced him to take heed of a hitherto concealed current of basic beliefs and sentiments. Most significant, of course, was the fact that the Dreyfus Affair naturally brought him to acknowledge that he was, in part at least, Jewish. Yet unlike his Dreyfusard companions, André Spire or Julien Benda, whose allegiance to the revisionist camp was largely determined by their Jewish origins, there was nothing in Halévy's past which made such a commitment inevitable. His case, indeed, bears more resemblance to that of Proust in that he too belonged to a completely

[14] Cited in Cecile Delhorbe, *Les Ecrivains français et l'Affaire Dreyfus* (Paris, 1932), 302.

assimilated upper-class Jewish society. Both were only partly of Jewish extraction—Proust on his mother's side, Halévy on his father's—and it was only the wave of anti-Semitism unleashed by the Affair which forced them to come to terms with their half-forgotten Jewish heredity.[15]

In fact, the very eclecticism of Halévy's milieu promoted a natural indifference to attachments of any sort. The peculiar character of his upbringing in a family whose Jewishness was by now only skin-deep was admirably expressed by Mme Straus when she prided herself on an inbred tolerance entirely in keeping "with the tradition of the Halévy family where all religions are intermingled." [16] In her salon, where Anatole France rubbed shoulders with Jules Lemaître and Paul Bourget, the young Halévy had been exposed to a climate of free inquiry uninhibited by any dogmatism. The Dreyfus Affair, which made such rigid demands on one's loyalties, was therefore doubly distasteful for a person in Halévy's position. It forced him, for the first time in his life, to make a clear-cut choice, and this choice, in turn, was dictated by a certain racial origin hitherto ignored. Utterly alien to his Jewish past, he even betrayed a streak of anti-Semitism, confessing in his journal the sense of relief at having been spared "the tainted idiosyncracies of my race." [17] He could never abide Bernard Lazare whose very Jewishness had attracted his friend, Péguy, and in his "Apologie" he even goes as far as to write that "anti-Semitism is a very plausible and, to a large extent, prudent attitude,"—a state-

[15] Julien Benda, La Jeunesse d'un clerc (Paris, 1936), 38 ff.; Benda, Les Cahiers d'un clerc: 1936–1949 (Paris, 1950), 156; André Wurmser, "Souvenirs sur Julien Benda," Europe, Sept., 1961, 3–13; André Spire, "Le Problème juif dans la littérature," in Georges Guy-Grand (ed.), La Renaissance religieuse (Paris, 1928), 99; André Maurois, A la Recherche de Marcel Proust (Paris, 1949), 94; Jacques Emile Blanche, Mes Modèles: Barrès, Proust, James, Moore (Paris, 1928), 112–119.

[16] Cited in Maurois, loc. cit. Cf. George D. Painter, Proust: The Later Years (Boston and Toronto, 1965), 108.

[17] Entry for Dec. 2, 1898.

ment which betrays rather crudely the feelings of many assimilated Jews who feared that the Affair would jeopardize their precarious niche within the upper bourgeoisie.[18]

To this apparently stable society the Affair soon became a "dividing sword," replacing many a warm friendship with animosities which never quite healed.[19] For Halévy, the feuding spirit of this civil war was particularly painful in that it revealed Degas to be an anti-Semite of the first water. The petulant recluse of Montmartre could not tolerate the younger man's slurs on established authority. Degas's visits to the Halévys' ended abruptly. "This is the last of our delightful chats," lamented Daniel in 1897. "The bond is broken—our friendship perishes." Yet although the rupture caused Halévy untold agonies, it did not prevent him from turning all his youthful energies to fighting for the good cause. The following week he banished Degas from his mind and passionately jotted down in his diary:

This Affair has violently shaken my life. I am now certain of my political convictions: I am a Republican, an individualist. I loathe demagoguery which is the reverse of liberty. . . . I no longer have the time to write, totally absorbed as I am with drafting the petition of protest. . . . We are witnessing the dreadful spectacle of a nation losing its honor, degrading itself and us—this is France's gravest hour.[20]

IV

After a summary court-martial held *in camera*, Dreyfus had been found guilty and sentenced to life imprisonment on Devil's Island. There he languished for over four years, forgotten by all save his family. Only his wife and brother were convinced of his innocence, but public opinion greeted

---

[18] Halévy, *Luttes et problèmes* (Paris, 1911), 99. Cf. Hannah Arendt, *The Origins of Totalitarianism*, 97 ff.; Fernand Gregh, *L'Age d'or* (Paris, 1947), 288; Jean Variot, *Propos de Georges Sorel* (Paris, 1935), 150.

[19] Brogan, *op. cit.*, 341.

[20] Entry for Nov. 14, 1897, reprinted in Halévy, *Degas parle*, 137.

the verdict as a just retribution, and the Jews heaved a sigh of relief and hoped that the embarrassing case would soon be forgotten.

It was Colonel Picquart who, replacing Sandherr at the head of the Statistical Section of the General Staff, first discovered that the *bordereau* that had served as the principal evidence against the Captain at his trial was, in fact, a forgery. His suspicions were further aroused when a charwoman, employed by the German Embassy but in the pay of French counter-intelligence, produced a torn section of the *petit bleu,* a letter that she had recovered from the wastepaper basket of the German military attaché. The message was addressed to a certain Commandant Esterhazy, a French infantry officer. At first, Picquart thought that Esterhazy was yet another spy, but further investigation revealed the remarkable fact that his handwriting was identical to that of the *bordereau* allegedly written by Dreyfus. Upon examining this *bordereau,* he discovered that it was padded with additional forgeries, which he ultimately traced to his own subordinate, Captain Henry. He notified his immediate superior, General Gonse, only to be told that the Army had no desire to review the case.

Working independently, Mathieu Dreyfus, persuaded of his brother's innocence, had with the help of Bernard Lazare also arrived at the conclusion that the real culprit was Esterhazy. On November 10, 1897, he published facsimiles of the *bordereau* in *Le Matin* and, a few days later, he publicly denounced Esterhazy as its author. His case was reinforced when *Le Figaro* reproduced photographs of the *bordereau* accompanied with a letter by Esterhazy to his mistress: the handwriting was the same. It was at this point that Clemenceau's *L'Aurore* demanded a revision of the court-martial and an investigation of the charges against Esterhazy. The Affair, now taken up by the press, had at last fallen into the public domain.

Events soon followed each other in rapid succession. On January 11, 1898, Esterhazy was brought to trial and promptly acquitted amidst wild popular rejoicing and a recrudescence of a violent anti-Semitic campaign launched by the nationalist press. Two days later, Picquart, who had been assigned to colonial duty, was recalled to Paris and placed under arrest. On the same day, *L'Aurore* published "J'Accuse," and on the fourteenth, Clemenceau's Radical paper printed the first installment of the "Manifesto of the Intellectuals" with Daniel Halévy's name heading the list of petitioners demanding revision.

Halévy's role during these hectic months was merely that of a bystander. It amounted to little more than observing the unfolding of the dramatic events, pouring over the newspapers and engaging in heated discussions.[21] With Proust, Bizet, Gregh, Robert Dreyfus, and others, he joined his brother's friends in nightly gatherings at the Café des Variétés, which soon became an unofficial Dreyfusard headquarters. It was from this group of so-called dissidents that the idea of drawing up a petition demanding revision was first launched.[22] Like so many others, Halévy could not fail to notice that the *bordereau* facsimile published by the press was in Esterhazy's handwriting. His doubts were confirmed when Bernard Lazare's pamphlet exposed the irregularities of the court-martial. There was nothing to do now but demand a revision, and Halévy was among the first to approach Clemenceau to persuade him that the just cause should be taken up by his paper.[23]

One of the most revealing confessions contained in Halévy's "Apologie pour notre passé" was the extent of his procrastination before he finally took this decisive step. He makes it clear that commitment to the revisionist cause was

---

[21] *Ibid.*, 123; cf. Halévy, *Luttes*, 59.   [22] Gregh, *L'Age d'or*, 290.
[23] "Carnets," entry for Nov., 1897.

forced upon him and his friends: it was not they who sought the *engagement*, but their opponents who forced it on them. "With no thought of civil war," he writes, "we were on the threshold of a life dedicated to the preservation of a culture that was our legacy, our passion and our honor." [24] The sacrifices imposed by the Affair destroyed these buoyant expectations. "It fell upon us in the sweetness of our youth, deflected the course of our lives, deprived us of that calm which any civilized country owes to its young. . . ." [25]

Reflections such as these inevitably reinforced his reluctance to jump into the fray, and his decision to intervene came only after the logic of the facts had compelled all men of good will to protest against the patent iniquity. Halévy notes that even as early as 1896, an obscure newspaper, *L'Eclair*, had disclosed that the military tribunal had reached its verdict on the basis of secret evidence withheld from the defense, but even this revelation failed to provoke the slightest stir. "We refused," he confesses, "to be shaken from our natural prudence." [26] He even admits that, placing his trust in the good faith of the General Staff, he believed in the existence of the celebrated secret memorandum allegedly annotated in the Kaiser's own hand—a fraudulent fabrication circulated by the Army to silence its opponents. Next, came Lazare's tract, written at the bidding of Dreyfus' family, comparing the handwritings and proving beyond any reasonable doubt that Dreyfus could not possibly be the traitor. Yet even this famous pamphlet which aroused Péguy's combative ardor merely filled Halévy with premonitions, and he recalls how, still prompted by caution, he replaced it on his desk and turned away from "the hatred contained in these formidable pages." [27] Finally, Mathieu Dreyfus' revelations in *Le Matin* brought the whole sordid matter into the open. The truth could no longer be evaded—

[24] Halévy, *Luttes*, 113.   [25] *Ibid.*, 47.   [26] *Ibid.*, 37.   [27] *Ibid.*

"reluctantly," recalled Halévy, "we were entangled in the Affair." [28]

V

Proust once boasted: "I was the first Dreyfusard, for it was I who went to ask Anatole France for his signature." [29] In fact, France had already pledged his name to Halévy at a dinner party, also attended by Proust, at Ludovic's. The following morning, accompanied by his brother and by Proust, Daniel Halévy called on the novelist, who warmly greeted the youngsters and, true to his word, "signed passionately—with one bold stroke of the pen." [30] Halévy was instrumental in soliciting further signatures for the petition, an intellectuals' revisionist protest, which, now adorned with Anatole France's name, shook others out of their lethargy. But the self-styled intellectuals did not have the whole field to themselves. Dismayed by the unwarranted connotation which Halévy and his friends had succeeded in giving to the word "intellectual," Barrès retorted in *Le Journal* on February 1, 1898, with an emphatic antirevisionist "*Protestation des intellectuels*" that was rapidly endorsed by an equally impressive array of writers, professors, and academicians. The issue was now joined on the plane that the Dreyfusards had deliberately chosen, and Halévy was to confront his adversaries—and later his allies—over the essentially intellectual and moral problems raised by the Affair.[31]

The *Aurore* petition appeared on the fourteenth of January. On the seventeenth, Halévy added his signature to a similar petition printed in Jaurès' Socialist daily, *La Petite*

[28] *Ibid.*, 38.
[29] Cited in Painter, *Proust: The Early Years*, 273–274.
[30] "Carnets," entry for Jan. 21, 1898. Cf. Delhorbe, *op. cit.*, 95–96.
[31] Cf. Rémond, *op. cit.*, 868; cf. Victor Brombert, *The Intellectual Hero* (Philadelphia and New York, 1960), 23; Georges Charensol, *L'Affaire Dreyfus et la Troisième République* (Paris, 1930), 170.

République. It was on this occasion that his name appeared for the first time beside Péguy's.[32] The date is important, for it marks a turning point in Halévy's life: with the revisionist campaign he emerged from his sheltered right bank milieu into the more purposeful atmosphere of the Latin Quarter. Through Péguy and his Normale circle, which included Léon Blum, the Tharauds, Mario Roquès, and others, he was irresistibly drawn by Jaurès into the great current of social reformism. Under the aegis of the great Socialist tribune, these young men of different backgrounds buried their differences in the face of an immediate peril that demanded prompt action and quick decisions. Momentarily achieving a harmony of views and a singleness of purpose dictated by the urgency of the situation, they hardly formed a homogeneous group, however. A well-informed English correspondent, observing them in the heat of the civil war, accurately described them as follows:

They come from political parties and religious communities who have nothing in common, who are even in conflict with each other. . . . They have fought and on occasion will fight again. Do not deceive yourselves; these are the elite of the French democracy.[33]

The following month—February—was taken up by Emile Zola's trial. From the public gallery of the Palais de Justice, next door to his home on the Place Dauphine, Halévy watched the dramatic proceedings, later to be recounted in *Jean Santeuil*, where Proust immortalized his Dreyfusard companion as the earnest Henri Durrieux.[34] The prosecution, seeking to evade the subject of Dreyfus' court-martial, had limited the charges against Zola to defamation, indicting

[32] Cf. Reprinted petition in *Feuillets*, no. 60, 11.
[33] K.V.T., "The Dreyfus Case: A Study of French opinion," *Contemporary Review*, Oct., 1898, 608.
[34] Marcel Proust, *Jean Santeuil*, trans. by Gerard Hopkins (New York, 1956), 319 ff.

him only for those passages in "J'Accuse" which had in-
criminated the Army's intervention in securing Esterhazy's
acquittal. Yet they could scarcely prevent Zola from proclaiming in the course of his trial what the revisionists had
sought to force the Government to acknowledge from the
start, namely, that Dreyfus' court-martial had been a mistrial
on procedural grounds. Dreyfus, asserted Zola, had been
wrongly condemned since part of the evidence used against
him had been concealed from his own defense. General
Boisdeffre, chief of the General Staff, retorted by testifying
that the *faux Henry* was a genuine document. Yet it was not
so much the niceties of procedure but rather the General's
threat that if Zola were acquitted he would resign that
persuaded the court to convict Zola—a blatantly political
verdict.[35]

At this juncture, the Dreyfus Affair had passed its heroic
stage. Boisdeffre's ultimatum had subordinated the question
of justice to the more immediate issue of the Army's role in
the nation. The Affair had fallen into the realm of politics.
What had begun as a collective protest against a miscarriage
of justice was now to be exploited by those whom Proust was
to call "the Dreyfusards of the eleventh hour"—the radical
and Socialist politicians dismissed by Péguy as the *petits
arrivistes ultérieurs*. The aim of the "Dreyfusards of the first
hour" was stated by Péguy in the plainest terms:

The anti-Dreyfusards said: military treachery is a crime and
Dreyfus is a military traitor. We said: military treachery is a
crime and Dreyfus is not a traitor. He is innocent of that crime.
Since Hervé has come on the scene, there has been an about-
face.[36]

In the hands of Hervé, and of Jaurès too, the initial impulse
of Dreyfusism was to be transformed into a political revolu-

[35] Miquel, *op. cit.*, 61–65.
[36] Péguy, *Notre Jeunesse* (Gallimard ed.; Paris, 1933), 151.

tion culminating in the "Combist tyranny." The genuine outcry of moral indignation was submerged by a vast political maneuver in which the organizers of the petition campaign felt increasingly out of their element.[37]

Halévy later traced this turning point to the period between the launching of the *Aurore* petition and Zola's escape to London in July 1898. During these crucial months he was more assiduous than ever in attending Mme Straus's salon, which had now become the center of the revisionist faction. The main attraction at his aunt's was Joseph Reinach, the nephew of the Baron of Panama fame and the principal architect of the coalition which ultimately forced the Government to reopen the Dreyfus case. Through his connections with Scheurer-Kestner on the one hand, and Bernard Lazare on the other, it was Reinach who brought together the two sides that had been working independently for revision in the dark hours before Zola's trial.[38] But Reinach, as one of the leaders of the Opportunist clique discredited by Panama, was also determined to turn the Affair to his party's advantage. To Halévy, whom he had fired with enthusiasm at the height of the Affair, it was he who came to incarnate in retrospect the decomposition of Dreyfusism, for it was through Reinach's good offices that the Opportunists joined hands with Jaurès and the Radicals to exploit the Dreyfus Affair for political ends.[39]

As early as 1899 Halévy had anticipated the equivocal character that Dreyfusism was bound to assume in the hands of such widely divergent groups. Already during the early years of the *Cahiers de la Quinzaine* he had noted that the unanimity which a civil war of this kind imposed on each of the two feuding factions would inevitably give way,

[37] *Ibid.*, 93–121.

[38] Halévy, *Luttes*, 28–31; cf. Painter, *Proust: The Early Years*, 278–279.

[39] Halévy, *Luttes*, 86–89. See also Guy Chapman, *The Dreyfus Case: A Reassessment* (London, 1955), 321–341.

once the immediate peril had passed, to varying shades of meaning. For his part, he had fought the real battle not so much in the campaign for petitions or the street fights, but within himself, in the privacy of his study. After allowing himself a respite for reflection, he chose the occasion of the tenth anniversary of the Affair to take stock of its effect on himself and his generation, and to present his verdict in the form of a long essay, "Apologie pour notre passé," which Péguy published in his *Cahiers* in 1910.[40]

This essay is a document unique in its kind—a candid appraisal of his decisive *engagement*, vividly reflecting the strains and stresses that the strife had provoked. In it, Halévy attempted to sort out his motives and define the precise character of his Dreyfusard creed. Adopting an analytical method superimposed on a clear narrative of events, he sought to reverse a kind of intellectual rake's progress. Undeterred by the risk of abuse to which such a profession of remorse would doubtless expose him from his former companions, he gave free rein to his misgivings and seemed to leave little doubt as to where his real sentiments lay.

The "Apologie" provoked an immediate reaction from Péguy, who retorted in another *Cahier* with "Notre Jeunesse," a passionate disclaimer of his friend's manifest contrition. Halévy had expected that his "Apologie" would, as he put it, "get me in trouble in some quarters,"[41] but Péguy's rejoinder was the unkindest cut of all and he never recovered from the way in which his former companion made him the scapegoat for all those who sought to destroy the purity of their youthful ideals. In "Victor-Marie, Comte Hugo," an open letter to Halévy that appeared the following

---

[40] 10ème cahier de la 11ème série, Apr. 10, 1910, later reprinted in Halévy, *Luttes*; all references are to this second impression.

[41] Halévy, *Péguy and "Les Cahiers de la Quinzaine,"* trans. by Ruth Bethell (London, 1946), 109.

THE AFFAIR

year in another issue of the *Cahiers*, Péguy, regretting his earlier impetuosity, sought to make amends to his offended friend. This trilogy of *Cahiers* forms a unique chapter in a stirring dialogue on the nature of the Dreyfus Affair.[42]

By 1910 Halévy sensed that the Affair had reached, as he wrote, "a dead moment"; its anniversary had been greeted with a "blank and unbroken silence" which he interpreted as a sign that all was not well.[43] Like many who had rallied to Péguy's *boutique*, he felt uneasy about the turn of events that had followed the Dreyfusard triumph and could scarcely conceal his dismay before the spectacle of the abuses of Combism which, justifying itself as the rightful heir of Dreyfusism, had put the original champions of Dreyfus' innocence to shame. Sorel, Spire, the Tharauds, and many others who had belonged to the little band of the "Dreyfusards of the first hour" shared his concern, and even Romain Rolland had descended from his ivory tower to join in the general indignation.[44] As early as 1903 Dreyfus' own attorney, Maître Labori, had conceded that nothing good had come out of the Affair, denouncing in the liberal *Journal des Débats* the Combist "degradation of political morality as the most complete moral anarchy."[45] Even Lagardelle's *Le Mouvement Socialiste*, whose Dreyfusism was beyond

---

[42] *Ibid.*, 227; cf. Péguy, *Victor-Marie, Comte Hugo* (Paris, 1934), 233. Roger Martin du Gard used Halévy as a model for the character of Luce in his *Jean Barois* (personal communication: Henri Clouard, confirmed by Gabriel Marcel). For some of Luce's reflections which are pure Halévy, see *Jean Barois*, trans. by Stuart Gilbert (New York, 1949), 169 ff., 266–272. See also Delhorbe, *op. cit.*, 321–326.

[43] Péguy, 208–209.

[44] Sorel, *La Révolution dreyfusienne*, 54 ff.; Jean and Jérôme Tharaud, *Notre Cher Péguy* (Paris, 1926), II, 156: Spire, *Souvenirs à bâtons rompus* (Paris, 1959), 12 ff.; Romain Rolland, *Péguy* (Paris, 1944), I, 222 ff.; see also André de Fouquières, *Mon Paris et ses parisiens* (Paris, 1953), II, 245.

[45] Fernand Labori in *Le Journal des Débats*, Aug. 21, 1903.

reproach, could publish an article in 1906 entitled: "The bankruptcy of Dreyfusism, or the triumph of the Jews."[46]

Halévy's reflections voiced this widespread uneasiness, but they were also affected by a resurgence of the passions originally aroused by the Affair. In July 1906, a decision of the Cour de Cassation, under strong pressure from the new premier, Clemenceau, had quashed the Rennes verdict without right of appeal and completely rehabilitated Dreyfus. The militants of the Right were quick to seize their chance, protesting the validity of a legal subterfuge behind which they rightly discerned the vengeance of their opponents, while Clemenceau's well-meaning but tactless intercession placed his own followers in an awkward position.[47] The old Dreyfusards were hard put to it to justify what was clearly a violation of the letter of the law, of that same law that they themselves had championed some years before. That a civilian court could flout that law with as much impunity as the military tribunals seemed to make a mockery of the entire Dreyfusard position. While providing the nationalists with further proof of Republican perversion, it placed such pure Dreyfusards as Péguy and Halévy—who throughout the Affair had demanded nothing more than that Dreyfus be given a fair trial—in the predicament of having to condone a compromise that undermined the righteousness of their cause. It was in such an atmosphere of general discontent, further aggravated by a feeling of revulsion against this distortion of legal procedure, that Halévy's book appeared.[48]

The "Apologie" was greeted with mixed feelings. Péguy, as we have seen, reserved judgment, maintained an ominous silence for two months, and then replied abruptly with

[46] Cf. Sorel, *La Révolution dreyfusienne*, 54.

[47] Louis Dimier, *Vingt Ans d'Action Française* (Paris, 1926), 106–109, 114.

[48] Halévy, *Luttes*, 110; cf. Sorel, *La Révolution dreyfusienne*, 3, 39; but see André Zévaès, *L'Affaire Dreyfus* (Paris, 1931), 200–214.

"Notre Jeunesse." Yet Halévy's book was, in general, favorably received, particularly among such groups as the *Nouvelle Revue française* who commended him for his courage in reopening the case, the case which had launched them all on their careers. "The awkward harmony which reigns among us," wrote Jean Schlumberger, André Gide's official spokesman at the *Revue,* "conceals a serious misunderstanding, and it is imperative that our whole generation take its cue from Daniel Halévy's *examen de conscience* to examine afresh its past conduct." [49] From the Right came even more emphatic praise for Halévy's intrepidity in reviving their past. René de Kérallain, with whom Halévy had parted company during the Affair, congratulated him for a "memorable psychological achievement." [50] Jean Variot, Sorel's closest disciple, hailed the "Apologie" as "a masterpiece of sanity, clarity and balance," [51] while Maurras in *L'Action française* welcomed Halévy's "change of heart where anxiety creeps through the pride of mourning." [52] But the opinion which Halévy respected most was that of an older man. Writing in *L'Indépendance,* a new review with Maurrassien overtones, Georges Sorel commended him for his courage in challenging accepted opinion and for applying a "psychological" rather than the despicable current "sociological" approach in elucidating the significance of the Affair.

His noble sentiments and intellectual integrity give Halévy's investigations the tone of a rational confession. His most remarkable literary skill has enabled him to overcome the enormous difficulties that beset all those who attempt to narrate matters pertaining to the most profound psychology.[53]

[49] Jean Schlumberger in *Nouvelle Revue française,* June 1, 1910, 787.
[50] Kérallain, *Correspondence* (Quimper, 1933–1935), III, 286.
[51] Variot, *Propos,* 264.
[52] *L'Action française,* May 7, 1911; cf. Henry de Bruchard, "Le Cas de Daniel Halévy," *La Revue critique des Idées et des Livres,* Sept. 10, 1910, 424.
[53] Sorel, "Trois Problèmes," *L'Indépendance,* Dec. 15, 1911, 222.

And in the following year he seized the opportunity offered
by the publication of the second edition of his own *Révolution dreyfusienne* to add a new preface in which he hailed
Halévy's "Apologie" as "not only a literary masterpiece but a
piece of work which must be counted among the most
indispensable documents of our contemporary history." [54]

The tone of the "Apologie," as its title implies, is one of
repentance. Speaking in the name of the French liberal
tradition—from Mme de Staël through Prévost-Paradol to
Renan—Halévy argued that Dreyfusards like himself were
above all liberals who had rallied to the Captain's defense
not only to proclaim his innocence but also to vindicate the
nation's crumbling liberties.[55] These two tendencies, however, converged into one single purpose for which the
Dreyfusards fought with the utmost resolution. But in the
turmoil of the fight, the intellectuals of liberal persuasion
found themselves allied with others whose aim—a radical
transformation of French society—was utterly alien to the
real purpose of all true Dreyfusards. Halévy accuses the
Moderates and the Ralliés for having by their ineptitude
forced their supporters into this unholy alliance. For by
failing to uphold the principles of justice in the Republic,
the liberal parties had left the younger generation with no
choice but to join hands with their enemies to defend the
nation's imperilled liberties.

This circuitous analysis is based on the premise that there
were at least two separate Dreyfus cases.[56] The first, primarily
a juridical matter, arose from a miscarriage of justice. The
second was a deliberate exploitation of the iniquity inflicted
on Dreyfus by political opportunists. The domination of
these Radicals and Socialists over French politics was,

[54] Sorel, *La Révolution dreyfusienne* (2d ed.; Paris, 1911), 3; cf.
Delhorbe, *op. cit.*, 321.
[55] Halévy, *Luttes*, 50 ff.
[56] *Ibid.*, 44.

contended Halévy, the inevitable consequence of the collapse of the liberals as a responsible political party.[57] After
more than half a century of further reflection, Halévy did
not find that this interpretation needed any substantial
revision. In his last book, where he once again came to grips
with the issues raised in his first, he endorsed his earlier
judgment.[58] Indeed, the passage of time had only convinced
him that all the evils that had befallen his country, from
Combes through the Popular Front to the Occupation,
could be traced to this initial blunder. To the extent that he
had contributed to this disastrous state of affairs he was to
remain inconsolable. He looked back to his participation in
the events at the turn of the century as a grievous fault, a
blemish on his record; yet he always believed that the
"Apologie," by laying bare his *crise de conscience*, had
sufficed to redress the balance in his favor.[59]

By 1960, as he reconsidered his past, he perceived even
more clearly that the abuses resulting from the Affair had
been the responsibility of Jaurès and his lieutenant, Lucien
Herr. The latter, in particular, combining the strategic post
of librarian at the Ecole Normale with that of literary editor
of *La Revue de Paris*, was admirably placed to recruit to his
revolutionary party both the university youth and their right
bank counterparts like Halévy. One of the main tenets of his
Socialist party was its antimilitarism, and it was with the
deliberate purpose of discrediting the military establishment
that Herr had launched his Dreyfusard forces to the attack.[60]
The original legal case served merely as a pretext to destroy
the generals, and through them, the Church and Judiciary,

[57] Cf. Thibaudet, "Les Partis politiques en France," *Nouvelle Revue
française*, Dec. 1, 1934, 894–900.
[58] Halévy, *Degas parle*, 123–126.
[59] Pierre Dominique in *Rivarol*, Jan. 28, 1960, 14.
[60] Cf. Hubert Bourgin, *De Jaurès à Léon Blum: L'Ecole Normale et la
politique* (Paris, 1934), 138 ff.; Chapman, *The Dreyfus Case*, 359.

the whole social and political order. But the very ambiguity of the conflicting tendencies in the revisionist camp and the momentary convergence of Dreyfus as fact and Dreyfus as symbol reinforced Herr's hold on all those whose real intentions went no further than to redress a violation of justice. Moreover, any divergence of views among the revisionists was concealed by the singleness of purpose dictated by events, so that Halévy had found himself swept into an alliance with a cause whose ultimate purpose he would not normally have sanctioned. Indeed, it was precisely the evils that Halévy attributed to his anti-Dreyfusard foes that his own allies were to exhibit after their victory. "What had been our greatest fear during the Affair?" he asked in the "Apologie."

We feared the rise of a demagogic bloc, ruining under its inane authority the last remaining liberties of the country. And we saw precisely, at the end of our struggle, on the morrow of our victory, an analogous bloc arising from our side, emerging from our midst, and thriving from our efforts.[61]

Halévy discerned a patent proof of the Socialists' duplicity in the titles of the two works which Jaurès devoted to the Affair. The first, dealing with the irregularities of the court-martial, was called Les Preuves. The second, published after Dreyfus' pardon, was entitled Les Conséquences. And Halévy observed ironically: "A simple soul would have assumed that the only consequence of Dreyfus' innocence would have been to set him free." [62] Halévy's trust in the good faith of Jaurès and Herr was to be his undoing. Even before Clemenceau's amnesty, he had discovered to his dismay that by contributing to their party's triumph, he had helped to carry out a revolutionary program whose principles had proved to be the very negation of his own cherished

[61] Luttes, 94.
[62] Ibid., 41; Halévy, Degas parle, 125.

beliefs: his socialism was of an entirely different order.

And so was his patriotism. Crushing the religious orders or separating Church and State did not disturb Halévy (who never concealed his anticlericalism) as much as did Combes's systematic policy of crippling the nation's strength. To deprive France of its military power in the name of vague principles of international solidarity did not necessarily follow as a natural consequence of Halévy's Dreyfusism. In fact, it was largely because he had felt that the national honor on which such power rested had been jeopardized by the ineptitude of the General Staff that he had become a Dreyfusard. The Moroccan crisis, by exposing his country to German provocations, served to strengthen his belief that his Dreyfusard commitment had rested on more than simply one ambiguity. Its effect, like the Affaire des Fiches and the dubious verdict of the Court of Appeals, was to spread disillusionment in the ranks of the Dreyfusards. It seemed to confirm the contention of the nationalists that the Dreyfusard Republic was not merely capable of distorting legal procedure, but that it was also the source of national disgrace.

Halévy was not alone in feeling profound shame over his country's humiliation after 1905. Coming from entirely opposite directions, Péguy in "Notre Patrie," and Maurras in a series of essays culminating in *Kiel et Tanger*, reached conclusions analogous to Halévy's. But whereas Maurras, who from the very outset had never ceased to proclaim that revisionism would undermine the national security, could now point to the greater wisdom of his cause, Péguy, no less alarmed by the German menace, could not quite bring himself to admit that by demoralizing the Army he had contributed to his country's present plight. Halévy's position in this context was significant, for he was one of the first "Dreyfusards of the first hour" to proclaim his complete conversion on this issue. Sharing Péguy's premonition of impending war, he did not hesitate to assume the blame for France's misfortunes. Such a confession inevitably drew him closer to Maurras, who welcomed the public expression of remorse from Péguy's closest collaborator, professing to speak in the name of the *Cahiers,* and making public penance for their past conduct.[63]

<h1 style="text-align:center">VI</h1>

The "Apologie" starts off on a note of remorse which runs right through it only to give way at the very end to a rather contrived challenge directed against the Right—a prudent rhetorical flourish, which offended Maurras but failed to reassure Péguy. Admittedly, the conclusion does not ring true, yet such is the paradox of Halévy's personality that he deemed it sufficiently emphatic to persuade himself not only that "there is no faltering in this stern small document of mine," but also that he could still maintain his ties with a cause whose decomposition he had so devastatingly exposed.[64]

That Halévy was seeking to break away from an awkward past was clear to any careful reader of the "Apologie." The burden of his book is a confession that his great expectations had turned to despair. Combism gave the lie to the fond hopes of creating a new order. It was the end of an illusion.[65] Agreeing with Péguy that Halévy's impressionistic account was made up of a medley of contradictory impulses, Sorel found the "Apologie" "the work of a man trying to make up for some of his Dreyfusard indiscretions," [66] whereas Pierre Andreu called it "a stirring farewell to Dreyfusism," comparable in its sober grandeur to the spirit of Sorel's own

---

[63] Halévy, *Luttes,* 14; Maurras in *L'Action française,* May 7, 1911.

[64] Halévy, *Péguy,* 109.

[65] Cf. André Beaumier, "Un Essayiste: Daniel Halévy," *La Revue des Deux Mondes,* Sept. 1, 1923, 227.

[66] Cited in Sorel, *Lettres à Paul Delesalle* (Paris, 1947), 233.

defection during these years from the cause of revolutionary syndicalism.[67] Romain Rolland interpreted it as "a plea for forgiveness," but he also noted that if the "Apologie" was marred by inconsistencies, this was because its author was seeking to convey the precise nature of the strain imposed by the Affair on all his fellow Dreyfusards.[68] In Rolland's view, Halévy was admirably suited, because of his own vacillating character—"perpetually lucid and uncertain, beset by doubts and remorse"—to epitomize the essential confusion of his whole generation.[69]

The mood of the "Apologie" is fixed in the very first pages, where, by the skillful use of literary artifice, Halévy embroidered on the theme of "an unconfessed remorse." "These are splendid memories," he recalled with melancholy, "yet they no longer fill us with joy." And, on an even more mournful note, he wrote:

Why do we shun each other and avoid our friends' gaze? . . . Does the truth disturb us? Then, let us seek it. May this arduous Affair, which for so many of us has become a school of misfortune, remain what it was at first, a school of truth. Let us remain as we were, and commemorate our anniversaries by defining our thoughts in spite of our embarrassment and our shame.[70]

Halévy traced their present predicament not only to the very completeness of their triumph but also to the absolute stand they had been forced to take, for by making an irrevocable choice in 1898, they had, in fact, disqualified themselves in case of error. But after a lapse of ten years, the harm had been done: "It is all over. The disturbance is beyond remedy. We bear within ourselves the same rifts which divide our country." [71] And then, suddenly, as if ashamed of such an

[67] Andreu, *Notre Maître, M. Sorel* (Paris, 1953), 70.
[68] Rolland, *Péguy*, II, 129.   [69] Rolland, *Péguy*, I, 222.
[70] *Luttes*, 16, 13.   [71] *Ibid.*, 116.

obvious confession of remorse, he once more evoked the revulsion which inspired them all to protest against the folly of the Right: "But enough, enough of this. . . . These memories bring back the fit of passion provoked by our opponents, and which makes it so hard for us to be fair." [72]

Halévy reproached the Conservatives for having disappointed the fond hopes that he and his generation had placed in their sagacity by relinquishing their authority. Assured of a comfortable electoral majority and enjoying the confidence of all the nation's elites, they could have successfully steered the Republic through the perils which lay ahead. The conservative tradition with which they were entrusted was a sacred heritage, a national legacy; it was their responsibility, and theirs alone, to preserve it intact. By a devious argument, Halévy maintained that theirs was a tradition which was also dear to his heart, for he regarded conservatism as a valuable ingredient in his own eclectic creed.[73] By defaulting before "the supreme test," the Conservatives discredited a tradition placed in their trust, which was not theirs alone, but of all France—and even of some of their opponents. "Men of the Right," exclaimed Halévy, "you should have defended it with your deeds, honored it with your lives. Instead, you dishonored yourselves and your tradition. This is a national calamity. . . . You have disqualified yourselves; you are guilty of our own guilt." [74]

Such a contention could hardly fail to disturb Maurras, who from the start had warned that by challenging the courts the Dreyfusards were guilty of provoking "a grave national disorder." [75] Halévy, however, dismissed this explanation as inadequate, for it failed to take into account the "sublime nature" of the Affair: "the prodigious cataclysm" feared by Maurras grew precisely from the symbolical char-

---

[72] *Ibid.*, 116.   [73] *Ibid.*, 117.   [74] *Ibid.*, 121.   [75] *Ibid.*, 45.

acter assumed by the Jewish captain.[76] The Dreyfusards identified him with a "certain race" which they sought to defend against the false accusations of a "certain caste"— their reactionary opponents. The question of Dreyfus' guilt was overlaid with a deeper significance; and if his trial threatened to disrupt the very foundations of society it was because it revived a debate which had divided Frenchmen for more than a hundred years.[77]

Halévy's argument, forcefully presented in his "Apologie," sheds further light on the general character of the Affair. Both sides did not hesitate to use Dreyfus as a pretext to crush their traditional opponents. To Barrès—who proclaimed that it was the Rubicon itself which flowed through Rennes—the choice lay between Dreyfus and the generals, "the great leaders of France," while Mercier, the Minister of War, placed all patriots before a dilemma when he declared with disarming simplicity that the culprit was either Dreyfus or himself.[78] Moreover, the antirevisionists were not merely concerned with defending the Army. They were also defending one of the bulwarks of bourgeois society against those who challenged the generals as the last line of resistance of the *notables*. Similarly, the Church also stood for tradition and social order; and there were many "cerebral Catholics," as Bernanos called them, who like Brunetière and others had reverted to their faith only because it had become the only remaining refuge for all those champions of the *status quo* who could not tolerate a godless and egalitarian Republic. *La Croix*, for instance, the official organ of the Assumptionists, fostered the wave of conversions by urging all believers to rally behind the sacred union of Army and Altar

[76] *Ibid.*, 43, 21.
[77] Cf. Variot, *Propos*, 147; Maurice Reclus, *Grandeur de la Troisième de Gambetta à Poincaré* (Paris, 1948), 240 ff.
[78] Miquel, *op. cit.*, 107.

and by evoking the sinister menace of the international
Jewish syndicate which was bent on destroying the moral
basis of the established order.[79]

To the enemies of "the sword and the holy water
sprinkler," the fate of Captain Dreyfus was also overshadowed by larger issues. The Ligue des Droits de
l'Homme, the Republican counterpart of Barrès' Ligue de la
Patrie française, proudly traced its origins to the great
national crisis associated with "all that is noblest in the
Revolution." [80] To Julien Benda, a typical example of so
many Dreyfusards of the Jacobin variety, the Affair resurrected a vaster conflict "which has brought to grips two
schools of thought that have been at loggerheads since the
Revolution: those who believe in an egalitarian form of
society [and] those who conceive it as hierarchical." Fifty
years later, on the eve of the Republic's fall, he spoke for
many when he still maintained that the principles of '89
should remain the rallying cry of all those who claimed to
have been the real Dreyfusards.[81]

The peculiarity of Halévy's Dreyfusism was that with
strong affinities for the opposite side, he nevertheless found
himself committed to the revolutionary camp. His native
Orleanism, his deference to tradition, his loathing for Jacobinism in all its forms, were so many traits in his character
that should have inclined him to rally to the antirevisionists.
Yet the "Apologie" makes it clear that although he regarded
all those who persisted in the face of incontrovertible
evidence to proclaim that Dreyfus was a traitor as either
fools or knaves, he also subscribed to Maurras's thesis that
the Affair by its tragic simplicity demanded an equally

[79] Georges Bernanos, *La Grande Peur des biens pensants* (10th ed.; Paris, 1931), 127.

[80] Henri Sée, *Histoire de la Ligue des Droits de l'Homme* (Paris, 1927), 65.

[81] Benda, *Les Cahiers d'un clerc*, 156.

simple commitment.[82] With the social order itself at stake, a single injustice should perhaps have been condoned to preserve the nation from catastrophe, for to rehabilitate Dreyfus was tantamount to delivering "a shattering blow against French society." [83] There were thus not one but two culprits to be considered, argued Halévy, the wronged Captain, and also the Establishment. The tragedy of the Affair was that if one was guilty, the other must be innocent. Seen in this light, the Affair should have been approached with the utmost discretion; yet Halévy admits that in the frenzied passion which the mistrial aroused, he had thrown all caution to the winds—"we should have been prudent, yet we acted with the most intemperate temerity." [84]

Halévy pursued the argument by contrasting the character of the two contending factions. He traced their divisions to the great issues of the Revolution which had virtually split the country into two incompatible blocs, the one authoritarian and elitist and resting on discipline and order, the other libertarian and democratic. To Halévy the chronicler, the Affair resurrected this old conflict and gave a new dimension to the central division in his country's past. But to Halévy the Dreyfusard, this neat division was upset by the fact that, while his sympathies inclined him toward the elitist tradition, his decisive *engagement* shifted him to the other.[85]

By the nineties, Halévy contended, the ideas propounded by the conservatives did in fact command a wide hearing. The masters of his generation, Taine and Renan, had condemned the legacy of the Revolution, forging a devastating critique of the almost sacrosanct principles of '89. But to tamper with what amounted to a national dogma was to run counter to the most strongly rooted tradition in the national

[82] *Luttes*, 115.
[83] Cf. Pierre Lasserre, *Mise au point* (Paris, 1931), 119.
[84] *Luttes*, 22.   [85] Bruchard, "Le Cas de Daniel Halévy," 424.

sentiment. Only intelligent opinion, oblivious to popular susceptibilities, had dared to condemn the dangers of a moral rationalism which had been invalidated by the course of events. The literary elite, to which Halévy belonged by birth and tradition, had moved in the direction of a conservative ideal, which stressed those tangible aspects of the French past that alone seemed capable of serving as a foundation for political stability and moral progress. Tradition, founded on concrete experience, offered a safer guide for action than any hazardous experimentation based on the vague abstractions of revolutionary dogma. Prévost-Paradol had dismissed the Revolution as a folly perpetrated by fanatics swept by an "entraînement d'artistes," and Renan had conclusively demonstrated that a principle that in the course of a century had exhausted the nation's creative energies could not possibly be sound.[86]

Halévy deplored the fact that this conservative tradition, logically consistent and intellectually satisfying, should, at the same time, be so politically inept. By condoning the iniquity inflicted upon Dreyfus, its parliamentary leaders discredited the tradition, impaired its great practical value, and confounded its champions. Thus, Maurras's dilemma, perhaps valid in 1895, was mere sophistry in 1898, for by then it had become clear that if what was at stake was indeed "the temporal salvation of France," it was only the folly of the Right which had placed the national honor in jeopardy.[87] The upper bourgeoisie, allied with the Jesuits and abetting the anti-Semitic demagogues were no match for Waldeck-Rousseau's supporters, who, for all their shortcomings, displayed at least the courage and wisdom to come

[86] Halévy, *Luttes*, 55; cf. Halévy, *Histoire d'une histoire* (Paris, 1939), 24–28, 41–46; see also Pieter Geyl, *Debates with Historians* (New York, 1958), 107–108.

[87] Halévy, *Luttes*, 44–48.

to grips with the Affair and rescue the nation from dishonor.[88]

Yet, if Halévy sought to mitigate his past by blaming the other side for his errors, he was also reluctant to forsake his "revolutionary hope." For all his "conservative instincts," he confessed that he succumbed during the Affair to what he called "a muddled love of humanity." Such vague sympathies, he admitted, constituted a fragile doctrine, resting largely on emotion and totally devoid of any systematic coherence. He tells us that he shared with his friends a juvenile devotion for Proudhon and "that noble race of men, the French Republicans of the nineteenth century." [89] Like their master, they rejected the term democrat, professing themselves "démopédistes," which they defined as idealists with "a tender passion for popular liberties." Confident in the purity of their motives, steering clear of all doctrinaire loyalties, they sought, often awkwardly and hesitantly, to define their purpose in a pragmatic way. With this force as their guide, they faced the future with the assurance that experience alone would unravel their instincts.[90]

This definition of the source of his Dreyfusard creed goes a long way to explain why Halévy had as little in common with the Radicals as he did with Maurras and his followers. The Radicals' Jacobin convictions were as alien to his deeper sympathies as the Action Française's repudiation of sentiment as a guide for action. That the sentimental force that Halévy invoked as the basis of his Dreyfusism should be excluded from Maurras's definition of "integral nationalism" was, he contended, a disaster for the cause which the Action Française claimed to embody. For to reject the "generous impulse" that prompted so many Dreyfusards impoverished the national ideal by neglecting "one of the moral riches of

---

[88] *Ibid.*, 69, 89, 121.   [89] *Ibid.*, 98.   [90] *Ibid.*, 100.

our race." [91] Love, protested Halévy, is a better motive than Maurras's "politics of hate." "The muddled love of humanity" which governed his actions in 1898 could perhaps provoke disorder, but it could not destroy the spirit of justice without which no civilized society can survive. Rejecting the charge that his cause was unpatriotic, Halévy maintained that the first Dreyfusards had a keener sense of French honor than those who placed reason of state above justice. It was not the antirevisionists, but Péguy, himself, and their companions, who were inspired by the right conception of national salvation.[92]

Here, Halévy anticipated the arguments set forth in "Notre Jeunesse," where Péguy asserted with still more fervor that the aim of the Dreyfusards was to preserve France from a state of mortal sin. In a moving passage which echoes his friend's sentiments, Péguy exclaimed:

And we, what did we say? We said that a single injustice, a single wrong to humanity, a single crime shatters the whole social pact, a single dishonorable act will dishonor a whole people. It is a touch of gangrene that corrupts the entire body. What we defend is not our honor alone . . . it is the historical honor of our people, all the historical honor of our whole race . . . all history, all the ascent, all the urge forward, all the past, all the future, all the promise of a people; all that is inestimable, incalculable, of infinite value . . . because it is a unique achievement. . . . At bottom, we did not want France to be placed in a state of mortal sin.[93]

Despite his admiration for Maurras's rhetoric, Halévy subscribed to this vision of France's eternal salvation. It is this fundamental affinity with Péguy, and not the surface differences that provoked "Notre Jeunesse," which has been stressed by all the chroniclers of the *Cahiers de la Quinzaine.*

[91] *Ibid.*   [92] *Ibid.*, 99.
[93] *Notre Jeunesse*, 205–207, adapted from the translation by Julian Green, *Charles Péguy: Men and Saints* (New York, 1944), II, 109–111.

Thus, Vernon Lee, shrewd observer of Péguy's *boutique,*
could still assert more than a year after their quarrel, that
Péguy and Halévy remained as united in the common
struggle against the decomposition of Dreyfusism as they
had been at the height of the Affair.[94]

VII

Certainly not Jacobin, not quite Maurrassien—where then
did Halévy's allegiance lie? His "Apologie," the most introspective of his writings, furnishes us with a better definition
of the objects of his hatred than with any clear statement of
his political loyalties. Yet it is precisely the vagueness in
which he himself shrouded his beliefs that provides us with a
clue. Halévy, in fact, belonged to the most elusive of French
traditions—he was an Orleanist. And here again, it is the
"Apologie" which illustrates the manner in which his latent
Orleanism was revealed to him.

At the root of Halévy's Dreyfusard creed was a dual
loyalty: a love of France combined with a love for humanity,
a form of patriotism embedded in a larger humanism.
During the Affair he sacrificed the former to the latter, and
the gist of the "Apologie" is that now, after the Combist
interlude, the balance must somehow be redressed. But by
stressing the theme of repentance, Halévy at long last
explicitly placed himself in line with Orleanism, regarding it
as the only solid basis for a national restoration. Orleanism,
he admitted, is not without its faults: it is distinguished by a
kind of schizophrenia, alternating between the extremes of
reckless action and subsequent remorse. All liberals, from
Mme de Staël to Paradol and Renan, he tells us, have this in
common: after being swept by revolutionary enthusiasm
they inevitably succumb to self-reproach. Their causes are

[94] "M. Sorel and the Syndicalist Myth," *Fortnightly Review,* Oct., 1911,
668.

always lost causes. Halévy sought some consolation from his present plight in an Orleanist record marked by the same tendency to mitigate the past and build anew on the ruins of lost illusions. He inferred that his own post-Dreyfusard remorse was a clear sign of a hitherto ill-defined and vaguely sensed allegiance, and he rejoiced to discover that the Affair had at last revealed to him the true character of his liberalism. It is this kind of allegiance which was to provoke Péguy's despair with his friend's equivocations. Sorel, who scorned Orleanism as a form of irresponsible dilettantism both politically inept and intellectually shallow, also deplored this aspect of Halévy's attachments. In his final verdict on the "Apologie," he joined Péguy in reproaching him for exhibiting a self-righteousness typical of the Orleanist "pride of mandarins." [95]

But to deduce Halévy's political bearings from a single psychological attribute is inadequate, for the "Apologie" itself attests to a more complex personality, revealing another, equally significant, attachment. Awakened by the Affair and its aftermath, his curiosity was steered in a direction far removed from his avowed Orleanism. The most valuable and enduring of his discoveries were Péguy—and through Péguy—the "nation ouvrière et paysanne" in which he discerned an abiding source of national strength. After his hectic journey through the Affair, he fancifully recounted how he disembarked in this terra incognita inhabited by a breed of men embodying a libertarian vigor, which long concealed from his liberal forbears, was utterly alien to him. [96] It was regrettable that the Orleanists of the past, living in their splendid isolation, had been oblivious to this rich vein of sentiment, which would fulfill their fondest

[95] Péguy, *Solvuntur objecta* (Gallimard ed.; Paris, 1934), 32, 54; Péguy, *Hugo*, 233; Sorel, *Matériaux d'une théorie du prolétariat* (2d ed.; Paris, 1921), 246–247.

[96] Halévy, *Luttes*, 78–82.

hopes. The gulf that separated them from the living reality of artisans and peasants had distorted their sense of the past and their vision of the future. It was necessary to step down from remote armchair speculations and to bridge the gap between the two cultures by relating both levels of liberal achievement. To reconcile the Orleanist and the popular strains of the liberal tradition into an enduring ideal resting on common elitist principles would be the task Halévy would set himself.

Thus the "Apologie," standing in a class apart from Halévy's other works, already revealed the whole gamut of its author's disposition. The futility of political action, the curiosity for the man of the people, the deference to Orleanism coupled with the timid admission of susceptibility to the allurements of "revolutionary hope" (which, in Halévy's as well as Péguy's view belonged to the realm of *mystique*)—all these themes, inextricably intertwined in his first significant book, constituted the principal elements that shaped the course of his maturing ideas. Provoked by a single event of unique intensity, the "Apologie" foreshadowed the course of his future commitments.[97]

In a more immediate sense, the "Apologie" remains one of the most penetrating commentaries on the Dreyfus Affair, reflecting, through the experience of one man endowed with rare sensitivity, the transformations in the ideas and sentiments of a whole generation. Its character as a *témoignage* is dramatically conveyed by the halting style, interspersed with dialogue, digressions, and flash-backs, for it was only by means of such literary devices that Halévy could evoke the medley of contradictory impulses to which he and his friends succumbed. By his own admission, his purpose was not so much to attempt a critique of the Affair, as to present a

[97] See, *inter alia*, Halévy, *Les Trois Epreuves* (Paris, 1941), 72 ff.; and Halévy, *Décadence de la liberté* (Paris, 1931), especially the two sections "Vox populi" and "De re gallica."

chronicle of the turning point in his life, the central chapter in his autobiography. "This is a reconstruction," he wrote, "whose object is to evoke our very disorder."[98] Hence the confusion of themes, the paradoxes, the disparity between reason and emotion are laid bare before the reader.

The "Apologie," the fruit of a decade of reflection on the most important single event in Halévy's life, is a psychological self-analysis, a chronicle, and a polemical tract all in one. As a personal confession it is often puzzling and contradictory, but never tedious or insincere. Halévy's remorse was offset by sudden outbursts of reawakened vehemence against Dreyfus' detractors, his former enemies who then sought his friendship. Now accusing himself, then denouncing his accusers, Halévy sought to convey the pulse and throb of the dramatic events themselves. The "Apologie" is a plea for the virtues of liberalism and at the same time an avowal that "revolutionary hope," also a progressive force, can complement the liberal tradition to enrich the national heritage. It is an account of the Affair in which all its intricacies are scrupulously exposed in the light of later revelations, but also as they were seen at the time. It is a convincing portrait of "a Dreyfusard of the first hour," the tale of an intellectual adventure told with all the zest of the neophyte but also tempered by reflection. It is thus a composite picture of two different levels of reality, for although it succeeds in recapturing the original intensity of the struggle, Halévy's narrative is also overlaid with critical hindsight. It is a remembrance of things past, as though Halévy had revised a contemporary diary, which we are invited to read over his shoulder while he adds his marginal comments. Together with "Notre Jeunesse," which serves as its natural complement, the "Apologie pour notre passé" is

[98] *Luttes*, 97. Cf. René Johannet, *Péguy et ses cahiers* (Paris, 1914), 138, n. 1.

one of the most memorable *témoignages* on the Dreyfus Affair.

VIII

It would be only partly true to say that, of the two companions, Péguy alone was capable of grasping the tragic grandeur of the Affair. The difference in their attitudes was mainly one of temperament—both men sensed the same thing but they translated it in a manner that was in keeping with their contrasting characters. It is hard not to believe Halévy when he tells us that the popular rally of "Le Triomphe de la République," which furnished Péguy with the stirring theme of his opening *Cahier de la Quinzaine*, made an equally "strong impression" on him.[99] Yet if, unlike the son of the chairmender of Orléans, Halévy was not part of that mighty crowd which surged out of the Faubourg Saint-Antoine to the tune of the Marseillaise, it was because he already displayed a characteristic predilection for detachment, for stepping out of the main stream from which he had just emerged so as to be better able to observe it. He recalls how, on that memorable day, standing beside Paul Desjardins, intently watching Péguy immersed in the vast crowd, he discerned that at that moment "something else was on foot, sprung from the Affair, but no longer part of it: the Dreyfus revolution. Let me repeat once more that the *Affaire Dreyfus* was over." [100]

His "Apologie," appearing ten years later, was written in this spirit. As a chronicler he sought to evoke its peculiar temper, but as a *moraliste* he also attempted to bring out the contrast between the original loftiness of the Dreyfusard ideal and its subsequent decomposition. In the process, he inevitably dissected the motives and sorted out the feelings of those who had been blind to the consequences provoked by a civil war that they had precipitated. Péguy could not

[99] Halévy, *Péguy*, 47.   [100] *Ibid.*, 46.

tolerate such tampering with the purity of his youthful zeal to which, by 1910, he had returned with the renewed fervor of a reconverted Christian. To believe that the Affair could be placed, as Halévy claimed, in its "historical setting," was to miss its point altogether, to overlook the essential *mystique*, which to Péguy had been its sole *raison d'être.*[101]

Péguy took a dim view of any kind of reconstruction based on the pretensions of a "scientific method" professing historical accuracy, and it is hardly surprising that Halévy's contention that he could recapture in this manner the sentiments which they had shared ten years before should be anathema to him. In his "Clio" as well as in a doctoral dissertation entitled "Dialogue de l'histoire et de l'âme charnelle," which, significantly, he had written in the form of a rambling dialogue with Halévy, Péguy had—as a faithful disciple of Bergson—contrasted the notion of time as duration with time as the barren reconstruction of history.[102] The former expressed a spiritual tension of the eternal spirit that strove for justice; the latter was an inferior thing, a fruitless endeavor, for to Péguy history was "this *évanouissement,* this inevitable obliteration which comes with the passing of years." [103] In other words, Péguy the poet abhorred historical vanity as an aberration conforming to the sociological approach of "the new Sorbonne," which he condemned as the principal vice of the modern world, "le monde qui fait le malin." Protesting that we must first murder to dissect, he could not sanction any tampering in

---

[101] *Ibid.,* 109. Cf. Marjorie Villiers, *Charles Péguy: A Study in Integrity* (London, 1965), 250–254.

[102] Fragments from the thesis were posthumously published by Gallimard in *La Thèse* (Paris, 1955), but Péguy kept Halévy abreast of its progress, cf. Péguy, *Notre Jeunesse,* 22 ff., 58 ff.; Péguy, *Solvuntur objecta,* 55 ff. See also the glossary by André Fossier, *Tables analytiques des oeuvres de Péguy* (Paris, 1947).

[103] Thibaudet, "Péguy et Bergson," *Nouvelle Revue française,* Apr. 1, 1931, 592; Delhorbe, *op. cit.,* 279.

the name of history with the uniqueness of a past that
nothing could recapture. Because that past was itself duration, not history, he would not, he could not, Péguy
proclaimed, "deny a single atom of my past." [104]

In the "Apologie," Péguy discerned not only a trace of this
historical pretension that he despised, but also a pernicious
illustration of what it meant to grow old. For him, the
notion of aging, of being relegated to the dry dust of
archives, implied betrayal.[105] It was tantamount, again in the
Bergsonian sense, to submitting to the laws of matter, to
becoming a conformist, to forsaking that vital, intuitive
spark that alone could invest the initial experience with its
real and true meaning. As a good disciple of Bergson, Péguy
conceived time as a continuous flow, as the continuity of
consciousness. To step aside from one's stream of memories
was to sin against one's *jeunesse*; to forsake one's youth was
to deny it, to be a traitor. The core of Péguy's belief was an
eternal *engagement*. From the tone of the "Apologie" he
surmised that Halévy had betrayed his past by slipping down
(in Péguy's phrase) "the historical slope," which was temporal, not eternal. Nor could he subscribe to Halévy's
implication that their past could have been an error, for
Péguy saw it instead as the organic culmination of all the
French past, as something solidly rooted in the national
mystique. In his own terminology, their Dreyfusism had
been an *époque* in the main stream of the French past while
Combism was the degeneration of that *époque* into a
période.[106] Against what he alleged was the mechanical
memory of Halévy, the chronicler, he presented his own
living memory, his own vision of the eternal duration and
not merely the historical reconstruction of what he regarded
as a sublime moment in French history, of a national epic

[104] *La Thèse*, 60; *Notre Jeunesse*, 14, 89–90.
[105] Péguy, *Clio* (Gallimard ed.; Paris, 1932), 255.
[106] Péguy, *Notre Jeunesse*, 21.

that had crystallized the Republican, Christian, and Jewish *mystiques* into one great spiritual upsurge. No historical analysis, however sincere, could possibly do justice to such a unique event.[107]

Halévy was quite aware of this fundamental difference in their approach. He realized that the poet, captivated by their "generous impulse," could only convey the "heroic and saintly" virtues of their combat. But for that same reason, he also realized that Péguy was incapable of seeing "the ground strewn with wreckage." [108] For Péguy, on the other hand, the tone of remorse in the "Apologie" implied a betrayal which he, for his part, could not possibly sanction, since it amounted to denying the reality of the Dreyfusard *mystique*. To the extent that Halévy, like Maurras, had deplored the ravages of the Affair, he was equally guilty, in Péguy's eyes, of having destroyed the *mystique* of their cause, of capitulating to the *politique* of their opponents.

"Notre Jeunesse" contains a devastating attack against the sophistries of the Action Française. That this should appear in what was virtually an open letter to Halévy, whom Péguy implicitly identified with the opponents of his *mystique*, seemed not only an insult but an injustice to his offended friend. For what Maurras had maintained from the outset was that the Dreyfusards were tainted by their origins, whereas the "Apologie" had demonstrated quite the opposite view, namely, that the purity of their "generous impulse" had only subsequently been corrupted by the politicians. In his passionate indignation against his collaborator's remorse, Péguy seems to have overlooked the fact that Halévy's argument was essentially analogous to his own theory about the "decomposition" of Dreyfusism. It seems likely that, shocked by those passages in the "Apologie" which seemed flattering to Maurras, he jumped to the

[107] Thibaudet, "Péguy et Bergson," 584, 591.
[108] Halévy, *Péguy*, 111.

conclusion that Halévy had completely defected to the other side.[109]

In fact, the "Apologie" had much more in common with "Notre Jeunesse" than with the ideas professed by Maurras. The two disciples of Bergson stressed the inevitability of the transformation of the organic into the intellectual. Both distrusted the Action Française as a party of the same order as the Radicals—a faction of what Péguy called "le parti de l'intelligence." They shared the view that Maurras's positivism conformed to the same spirit as the Jacobin abstractions, and they rejected both these logical constructions because they rested on a misguided historicism that failed to take into account the tangible realities of the French past. That Péguy seemed to ignore this underlying identity in their views was most galling to his friend's pride.[110]

The liberal, Renanien tone of the "Apologie" was a further source of irritation to Péguy, for almost as repugnant as Maurras's positivism was Halévy's profession of Orleanism. This too was a form of betrayal, for to Péguy the Orleanists were as alien to the French tradition as he interpreted it as were the Combistes or the followers of Herr and Jaurès. In his personal scheme of French history, the July Monarchy, on which he conferred the label of a *période*, was but the pale reflection of what he grudgingly admitted had been the *époque* of the Old Regime. On this matter, admittedly, the two men were entirely at odds, but in a deeper sense, in their intuitive discernment rather than in their political loyalties, they were in harmony—if only because they both discerned by 1910 the limits of the validity of their Dreyfusism. "Notre Jeunesse" and the "Apologie" are in this sense complementary. Péguy the poet

---

[109] Péguy, *Notre Jeunesse*, 65 ff.; Péguy, *Hugo*, 234–236.
[110] Rolland, *Péguy*, I, 342. There were even rumors that Halévy had challenged Péguy to a duel, cf. Rolland, *Péguy*, I, 225; Halévy, *Péguy*, 110, n. 1.

sang the epic of their selfless devotion to the noble cause. Halévy wrote a chronicle of the drama, and as a good Orleanist, drew attention to their rashness. At bottom, the two friends shared a common devotion to the same *mystique*. Marcel Péguy's contention that their difference could be explained purely in terms of conflicting political sympathies is misleading.[111] Sorel was closer to the truth when he ascribed their quarrel to a clash of personalities: the "Apologie" in its essentials merely reiterated the doubts which Péguy himself had expressed in an earlier *Cahier*, "A Nos Amis, à nos abonnés"—but with the additional dimension of a certain remorse defined in Orleanist terms which Péguy could not tolerate.[112]

The two men were particularly intimate precisely at the time when Halévy was pondering over his "Apologie." By moving to Orsay, not far from Halévy's family estate in Jouy-en-Josase, Péguy had gained in Halévy a rural neighbor after his own heart. He declared: "We reside in the same Ile-de-France, we are now country neighbors—this begets real friendship." That is why, he explained, he listened to Halévy's confessions during their long walks across the plain of Saclay, as one peasant would have listened to another, and when his manuscript was completed, Péguy published it in his *Cahiers* without changing a single word.[113]

The unexpected outburst of "Notre Jeunesse" could therefore hardly fail to astonish Halévy. He later attributed it in part to what he discreetly called Péguy's "dérèglement de cœur." The object of Péguy's affections was Blanche Raphaël, an unrepentant Jewish Dreyfusard, who had never concealed her own resentment against the "Apologie" and

---

[111] Halévy, "Carnets," entries for June 20, 1927; Dec. 3, 1927.

[112] Variot, *Propos*, 254, 264; cf. Péguy, *Hugo*, 199.

[113] Péguy, *Hugo*, 11–12, 47; see also Halévy, "Carnets," entries for Jan., 1910; cf. André Spire in *Feuillets*, no. 40, 3; Jean Cocteau, *The Journals of Jean Cocteau*, ed. and trans. by Wallace Fowlie (New York, 1956), 187.

who, it seems, exerted pressure on Péguy to reply. The strident Dreyfusard tone of "Notre Jeunesse" was prompted by his love for her.[114]

Another explanation for a quarrel conducted on such a high moral plane can be traced to the more mundane considerations of Péguy's predicament as editor. His return to orthodox Dreyfusism was reinforced by the pressing necessity of preserving the economic solvency of his *Cahiers*. Since its foundation, the bulk of its subscribers had been Jews, most of whom, already dismayed by "A Nos Amis, à nos abonnés," now still further disturbed by the tone of the "Apologie," threatened to withdraw their support from a review which seemed to endorse Halévy's views. "Notre Jeunesse" was written in an effort to ward off this menace. Its moving eulogy to the memory of Bernard Lazare and its evocation of a Jewish *mystique* which Péguy generously ranked with his own were, it has been asserted, deliberately stressed to offset the passionately Christian tenor of his *Jeanne d'Arc* and regain the favor of his Jewish clientele.[115]

All those who frequented Péguy's *boutique* have confirmed that the Jews formed its principal element. René Johannet, one of Péguy's most ardent Catholic disciples, complained that "there was always a Jewish air" about the *Cahiers*, and the anti-Semitic Sorel, resenting Péguy's excessive attachment for his Jewish friends, also attributed "Notre Jeunesse" to economic expediency.[116] Péguy himself gave credence to his indebtedness to the Jews when he bluntly acknowledged: "It is they who provide me with a living."

[114] Madame Favre, "Souvenirs sur Péguy," *Europe*, Feb. 15, and Mar. 15, 1938, 324; Yvonne Servais, *Charles Péguy: The Pursuit of Salvation* (Oxford, 1953), 363; but see Villiers, *Péguy*, 250–251.
[115] Personal communication: Gabriel Marcel, confirmed by André Spire; René Johannet, *Péguy et ses cahiers*, 157.
[116] Variot, *Propos*, 263.

But another of his epigrams—"with the Jews I can be a
Christian to my heart's desire, with the Catholics, I could
not"—adds the proper nuance to this indebtedness.[117]
Among those who acted as a foil to his personality, he could
freely assert his highly individual Christian sentiments.

The rupture provoked by the "Apologie" can also be
traced to Péguy's growing resentment against "notre maître,
M. Sorel." Exasperated by the latter's increasing sympathy
for the Right, whose abusive anti-Semitism Péguy roundly
condemned, he believed, with some justice, that the "Apologie" had been inspired by Sorel's own *Révolution dreyfusienne*, published the year before. He could not tolerate the
intrusion of Sorel's ideas in his *Cahiers*. By his attack against
Sorel's disciple, the querulous Péguy, a stout peasant to the
core, meant to proclaim his intention that he alone would be
master of his house.[118]

Péguy's quarrel with Sorel, the immediate cause of which
was indeed too trivial to be taken at face value, was of the
same order as his break, two years earlier, with Halévy.[119] In
both cases, he could not bear to be identified with either of
his collaborators because the drift of their thinking and their
modes of feeling were, in fact, a shade too close to his own.
He was fonder of Halévy than of any other of his associates,
and he respected his literary gifts as well as his integrity; yet
the harmony of their views concealed radically divergent
temperaments. The "Apologie" gave rise to an ambiguity,
for its tone of remorse could easily be mistaken as Péguy's by

[117] Cited in MS letter from Halévy to Pierre Andreu, dated Feb. 11,
1951.
[118] Andreu, *Sorel*, 280; MS letter from Sorel to Halévy, dated June 15,
1913.
[119] Marcel Péguy, "La Rupture de Charles Péguy et de Georges Sorel,"
Cahiers de la Quinzaine (Paris, 1930), *passim*; Andreu, *op. cit.*, 271–288;
Georges Goriely, *Le Pluralisme dramatique de Georges Sorel* (Paris, 1962),
179–181.

the readers of the *Cahiers*. Moreover, Péguy, increasingly absorbed by his Catholic conversion, growing more irascible and uncompromising, could only welcome the collaboration of such people as Benda whose jesting impertinence would more suitably offset his own intransigence. It is ironical that while Benda's *La Trahison des clercs* arraigned Péguy as the arch foe of rationalism, as the chief culprit for transmitting Bergsonian vitalism to the nationalist revival on the eve of the war, it was Halévy, who, ostracized from the *Cahiers*, was to become the most sedulous propagandist of Péguy and his review.

Halévy's expulsion from the *boutique* coincided with the beginning of the *Cahiers'* decline. The golden age of Péguy's review came to an end after 1910. With Edouard Berth, André Spire, and a handful of other Sorelian disciples, Halévy followed the master to Paul Delesalle's book shop, while Péguy remained, as Halévy wrote, "virtually alone, greater than ever." [120] With the notable exception of the final installment of *Jean-Christophe*, the contents of the last years of the *Cahiers* were meager; and it is significant that after the parting shot of "Victor-Marie, Comte Hugo," Péguy never resumed the debate provoked by the "Apologie." Halévy's *Jeunesse de Proudhon*, his first *Visites aux paysans du Centre*, and his edition of the memoirs of Perdiguier, to say nothing of his *Quelques Nouveaux Maîtres*—all of which, being directly inspired by Péguy, deserved to appear under his auspices—were published elsewhere. Péguy's swan song was undoubtedly grandiose, and his lonely striving to recapture during his last remaining years the purity of his Republican and Christian ideal was not without pathos. But it was unfortunate that the one friend on whom he had made the greatest impact should have been forced to seek his destiny elsewhere—with De-

---

[120] MS letter from Halévy to Andreu, *supra*, n. 117.

lesalle, the provincial *Cahiers du Centre,* or the enterprising socialist editor, Marcel Rivière.

Of all the forces which influenced Halévy's thinking, those represented by Péguy most decisively shaped the course of his ideas. This influence took the form of a search for French values buried deep in the popular soul: in the syndicalist movement, which at least in its early stages reflected the peculiar libertarian temper embodied so eloquently in Péguy, and in its peasant roots, especially in the Centre from which Péguy had himself emerged. In Proudhon or Michelet, in the itinerant artisans and journeymen of the Compagnonnage du Tour de France, or in his younger contemporaries such as Jean Guéhenno and Robert Garric, Arnaud Dandieu or Pierre Hamp—in all these, Halévy found a trace of that living reality of a certain French past which Péguy had revealed to him.

He was not alone in identifying this national spirit with Péguy. Like him, Sorel had also been drawn to the *Cahiers* because he too felt that its editor more than any other living Frenchman epitomized, as he put it, "the ancestral soul of France—of that old France which is perishing." [121] Romain Rolland shared this admiration, and his monumental biography of his former pupil at the Ecole Normale is as much a study of his life as a panegyric of the "old France," which he had so splendidly incarnated. Halévy's sentiments were of the same order, but perhaps because he himself fell short of achieving a full-fledged creative talent of his own, his loyalty to Péguy was more persistent, more concentrated. With a greater readiness to subordinate his own personality to that of his friend, he proved to be the best equipped among Péguy's admirers to translate the unique flavor of his genius.

Péguy's influence is reflected in much of Halévy's work.

[121] MS letter by Sorel, dated Feb. 25, 1914, printed in *Feuillets,* no. 34, 13. See also Winfred Stephens, "Charles Péguy," *Living Age,* Jan., 1919, 89–91.

The two masterly volumes that he devoted to *La Fin des notables* are a penetrating account of the twilight zone between the Republican *mystique* and its resulting *politique*, while his diatribes against "la république des comités" bear the unmistakable mark of Péguy's own polemics against the "multicésarisme des comités." It was also Péguy who reminded Halévy that the great cleavage in the history of the Republic occurred in 1880. It was in that year, he told his friend, that the primary school made its first impact on French society, thus destroying consecrated custom and the popular fibre of old France—an insight, claims Halévy, "to which my historical work owes a lot." [122]

The effect which these and other simple verities—the result of Péguy's native intuition—had on Halévy's own thinking is incalculable. They added a new dimension to his liberal sensibilities and broadened the scope of his quest for French values. Péguy, in his conceit, never failed to stress the debt which his *notable* friend owed him for merely unveiling before his bewildered curiosity the mysterious resources of the old France which he so self-consciously incarnated. Nor was he unaware that his friend relished his company as a vicarious insight into a vast area of the national culture which was lacking in his own breeding, reminding him for instance, in that astonishing open letter, "Victor-Marie, Comte Hugo": "When you are with me, Halévy, when you are in my province, my province of thought and my province of conversation . . . , then you have in fact made the same journey as I. [123]

More discreetly, Halévy repaid this debt by devoting his life's work to the memory of his friend. Perhaps nowhere does he express his devotion with more feeling than in his

[122] Halévy, *Péguy*, 180; cf. Péguy, *Lettre à Franklin-Bouillon*, ed. Daniel Halévy (Paris, 1948), 16, 31. But see also Jean Onimus, *Incarnation: Essai sur la pensée de Charles Péguy* (Paris, 1952), 240.
[123] Péguy, *Hugo*, 37.

obituary in the Orleanist *Le Temps*. Here, breaking through his usual reserve, he resumes the unfinished dialogue of "Victor-Marie, Comte Hugo": "You were such a different person—so strongly rooted in realities. . . . Your life has captivated me." [124] Almost all his work was a commentary on this theme.

[124] *Le Temps*, Dec. 12, 1914, reprinted in *Le Divan*, Dec., 1916. Cf. Maurice Barrès, *Chronique de la Grande Guerre* (Paris, 1923), VIII, 403; and Barrès, *Mes Cahiers* (Paris, 1929–1957), II, 163.

CHAPTER IV

The Socialist Militant

ONE of the most important results of the Dreyfus Affair was the revelation of the inadequacies of parliamentary democracy and of the social order on which it rested. Discredited by its alliance with the defeated supporters of antirevisionism, the bourgeoisie was regarded as a spent force:

Yesterday still Voltairian . . . , today clerical while anxiously asking the reactionary forces of the past for protection, now the bourgeoisie was no longer anything but a worn-out wheel, dilapidated through misuse of its strength. . . . Therefore, the strength of the future rested with the people; there was the dormant stock, the immense resources of latent intelligence, energy and individuality.[1]

With these words contained in his "Lettre à la jeunesse," Emile Zola pointed the way to many, like Halévy, who had emerged from the Affair scorning middle-class values and resolved to carry on the Dreyfusard struggle against the forces of reaction.

I

The "Dreyfus Revolution" had released a powerful cur-

[1] Cited in William Herzog, *From Dreyfus to Pétain* (New York, 1947), 132.

rent of humanitarian ardor, which swept many of the champions of Dreyfus into what one of them, André Spire, has called "a great wave of social solidarity." [2] This second phase of the Affair, which Halévy dates from the monster rally that had celebrated "The triumph of the Republic" at the Place de la Nation, was marked by energetic attempts to preserve the bonds that had been forged between intellectuals and their working-class companions in the thick of the fight. Elated by their victory, bourgeois and workers held their ranks to pursue together the social and economic implications of their Dreyfusism.

The triumph of Dreyfusism was also accompanied by an effervescence of socialist ideas breeding new hopes for a total reconstruction of French society. Exhilarated by the combative ardor shown by the working class for the good cause, the young Dreyfusards who gathered around the towering figure of Jaurès earnestly believed that their mission was to assist the masses in achieving their emancipation, and by raising their intellectual level, make them fit to take over the capitalist state. As befitted intellectuals, it was by the written and the spoken word that contact with the people was to be established, yet many of their efforts assumed an essentially practical form, largely empirical and sometimes even pioneering. Creating education institutes and sponsoring study groups, promoting popular magazines and joint cooperatives were the means by which the new utopia was to be revealed. But if "going to the people" was undoubtedly a genuine source of spiritual refreshment, it was also regarded by many as the essential condition for carrying out the revolution.[3]

This socialist fervor was at first identified with a Republican *mystique*, for Dreyfusism had also awakened a new loyalty for the faltering regime. The formation of Waldeck-

---

[2] In *Feuillets de l'amitié Charles Péguy*, no. 40, 3.

[3] Daniel Halévy, *Péguy and "Les Cahiers de la Quinzaine,"* trans. by Ruth Bethell (London, 1946), 47; D. W. Brogan, *France under the Republic: 1870–1939* (New York, 1940), 371–372.

Rousseau's revisionist government was hailed as the prelude to a renovated Republic, but in the first flush of victory, Halévy, like many others in Péguy's circle, looked to Jaurès as the real prophet of a new era that would regenerate the moribund Republic barely saved by their efforts. Jaurès incarnated the loftiest spirit of a militant Dreyfusism which aimed to reconcile a French socialist tradition with a progressive Republic into one great revolutionary upsurge. With all the resources of his intoxicating rhetoric, the great tribune held out the hope that the path to socialist reform lay through political action, justifying his participation in Combes's Délégation des Gauches as the first step toward the enactment of social reforms which would ultimately lead to the creation of a collectivist society. But by attaching the destinies of his party to an unholy alliance with the Radicals, his strategy tended to dilute socialism with timid reformism, so that his endorsement of the Bloc's persecution of their vanquished opponents was eventually repudiated by many of his supporters as a betrayal of socialist honor.

Halévy's disenchantment with Jaurès, however, came only gradually. Emerging from the Affair as a socialist only in the vaguest sense and with no precise doctrine, he was at first won over by Jaurès' moral conviction to subscribe to his brand of socialism. Jaurès' concern for social justice and his faith in the possibility of reforming society according to a strictly French revolutionary tradition were attitudes with which Halévy readily sympathized. With all the enthusiasm of a militant Dreyfusard, he had as early as 1899 hailed his courage in overcoming the hesitations of the Guesdists to commit the Socialists to the revisionist camp, and in the following years he welcomed his efforts to achieve Socialist solidarity.[4] An early convert to the humanitarian socialism which Jaurès incarnated, Halévy was easily drawn by an

[4] Halévy, *Essais sur le mouvement ouvrier en France* (Paris, 1901), 232 ff.; Halévy, "Avant le Congrès de Lyon," *Pages Libres*, Nov. 21, 1903, 712.

eclectic ideal, which sought to give French socialism its fullest measure of self-expression.

It was in this spirit that he responded to the generous impulse generated by Jaurès in the early party congresses, and it was with the same enthusiasm that he participated in launching *L'Humanité* which was originally conceived for the purpose of gathering all men of good will dedicated to transforming Dreyfusism into a great socialist crusade. Embarking on a career that was to carry him through many bewildering phases, Halévy found in Jaurès' newspaper a pragmatic ideal that sustained his hopes well into the years beyond the Affair. His accounts of the first labor congresses which he covered as a reporter reflect the perplexities of a rank-and-file socialist confronted by the tactical problems that divided the various factions. But they also reveal his conviction that those who plunged into the rough waters of politics were also assisting in the common endeavor to achieve a new order.[5]

The day would come when Halévy was to espouse the principle of a collectivism diametrically opposed to the form of socialism advocated by Jaurès. But before being swept by the currents of corporatism, which were already flowing through socialist thought at the turn of the century, he was still sufficiently imbued with the Dreyfusard vision of a Republican *mystique* to be drawn by a program conforming to the democratic process and which sought to integrate the laboring classes within the existing framework of Republican institutions. Once the Dreyfusard cause had prevailed and the Socialists had come into their own, however, he abandoned his earlier convictions and came to reject a political opportunism that seemed to recast Socialism in the image of Radicalism. Yet, characteristically, he never failed to react emotionally to the *élan* which Jaurès had given to his own

[5] MS letters from Halévy to Charles Guieysse, especially June 3, 1902, but also Feb. 7, 1905, and May 11, 1907.

idealism. Jaurèssism, like the Dreyfusism from which it had itself emerged, came to represent yet one more promise unfulfilled and hope deferred. But unlike Péguy who came to identify it with "the vilification of a great human love," [6] Halévy preserved to the end a distant admiration for "this endearing creature . . . , so splendidly keen and generous of speech." [7] With an eye for drama, he sympathized with the plight of a man who, before succumbing to party politics, "with no voice left for poetry," had incarnated some of the best in socialist sentiment. Jaurès' subsequent conduct, he maintained in retrospect, could never detract from the moral stature of the founder of L'Humanité. And long after Halévy himself had deserted the party, he did not conceal his veneration for the man whose prodigious energy and boundless enthusiasm had, in his words, "alone created and kept together a party which was cast in his own image." [8]

The new direction of Halévy's interests was in keeping with the general sentiment that prevailed among many men of letters whose political consciousness, only temporarily awakened by the Affair, soon gave way to the traditional scorn of their profession for politicians. Even many like Blum, whose loyalty to the party was beyond reproach, could never quite overcome their misgivings, and despite Jaurès' enormous prestige among university students, there were no more than a couple of Normale graduates who joined the ranks of the Socialists in the Assembly.[9] The niceties of constitutional reform or parliamentary tactics aroused little

[6] Halévy, Péguy, 66; Georges Goriely, Le Pluralisme dramatique de Georges Sorel (Paris, 1962), 177–178.

[7] Péguy, 225.

[8] Halévy, "Chronique nationale: France," La Revue de Genève, Mar., 1921, 421. Judging by Jean Santeuil, Proust also shared these sentiments, cf. Philip Kolb, "Proust's Portrait of Jaurès," French Studies, Oct., 1961, 338–349.

[9] Hubert Bourgin, De Jaurès à Léon Blum: L'Ecole Normale et la politique (Paris, 1938), 190 ff.; cf. Charles Andler, Vie de Lucien Herr: 1864–1926 (Paris, 1932), 118, 137; Gonzague Truc, "Un Penseur d'extrême-gauche: Lucien Herr," L'Opinion, July 30, 1932, 19.

interest among most intellectuals, while authors and critics joined in a campaign of denigration against a political system which, itself suffering from atrophy and corruption, was denounced as incapable of remedying the social malaise besetting French democracy. A constant flow of polemical literature ranging in quality from Paul Bourget's *Le Tribun* to the more substantial criticism of Emile Faguet's *Le Culte de l'incompétence* and its natural sequel, *L'Horreur des responsabilités*, exposed the chicanery of self-seeking politicians, stressing the futility of entrusting responsibility to a discredited political system.[10]

This widespread hostility, only partly the consequence of a general reaction against the more blatant abuses of Combism, was accompanied by an intense curiosity about social problems. After the dry positivism of Renan and Taine, the sympathy for the oppressed, which ran so deep in the wake of the Affair, provided a greater inspiration than party platforms. Largely as a result of the Affair, but also under the impact of a humanitarian current derived from Tolstoy, the Parisian litterati emerged from their seclusion to turn their attention to rural poverty and proletarian distress. This trend was reinforced by a revival of provincial and working-class literature. Such works as Pierre Hamp's *Le Rail*, the class-conscious reminiscences of Charles-Louis Philippe, and a whole genre of novels like J. H. Rosny's *Sous le Fardeau* reflected a new spirit in French literature, giving a fresh impulse to the social conscience of many a young author. At the same time, a spate of *enquêtes* devoted to labor conditions in town and village marked an increasing concern for what Fernand Gregh called "the human poetry of the toiling multitude." [11]

[10] Fernand Baldensperger, *L'Avant-Guerre dans la littérature française: 1900–1914* (Paris, 1919), 49–60.
[11] Romain Rolland, *Péguy* (Paris, 1944), I, 15 ff.; Baldensperger, *op. cit.*, 68–69.

Still wedded to the world of letters, Halévy's interests conformed to this prevailing trend. It was during the next decade that he achieved a literary reputation for his sympathetic social studies. His *Essais sur le mouvement ouvrier*, published in 1901, is not only a significant contribution to labor history but almost a literary masterpiece—in Val Lorwin's opinion, "a beautifully written and perceptive work . . . perhaps still the best guide to the social problems at the turn of the century." This was followed in 1904 by the first installment of his celebrated *Visites aux paysans du Centre*, a book of vibrant delight and great literary charm, still valuable for its illuminating glimpses into the rural cooperative movement.[12] Halévy's thumbnail sketches of syndicalist leaders, his first essays on Proudhon and other nineteenth-century libertarians, and a variety of fictional and imaginative works such as the novel "Un Episode" (1907) and that bizarre fable of a proletarian utopia, "Histoire de quatre ans" (1904), also date from this period.

II

As Halévy entered the next phase of his career—a phase which was to shape the course of his beliefs even more decisively than the Affair itself—he naturally turned to his elders for guidance. And it is significant that the two men who exercised the greatest attraction on a Dreyfusard whose curiosity was gradually shifting from an exclusive interest in letters should have been Maurice Barrès and Georges Sorel. *Le père* Sorel, as Péguy called him, soon came to be acknowledged as *notre maître* by the small group of the *Cahiers de la Quinzaine*, but it was undoubtedly Barrès who

[12] Val Lorwin, *The French Labor Movement* (Cambridge, Mass., 1954), 330. Paul Souday in *Le Temps*, Sept. 8, 1921; André Thérive in *Le Temps*, Aug. 22, 1935; Thierry Maulnier, "La Tragédie paysanne," *La Revue Universelle*, May 1, 1935, 371–375.

—despite the active antirevisionist stand that he had taken during the Affair—stood out as the undisputed master, maintaining his ascendancy over the minds of the generation that had made its literary debut in *La Revue Blanche*. This elegant purveyor of rare sensations, whose dandyism verging on anarchism had scandalized the staid Parisian bourgeoisie, had already in the nineties become the literary idol of the students at Condorcet. At a time when the younger writers were already questioning the intellectual values of their elders, Barrès was worshipped as a sort of *princeps juventutis* whose shadow was cast well into the years beyond the Affair.

As late as 1921, Halévy contended that Barrès had achieved the rare feat of being the *directeur de conscience* of two successive generations, his own and that of Henri Massis, which, too young to have participated in the Affair, succumbed as much to the lingering charm of Barrès as to the new trends represented by Péguy and Maurras.[13] Indeed, his influence, "ondoyant et divers," was deep and far-reaching. Only recently, Fernand Gregh has reminded his juniors that "the young men of today cannot possibly conceive what Barrès meant for my generation," while Proust in *Jean Santeuil*—that admirable chronicle of these crucial years— evokes the overpowering impression made by Barrès on all his schoolmates.[14] Léon Blum, in his *Souvenirs sur l'Affaire*, recounts the anguish endured by his Dreyfusard companions when Barrès proclaimed that he was rallying to antirevisionism: "something was shattered, broken; one of the avenues of my youth was closed—the Barrès drama was for me the

[13] Halévy, "Notes sur l'esprit publique," *La Revue de Genève*, Oct., 1921, 552. Cf. Julien Benda, "Regards sur le monde passé," *Nouvelle Revue française*, Sept. 1, 1935, 418–419.

[14] Fernand Gregh, "Barrès et Proust," *La Revue de Paris*, Nov., 1951, 64; cf. Pierre de Boisdeffre, *Métamorphose de la littérature française de Barrès à Malraux* (Paris, 1951), I, 54; see also Maurice Barrès, *Mes Cahiers* (Paris, 1929–1957), IX, 162.

most pathetic of all." [15] For Halévy, who emerged from the Affair somewhat less confident in the infallibility of his cause, there could scarcely be any question of a radical break with Barrès. In fact, he considered his continued deference to Barrès quite compatible not only with his Dreyfusard past, but also with his admiration for Sorel. Both men shared the same cult of heroic vitalism, and what one called the "national energy" was defined by the other as an integral element of his "social poetry." [16] Barrès' Lorraine, expanded into a cultural doctrine, was regarded by Halévy as merely a literary variant of the Sorelian myth. Halévy's penchant for ferreting out affinities transcending surface differences permitted him to be naturally drawn to both. Indeed, Barrès, being not only the more literary of the two, but also an *héritier* with a social conscience, was more likely to appeal at first to the young bourgeois of the Place Dauphine, naturally predisposed by his *notable* heredity to admire in Barrès the man of breeding and culture who was not blind to the social question.[17]

What endeared this "prince of youth" to Halévy was above all the *culte du moi*, the deliberate cultivation of the exalted self, the greedy craving for an experimental individualism that would enlarge his ego. The cult of the self was not merely a sentimental fad or a self-indulgent search for random pleasure. It was also a method for broadening one's experience, of establishing, as an enthusiastic Halévy asserted in his *Quelques Nouveaux Maîtres*, "a dialogue with all things and all beings." [18] If it smacked of dilettantism, it was a dilettantism of a nobler sort, doubly welcome because

[15] Paris, 1935, 88–89.
[16] Cf. Michael Curtis, *Three against the Republic: Sorel, Barrès and Maurras* (Princeton, N.J., 1959), 48–50.
[17] Albert Thibaudet, *La République des professeurs* (Paris, 1927), 6 ff. sets forth the famous distinction between *héritiers* and *bousiers*. Cf. R. K. Gooch, *Regionalism in France* (New York, 1931) 44, n. 1.
[18] Moulins, 1914, 149.

DANIEL HALÉVY AND HIS TIMES

it rejected the confining utilitarian values of a decadent bourgeois order while at the same time it steered one's curiosity in the direction of a disinterested idealism. The *culte du moi* provided an opportunity for combining aesthetic pleasure with purposeful endeavor. The youthful disciple of Renan could not fail to be drawn by a fellow admirer who had also started his literary career with his own *Huit Jours chez M. Renan*. For a Nietzschean enthusiast, who already before the Affair had succumbed to anarchist ideas, to abandon one's self to sensations need not be only sheer egoism. To assert one's *I* and cultivate one's feelings was not only the natural complement of that delicate Renanien skepticism and Nietzschean nihilism in which he had been bred. It was also a source of intellectual delight admirably suited to channel his desire for self-fulfillment.

Barrès' famous trilogy served Halévy's generation as handbooks of exquisite sensualism, as recipes for indulging an unbridled fancy by sallying forth on voyages abounding in gratifying experiences.[19] Appropriately enough, Halévy's first literary success, *Vénétie et Toscane*, was a rambling, introspective account of an Italian journey, suffused with the distinctive Barrèsien flavor of striving to reconcile the individual with the social.[20] This dainty pastiche is no mere imitation, however. In the opinion of at least one critic, *Vénétie et Toscane* possesses an originality of its own, combining an already mature, almost musical sensitivity with "a tender curiosity in discovering the unknown universe of the popular soul." [21]

In Halévy's view, these two tendencies need not necessarily be incompatible. Indeed, his fascination for what he

[19] Micheline Tison-Braun, *La Crise de l'humanisme* (Paris, 1958), I, 161.
[20] Appearing first in two installments in *La Revue de Paris*, Aug. 1 and Sept. 1, 1898, this essay was later privately printed for limited circulation.
[21] René Johannet in *La Minerve française*, Apr. 15, 1920, 189.

called "the popular soul" was derived from Barrès' proposi-
tion of an original solution for resolving the conflict between
tradition and the kind of individualism which sought to rise
above the *fin-de-siècle* nihilism besetting his generation. A
dilettante soon wearies of sensations, no matter how refined,
and must ultimately seek something outside his exalted self
that can become the center of his affections. By fastening his
curiosity on socialism Halévy was undoubtedly seeking to
project his personality beyond his confined Parisian milieu,
but he was also reacting to a force which was not totally
divorced from the principal concern of *Un Homme libre*.

As a self-styled socialist, Barrès—who had entered Parliament as a "National-Socialist" from Nancy—had turned his
disciples' attention to the stirrings of the proletarian soul,
which he regarded as a spontaneous reservoir of national
energy guided not by intelligence but by superior instinct
rooted in tradition. By placing sentiment above reason, the
people, he contended, were the real repositories of the
richest sentiments of the race. Adapting social emancipation
to the national fact, he advocated a policy that would be as
resolutely social as it was national, dedicated to both moral
progress and social preservation.[22] From Renan and Taine he
had adopted an organic theory of society determined by race,
time, and environment, and he rejected all abstractions
which distorted the continuity between past and present.
Deeply tinged with the powerful current of Tolstoian hu-
manitarianism, his early works—especially the blatantly
anarchist *L'Ennemi des lois*—are also impregnated with a
libertarianism that, in his view as well as Halévy's, constituted the most permanent strain in the French socialist
tradition.[23]

To be sure, the brand of socialism that he advocated

[22] Eugen Weber, "Nationalism, Socialism, and National-Socialism in
France," *French Historical Studies*, II (Fall, 1962), 274.
[23] Tison-Braun, *op. cit.*, I, 156 ff.

smacked of an archaic corporatism, having a certain air of unreality about it. Resulting from a dilettante's exasperation with bourgeois mediocrity and a disdain for heartless scientism, it also insisted on the positive value of exploring a popular ethic that could restore France to her ancient traditions and extirpate the evils of modern industrialism. Barrès' socialism took the form of a lyrical inspiration stressing the purity of provincial life and the regenerating virtues of a native libertarianism which could make way for something more broadly human than current collectivist dogma.

It was precisely this rare blend of an awareness of the resources of populism combined with a heightened literary sensibility which inevitably attracted Halévy. The groundwork for his conversion had already been laid by Barrès before the Dreyfus Affair. In its subject matter—a pleasure-seeking Italian princess converted to socialism by the social poetry revealed in the life of her tenant farmers—*Vénétie et Toscane*, first published in 1898, already foreshadowed the Barrèsien impulse that was to lead Halévy away from pure literature. Three years later, the publication of his *Essais sur le mouvement ouvrier* marked his resolution to become a free-lance explorer of proletarian life and to strengthen by his action a creative source of moral progress. To attach his loyalties to a cause that exhibited such courage and vigor could contribute as much to exalting his ego as to follow in Barrès' path to Venice or Toledo.[24] By participating in a great collective endeavor, which would merge his individualism with a genuine popular ethic, he could conveniently reconcile his growing concern for social questions with the requirements of the new literary mood.[25]

Like the author of *Sous l'Oeil des Barbares*, Halévy soon

[24] Cf. Christian Sénéchal, *Les Grands Courants de la littérature française contemporaine* (Paris, 1934), 77.

[25] Halévy, *Nouveaux Maîtres*, 4, 154.

discovered for himself the urgent need for preserving intact a popular culture rooted in regionalism from the encroachments of political parties and the routine of a centralized bureaucracy. For he shared Barrès' belief that such a culture was of value not only in its own right or as a literary curiosity but also as the source of all social transformations.[26] He also shared Barrès' anti-intellectualism, his disdain for bourgeois philistinism, his hostility to a sterile positivism that had distorted the real spirit of the national consciousness; and he detected in his own social explorations an encouraging basis for those "roots" without which, Barrès had warned, no political renaissance would ever be possible.[27]

Barrès' formulation of the problem of the *déracinés* in Republican and democratic France was also to become of crucial concern to Halévy, not only in the sense which Barrès attached to the plight of the "intellectual proletariate"—the alienation which threatened provincial youth corrupted by the capital—but also in the broader meaning that this question assumed for Halévy on the morrow of the Affair.[28] For Halévy the Parisian *notable*, the question of uprootedness took a dual form. In the first place, it was for him a matter of reversing the itinerary of the provincial intellectuals of Barrès' novel and of seeking his own roots in the French soil. In the second place, his personal craving for roots was merged with a larger preoccupation with the uprooted workmen and journeymen of the Paris *faubourgs* whose artisanal culture he somehow sought to integrate with his Orleanist legacy. Like Barrès, he too was distressed by the tragic anonymity of an emerging proletariate uprooted from

[26] *Ibid.*, 146.
[27] Henri Clouard, *Bilan de Barrès suivi de quelques essais et mises au point par Daniel Halévy, Claude Roy etc.*, "Hier et Demain," no. 3, (Paris, 1943), 40.
[28] *Ibid.*, 3, 18. Cf. Halévy, "Carnets," entries for May, 1901; Apr., 1903.

their native *pays* and cast adrift in industrial society.[29] It was this more immediate problem of reconciling a vanishing popular humanism with his own *notable* heritage, of acting as a link between his own French past and the forces of the future, which was to become his principal concern in the years which lay ahead.

Moreover, Barrès' evocation of his native Lorraine had obvious affinities with the innate provincialism of Péguy and also with the rough peasant manners of Sorel, which drew Halévy to both. Barrès resembled Sorel in his devotion to an indigenous form of socialism, and he also shared with the younger Péguy an attitude which, according to Halévy, "was determined by powerful feelings of a largely traditional character." [30] Like Halévy, he too admired that "croyant de la prairie" (as he once called Péguy), whose "racy, genial, medieval" genius he admired as the very incarnation of that genuine provincialism that could alone inspire a real national revival.[31] In their common cult for national roots, Halévy found a more meaningful ideal than the intellectual reconstructions of Maurras and his school. Although sometimes unable to resist Maurras's rhetorical verve, he was always repelled by the rigidity of a doctrine still too closely wedded to positivism to take into account the pragmatic realities of an artisanal and rural ethic.[32] And he rallied instead to the views of a true nationalist like Barrès when he dismissed the disciples of the Action Française as these "durs petits esprits." [33]

It was the Barrèsien image of the richness of regionalism

---

[29] Cf. Curtis, *op. cit.*, 110.

[30] Cf. Georges Sorel, "Socialismes nationaux," *Cahiers de la Quinzaine* (14ème cahier de la 3ème série, Apr. 15, 1902).

[31] Halévy, *Nouveaux Maîtres*, 145 ff.; Halévy, *Pays parisiens* (Paris, 1929), 286–288.

[32] Halévy, *Péguy*, 104–120.

[33] Cf. D. W. Brogan, *French Personalities and Problems* (New York, 1947), 113.

and the variety of the French experience, which in turn inspired Halévy's quest for more permanent roots. Lamenting in his autobiographical *Pays parisiens* the obvious limitations of a city childhood, he sought to compensate for what was inevitably lacking in the experience of a native Parisian by staking a claim to the Bourbonnais. In his successive *Visites aux paysans du Centre*, covering over half a century of sedulous exploration of the sheltered provinces of the Centre, neighboring Péguy's own ancestral Berry, he sought to create for himself a rural ancestry of sorts. There was something artificial and contrived about this deliberate provincialism, yet no less than with Barrès it was prompted by a genuine craving for an inspiration which could be found only in the French past and in the French soil.[34]

Halévy's reverence for Barrès was reinforced by a personal friendship, which, though severely tried by the rifts provoked by the Dreyfus Affair, stood the test of time. Through his cousin, André Berthelot, he was given an entree into the great man's circle. He played an important part in planning a memorable luncheon which brought Barrès and Sorel together, and it was he, no less than Jérôme Tharaud (for a time Barrès' secretary) who kept Barrès abreast of the vagaries of Péguy's *Cahiers*. When Péguy died in battle, Barrès asked Halévy to convey his condolences to his widow, and requested the younger man's permission to be the first to publish an obituary in *L'Echo de Paris*.[35]

By then, Halévy's political skepticism had found an echo in Barrès' *Leurs Figures*. But it was the earlier Barrès, the Barrès of *Un Homme libre*, whose lyricism had left a more

---

[34] Halévy, *Pays*, 7; "Fidus" (pseud.) "Daniel Halévy, un notable de Paris," *La Revue des Deux Mondes*, Dec. 15, 1936, 890; Henri Pourrat, "Daniel Halévy," *Nouvelle Revue française*, Oct. 1, 1932, 633; A. Albert-Petit, "Paris vu par un parisien," *Le Journal des Débats: Revue Hebdomadaire*, Jan. 15, 1932, 79.

[35] MS letter from Barrès to Halévy, undated.

lasting impression. His own investigations into the world of the laboring classes was prompted as much by the need for nourishing his sensibilities as they were by an equally genuine desire to banish poverty and carry out the implications of the Dreyfus revolution. Yet the patronizing attitude of the littérateur in search of bracing revelations usually prevailed over the dedication of the social reformer. Placing sentiment above reason, he was drawn by the modest grandeur of humble lives because he perceived that the toiling masses were a rich reservoir of emotions. The only real solution to the labor problem was to preserve them in the best tradition of the past, to keep the artisans bound to their craft and the peasants rooted to the soil so that their feelings would continue to flow in the right direction and serve as a fund of emotions in which the intellect of their betters could have its roots. For all its sincerity, Halévy's socialist fervor would betray more than a trace of the *culte du moi*.

III

Many years later, the youthful socialist enthusiast turned historian of the Third Republic recounted how "the most bourgeois of all French Republics" had established its authority by supplanting the *notables* while at the same time crushing the "red specter" of the Commune.[36] In *La Fin des notables*, Halévy evoked the plight of the rising proletariate during these dark days of middle-class supremacy, showing how a dispirited labor movement, deprived of its ablest leaders by the holocaust of the Commune and the subsequent proscription, gradually fell under the leadership of Jules Guesde. Although Marxist by persuasion, Guesdism was swayed by expediency to preach the political conquest of

[36] Halévy, *La République des ducs* (Paris, 1937), 334–339.

the state. Confronted by a hostile Assembly bent on eradicating all vestiges of working-class freedom, the Socialist leaders directed their efforts to aligning the labor vote with a political party that would triumph over their enemies through electoral tactics and parliamentary pressure.

Such a strategy, however, was carried out at the price of an almost total eclipse of the independent *militants*, who rebelled against the view that political maneuvers could in any way serve the interests of their class. Championing working-class autonomy, these precursors of syndicalism harked back to a spirit of French *ouvrièrisme* that challenged socialist orthodoxy by proclaiming that proletarian emancipation could only be achieved by direct action.[37] Although they accomplished little, such dedicated men could not fail to arouse Halévy's sympathy, and in his chronicle of the early years of the Republic, he could scarcely conceal his admiration for "these hardy individuals with passionate hearts who, here and there in the Paris *faubourgs*, dreamed of another society and another justice."[38]

The lingering flame of libertarian socialism seeking to build the good society by means of the workers' own efforts had survived into the twentieth century. Rekindled by such energetic leaders as Allemane and Griffuelhes—the only working-class organizers who were themselves commoners—it had become identified with a dissenting socialist faction dominated by men of "rare and ardent intelligence" in whom a Halévy emerging from the Dreyfus Affair discovered the most convincing manifestation of a genuine popular ethic.[39]

This revolutionary spirit, standing apart from the main current of socialist thought, was perhaps most vigorously

---

[37] Halévy, *Essais*, 281 ff.   [38] Halévy, *Ducs*, 335.
[39] Halévy, *Essais*, 284.

represented by the practical accomplishments of Fernand
Pelloutier. It was through their mutual friend, Sorel, that
Halévy first met in 1899 the consumptive bank clerk whose
federation of the Bourses du Travail was to become the
nucleus of the powerful Confédération Générale du Travail
(C.G.T.).[40] His conversion to Pelloutier's ideas was instanta-
neous. Like Sorel, he was captivated by the indomitable will
with which Pelloutier had succeeded in harnessing the
energies of the working class to the revolutionary forces of
the time.[41] After Pelloutier's premature death, Halévy followed Sorel to his disciple Paul Delesalle's book shop, there
to encounter some of the rank-and-file organizers of the
bourses who were to make such a significant contribution to
syndicalist endeavor in the years before the War.

Almost half a century later, long after the bourses had
declined, Halévy could still speak in a reverential tone of an
institution whose revival had been virtually the personal
achievement of Pelloutier. The greatest result of Pelloutier's
work, he maintained in 1947, was to have demonstrated the
enduring significance of Proudhon's socialist ideas. "By
typifying beyond doubt the most thoroughly Proudhonian
figure, in the militant sense of the word, of our times," he
had also inspired a whole generation of syndicalists with the
most vital legacy in the French socialist tradition.[42] This
preference for a libertarian brand of socialism was already
apparent in the first studies that Halévy published in 1901,
where surveying the whole field of working-class experiments
that had grown in the wake of the Affair he had singled out
the bourses as the most promising kind of labor organization.[43] These labor exchanges, springing from the workers'
own initiative, were modelled on the archaic *compagnon-*

[40] Halévy, "Carnets," entry for July 7, 1899.
[41] Halévy, *Essais*, 271, 283.
[42] Halévy, "Proudhon, Sorel, Péguy," *Fédération*, Nov., 1947, 13.
[43] *Essais*, 271.

nages, which brought together the elite of journeymen and artisans on the basis of superior skill and moral character. Emerging from the proletariate's own needs, the bourses possessed the unique advantage of being both traditional and revolutionary, and Pelloutier saw that by adapting these vestiges of an artisanal past to the conditions of modern industrialism he could channel a genuine working-class consciousness toward a new revolutionary ideal. His efforts bore fruit in the form of a national amalgamation of labor exchanges based on the principle of Proudhon's federal mutualism, which, at its peak, could claim over a quarter million members. Subordinating immediate economic advantages to the greater purpose of developing the moral capacities of the workingman, he laid the foundation of a vast popular movement, which could ultimately embrace all syndicalist organizations.[44]

Yet what Pelloutier stressed above all was the corporate sense of identity that would grow out of an independent labor movement. Group life, he contended, would foster an exclusive proletarian morality coming from within the syndicates and a self-reliance shaped by the very conditions of collective endeavor. The bourses were not merely labor exchanges, but also the purest expression of the popular will: because of their regional structure rooted in the ancient traditions of the *compagnonnages* they could appeal to a deeper sentiment than the trade-unions organized on a craft basis. To Pelloutier, their greatest strength lay in their value as centers of social life and moral education, where men drawn together by common interests could develop a common class consciousness. Combining an *élan des masses* with the industrial discipline of the new age, the bourses could

[44] Jean Maitron, "Le Mouvement anarchiste en France avant la première guerre mondiale," *Société d'Histoire de la Troisième République*, n.s., Oct., 1935, 299, 309. See also George Woodcock, *Anarchism: A History of Libertarian Ideas and Movements* (Cleveland and New York, 1962), 320.

serve as the model of the future proletarian state.[45] But as he himself warned, as he took stock of an achievement to be cut short by his untimely death, their principal aim should be to teach the proletariate not to lose sight of its moral purpose in its struggle for emancipation. By setting itself the task of preserving and cultivating a strictly proletarian self-sufficiency, the bourses would not only rescue the worker from his bondage to industrial capitalism, but would also serve to rebuild his character and elevate him from his function as a machine to "an intelligence manning and mastering the machine and rising above it." [46]

To the young Halévy, swept by the revolutionary current of Dreyfusism, Pelloutier's intransigence seemed to coincide with his own personal rebellion against his class. The Barrèsien dilettante, still a disciple of Nietzsche, could scarcely resist the attraction of an uncompromising populism which displayed such invigorating qualities of constant struggle and strife, while the spirit of the bourses' militants was admirably suited to stimulate the latent anarchist streak in his character. There could be no more exhilarating spectacle than the vehement nonconformity of these anarcho-syndicalists, and their almost lyrical bestiality—an "animalité fauve," as one observer described it,[47] recalling bygone aristocratic epochs and pointing to an heroic future —could not fail to arouse Halévy's enthusiasm. Yet Halévy also found a positive value in a movement which was capable of gathering the working-class elite around a clear-cut principle of action, and he detected in the bourses the vanguard of

[45] Edouard Dolléans, *Histoire du mouvement ouvrier en France* (Paris, 1947), I, 37.

[46] Fernand Pelloutier, *Histoire des Bourses du Travail* (Paris, 1902), xiii.

[47] Marius-Ary Leblond, *La Société française sous la Troisième République* (Paris, 1905), 294; cf. Paul Leroy-Beaulieu, "Le Syndicalisme," *La Revue des Deux Mondes*, Aug. 1, 1908, 492.

the syndicalist movement, foreshadowing the socialist wave of the future. Tracing in his early socialist studies the spectacular growth of Pelloutier's Federation, Halévy placed his heroic bands of militant craftsmen in a class apart and hailed them as "the true representatives of the people." To Halévy, they seemed the most "original and creative" institutions of his time, the breeding ground "for that great thing, a working-class self-consciousness." "Here," he noted, "the syndicalist movement reaches out beyond itself and holds out the hope of the new world to come." [48]

IV

Halévy's own hopes, clearly revealed in his account of the growth of syndicalism, steered his energies in the direction of the Universités Populaires, where he too could participate in the great endeavor which he enthusiastically chronicled in his *Essais sur le mouvement ouvrier.* The Universités Populaires were at first little more than a side show of the syndicalist movement, constituting as it were, the educational counterpart of Pelloutier's bourses. Tinged with a libertarian streak from the start, popular education reached back to the eighties and resulted from the initiative of workmen themselves, mostly of anarchist persuasion.[49] The first institute by that name had been launched by the notorious Auguste Vaillant, who in 1886 had established himself in the eighteenth *arrondissement,* not far from the Porte de la Chapelle, where more than a decade later Halévy was to inaugurate his own educational center. A similar establishment, growing out of what had originally been a soup kitchen, was founded by some earnest *normaliens* in 1891—the peak year of anarchist agitation—on the Rue

[48] *Essais,* 84.
[49] *Ibid.,* 282; Jean Maitron, *Histoire du mouvement anarchiste en France: 1880–1914* (Paris, 1951), 328–330.

Mouffetard, in the working-class district behind the Ecole Normale.[50]

It was the Dreyfus Affair, however, which gave a fresh impetus to the idea of popular education. After 1898, the movement gained in momentum, flourishing first in Paris, then spreading rapidly to the provinces. Anatole France and Jaurès gave it their blessings, and with the support of Allemane himself (who conceded that intellectuals could make a significant contribution to raising the intellectual level of the proletariate), exuberant Dreyfusards thrust themselves into what they regarded as a momentous experiment which would fuse the Dreyfusard spirit with proletarian *élan*. Georges Deherme, a self-taught typographer from Keufer's Fédération du Livre—the best disciplined of the trade-unions—revived Vaillant's moribund establishment by creating his celebrated Université Populaire on the Rue Paul Bert in 1898. The Co-opération des Idées, as it was ambitiously called, recruited its instructors from the Union pour l'Action Morale, an active Dreyfusard intellectuals' group. From here, Paul Desjardins, Halévy's old teacher and a recent convert to socialism, supplied Deherme with a constant flow of former students who dedicated themselves to what a contemporary popular manifesto called the workingman's "maisons philosophiques." [51]

The movement made spectacular progress in the following years, reaching its apogee in 1904 when delegates from all over the country assembled in the capital to constitute a national federation.[52] Many of the member institutes were exclusively educational endeavors, seeking to promote the workingman's desire for self-improvement. But there were

[50] Anatole France, *Trente Ans de vie sociale*, ed. Claude Aveline (Paris, 1944), I, 26.

[51] Halévy, *Essais*, 166.

[52] *Cahiers de la Quinzaine* (20ᵉᵐᵉ cahier de la 5ᵉᵐᵉ série, Dec. 15, 1904).

others of a radically different type. Some, sponsored mainly by wealthy Jews and Protestants, were really more philanthropic than educational in character, and soon became indistinguishable from mere charitable foundations. Others pursued strictly political ends, subsequently merging with the electoral committees of the Section Française de l'Internationale Ouvrière (S.F.I.O.), while most of them were eventually absorbed by the larger trade-unions or became identified with the Radical-Socialists, providing that party with a convenient platform for its program of the *école unique*. It is this last kind of *université*, based on the principle of free education for the masses, which survived into the thirties.[53]

The election of Gabriel Seailles, a prominent Sorbonne professor, as president of the Federation was interpreted by many in Péguy's circle as a sign that the movement had become too closely associated with Combism. As early as 1905, not only Péguy, but even Romain Rolland, one of the Université's staunchest supporters, voiced the fear that the Universités Populaires would become the instrument of Radical propaganda. Financial difficulties and the growing hostility of syndicalist leaders (who also came to resent Sorbonne encroachments) contributed to hastening its decline; by the end of the decade, this noble experiment—"the last vestige of the Dreyfusard spirit," as Halévy called it— had to all intents and purposes petered out.[54]

For Péguy, the Universités Populaires had become, like the Collège de France, just one more form of extramural education provided by the Radical Sorbonne—a far cry from its original purpose. Yet he echoed the sentiments of many who had devoted the best years of their lives to the movement when he recalled his nostalgia for what had been

[53] Sénéchal, *op. cit.*, 21.
[54] MS letter from Halévy to André Spire, dated Sept. 3, 1927.

un espoir infini,
une illusion infinie aussi,
et par suite, une déception peut-être une lassitude infinie.[55]

Although Halévy would one day come to share his companion's disillusionment, he remained to the end the most
stalwart champion of the Universités Populaires. Fondly
dwelling on the memories of the ten years he had spent in
daily contact with workmen, he still contended in old age
that it was this intimacy which, more than anything else,
had decisively shaped his socialist ideas.[56]

It was on November 22, 1898, that Halévy joined a
working-class Dreyfusard discussion club near his summer
home in Versailles. After serving his apprenticeship in
Deherme's institute, he proceeded the following year to
found his own Université Populaire on the Rue Saint-Martin,
in the heart of the popular district near the Porte de la
Chapelle. With him were his young wife and Charles
Guieysse, a graduate of the same *promotion* as Sorel's from
the Ecole Polytechnique and Halévy's collaborator in a
syndicalist review. They were soon joined by André Spire the
Jewish poet, and his former classmates from Condorcet,
Robert Dreyfus, and Fernand Gregh.[57]

These earnest reformers went about their mission with
commendable zeal. Their activities conformed to the usual
pattern of other Universités Populaires: there were nightly
lectures and debates, field trips and weekend picnics, poetry
readings and theater performances of plays especially written
by Gregh or from Romain Rolland's Théâtre Populaire

[55] Charles Péguy, *La Thèse* (Paris, 1955), 31.
[56] Paul Guth, "Daniel Halévy," *La Revue de Paris*, Jan., 1954, 142; André
Rousseaux, "Un Quart d'Heure avec M. Daniel Halévy," *Candide*, Apr. 17,
1930.
[57] Halévy, "Carnets," entries for Nov., 1898; Sept., 1900. Cf. Anatole
France, *Trente Ans de vie sociale*, I, 26 ff.

repertory.[58] Halévy's avowed aim was to rescue his students from their intellectual torpor and, by providing them with the rudiments of an education, to foster their desire for self-improvement. But here, also, Halévy could indulge in the fascination provided by the grandeur of humble lives, discerning in some of the robust individuals who were drawn to his locale those qualities of integrity and self-reliance that he could no longer find in his own class. Among those whom he befriended during these years, there were at least two who stood out from the rest of his students, fulfilling his fondest hopes by subsequently achieving a reputation for which they gave him credit. Pierre Hamp, a Proudhonian chronicler of syndicalism and the author of *La Peine des hommes*, and Ernest Guillaumin, who returned to his native Allier to launch one of the first agrarian cooperative movements in France, were good, solid, French workers, hewn out of native oak and displaying a sturdy populism which provided their bourgeois friend with a fresh source of enlightenment.[59]

But to probe the *moeurs* of these sturdy types who seemed to foreshadow the advent of a race of Nietzschean supermen was not merely to indulge in a dilettantist exercise. It could also contribute in a more practical way to strengthening a force which would bring socialism closer to its ultimate triumph.[60] Seeking to steer his educational institute in the direction of a larger syndicalist movement, Halévy affiliated his Enseignement Mutuel with the *bourse du travail* of his district, a fruitful association which lasted for almost a decade. His purpose was partly propagandist—to recruit for the local *bourse* those workers who had drifted to his locale.

[58] Cf. Halévy, *Nouveaux Maîtres*, 16–18; Halévy, "Carnets," entry for May, 1901.
[59] Halévy, *Lettres du Périgord* (Paris, 1930), 37 ff.; cf. preface by Guillaumin's daughter in Halévy, *Visites aux paysans du Centre* (Paris, 1934).
[60] Halévy, "Carnets," entries for Dec., 1898; Mar., 1899; Sept., 1902.

But transforming his establishment into a workers' clearing-house had the further advantage of enlarging its member-ship, and his Enseignement Mutuel, as its name implied, remained to the end a strictly educational undertaking.[61]

Halévy's perseverance in this self-appointed task was as-tonishing. While many of his associates—with the notable exception of Guieysse—gradually drifted away, he alone remained increasingly absorbed in an activity which set him further apart from most of his contemporaries.[62] His deliber-ate divorce from his own class and profession provoked the inevitable tensions within the family circle. Even his brother Elie, whose participation in the Universités Popu-laires went no further than what was regarded as suitable for any graduate of the Ecole Normale, could find no justifica-tion for Daniel's inordinate devotion to the cause.[63] His father shared Elie's exasperation; Proust and Gregh repeat-edly reproached him for what they regarded as his eccentric behavior, while the painter Jacques Emile Blanche, a trusted family friend, scolded him for wrecking his chances for a literary career. "I am astonished," he wrote, "that young independent men of talent like yourself, with no political ambitions . . . should regard the socialist ideal as worthy of such intense dedication." [64]

The remarkable obstinacy of Halévy's attachment to this enterprise can perhaps be traced to the very conditions of his upbringing. Not unlike his brother in this respect, he too had

[61] Halévy in "Opinions sur les Universités Populaires," *Pages Libres*, Aug. 27, 1904, 167.

[62] Cf. Halévy, *Courrier de Paris* (Paris, 1932), Appendix I.

[63] Elie, with Jacques Bardoux, furnished his brother with information on Toynbee Hall, but he always maintained that because he had entered *Normale* just shortly before Péguy's generation he had escaped the kind of socialist thrust that had affected his brother and his friends. See Elie Halévy, *L'Ere des tyrannies* (Paris, 1938), 211–217; cf. Ernest Dimnet, *France Herself Again* (London, 1914), 322.

[64] Blanche to Halévy, MS letter dated Nov. 5, 1901.

THE SOCIALIST MILITANT

been brought to reflect in time on the injustice of his own good fortune.[65] He tells us himself of his first premonition when still a youngster of "a lacuna to that existence in which I was bred," and how he came to suspect that there must certainly be "some grave echo to that absurd and delightful music which had deluded me." [66] Escaping from the idle seclusion of a well-to-do man of leisure, he undoubtedly felt that exploring the springs of proletarian life would gratify his humanitarian zeal no less than his taste for novelty.[67] Yet although his moral earnestness cannot be denied, it was never quite immune from a craving to seek in the enchanting allurements of this new universe his *culte du moi*.[68] There are many disturbing passages in his diary during these years that bear out Proust's reproach that his total absorption in working-class life was really prompted by his desire to escape from "sheer boredom and lassitude." [69] Nor is it surprising that it was precisely at this time that he was drawn to Sainte-Beuve, a literary critic like himself, who had not regarded the ideas of Saint-Simon as unworthy of his attention. In a revealing article, written in 1905, on the nineteenth-century author whom he resembled in many ways, he justified his own socialist loyalties by announcing his resolve that it would be in the same spirit that he would complete Sainte-Beuve's unfinished biography of Proudhon.[70]

The task that Halévy set himself was to become the

---

[65] Cf. J. Bartlet Brebner, "Elie Halévy," in *Some Modern Historians of Britain*, ed. Herman Ausubel (New York, 1951), 238.

[66] Halévy, *Pays*, cited by Gabriel Marcel in *L'Europe Nouvelle*, Aug. 1, 1932, 980.

[67] Robert de Traz, "Daniel Halévy," *La Revue de Paris*, Feb., 1934, 79.

[68] René de Kérallain, *Correspondence* (Quimper, 1933–1935), III, 140.

[69] Proust to Halévy, MS letter, undated.

[70] Halévy, "Note sur Sainte-Beuve et la démocratie," *Pages Libres*, Dec. 3, 1905, 465–485. Cf. Sorel, *Lettres à Paul Delesalle* (Paris, 1947), 189, 223. See also Marcel Proust, *Correspondence générale* (Paris, 1930–1936), III, 68.

interpreter of the "popular soul," and by acting as a link between the rising masses and his own class, to bridge the gulf between the two cultures. Having succeeded in establishing a rare intimacy with peasants and workmen, he conceived his aim as being to translate this solidarity in practical terms, vaguely hoping that the crude populism he had discovered could be merged with the greater traditions of the past.[71] Undaunted by the enormity of such an undertaking, he had no doubt that the venture represented the most decisive challenge of his times. "This is a solemn occasion," he insisted, "the most momentous experiment of our day," and he sought at the very least to communicate to others the great significance of what he had discovered.[72]

There is a recurrent note of irrepressible enthusiasm in the constant flow of articles and reportages that Halévy devoted to the growth of syndicalism during these years. The emergence of a new class was, indeed, for him, a stirring spectacle. "A sight such as this," he writes, "provides us with the bracing feeling that nature, constantly in a state of flux, is giving birth to a refreshingly new and heroic humanity." [73] He reassured his readers that "these robust individuals . . . these men of violence, are in fact really men of order, since they restore life to its proper equilibrium, giving it its noblest . . . expression." [74] Not only did he seek to mitigate the terror that they seemed to inspire; he also stressed the positive value of what he regarded as a salutary force:

Let us not belittle the times in which we live and let us admit that this is a great historical moment, pregnant in meaning and rich in promise, when men overwhelmed by tremendous odds, men who seemed incapable of effort and only worthy of pity succeed in conceiving an ideal and creating institutions. . . . Their labors hold out a rich promise and mark the beginning of a

---

[71] Halévy, *Essais*, 168. [72] *Ibid.*, 167. [73] *Ibid.*, 198.
[74] *Ibid.*, 294–295.

superior humanity. . . . Doubtless, they are few in numbers, but what is significant is that an elite has emerged from the deepest layers of the popular soul. Nothing is more instructive than to behold these men; to frequent them is to find the revelation of a new way of life.

And, with a passing reference to Barrès,

Some of our contemporaries cry out for *professeurs d'énergie;* here they are. Others complain that our times deprive us of heroes; here they are. Let us open our eyes. Is it not obvious that there is no purer glory than that of the proletarian Proudhon, of Bebel . . . Benoist Malon? If such individuals are the precursors of the world to come, then let us not despair . . . Socialism is a creator of men. There can be no more conclusive proof of its value than this.[75]

At the root of Halévy's dedication was his vision of a socialist utopia, a vision, he maintained, that was the common legacy of all men of good will, commoners and intellectuals alike. The Dreyfus Affair had not only revealed that the nineteenth century's "revolutionary hope" lingered on in the minds of an elite of the working class; it had also given him a glimpse of the lyrical quality of what Sorel called the "social poetry" in the popular soul.[76] The Universités Populaires, he insisted, were the logical outcome of his Dreyfusard principles, the natural culmination of the struggle which had banded together working-class militants and Dreyfusard intellectuals. Together they would evolve a new *mystique,* and by their common efforts finally build that heavenly city of peace and fraternity which was the dream of all mankind.[77]

From today's vantage point, it would scarcely be possible to look back to such generous sentiments with the same kind of optimism. The record of the past half century and the sobering spectacle of what mass culture has come to mean

[75] *Ibid.,* 198.　　[76] *Ibid.,* 168.
[77] "Fidus," "Daniel Halévy, un notable," 898.

would incline us to regard the Universités Populaires as the futile and pathetic vestiges of a distant and unreal past. That popular emancipation could lead to the planned society, the welfare state, "popular democracy"—or "organization man" —would have seemed inconceivable to those who devoted their best energies to stamping out poverty and creating a better world. Yet these great expectations cannot be dismissed as merely irrelevant. Seen against the background of an exciting decade when socialism aroused a remarkably intense debate among the French elite, the ephemeral episode of the Enseignement Mutuel illustrates the fact that lofty ideals did indeed prevail among many men of good will. Péguy spoke for Halévy and many others when, recalling with dim regret the great hopes they had all shared during these hectic years, he defined their purpose as having been nothing less than to build a glorious *cité*. "During these years of our apprenticeship, we believed, we hoped, that we could forge a new socialist culture, which would replace all other decaying cultures for the temporal salvation of all humanity" [78]

Like Péguy, Halévy would also one day look back with nostalgia to this utopian dream. As early as 1902, Sorel had cautioned his friend not to expect too much from his efforts, predicting that the disillusionment which would inevitably set in from such an unlikely fusion of cultures would have disastrous consequences for his working-class companions.[79] The hazards of his educational venture had, of course, been obvious to Halévy from the start, and for all his exuberance he had never really concealed his doubts on the uncertain results of such a precarious undertaking.[80] In retrospect, it

[78] Péguy, *Par Ce Demi-clair Matin*, cited in Jean Delaporte, *Connaissance de Péguy* (Paris, 1959), I, 168.
[79] Sorel to Halévy, MS letter dated May 2, 1902; cf. Pierre Andreu, *Notre Maître, M. Sorel* (Paris, 1953), 167–169.
[80] Halévy, "Carnets," entries of Nov., 1903; June, 1906.

would seem that the pioneering experiment inevitably yielded to a general disenchantment, and that all the dedicated effort which Halévy devoted to his labors merely contributed—as Sorel had anticipated—to diverting the proletariate from its true revolutionary vocation.[81]

Some of the staunchest advocates of the venture admitted that the Universités Populaires rested on an ambiguity that Sorel had been one of the first to detect. Guieysse, Halévy's colleague on the staff of *Pages Libres*, admitted that the movement from its very inception was torn between the ideas of two conflicting schools of thought. The first derived from the principle, held by most Dreyfusard intellectuals, that the Universités Populaires should seek to reconcile the two classes. But others, not infrequently the same men, held the opposite view that the first step toward popular emancipation was to promote the intellectual development of the proletarians so as to enable them to achieve the revolution against the old order by their own efforts. These two tendencies were clearly incompatible. In fact, by exposing their students to the delights and dilemmas of bourgeois culture, many of the altruistic intellectuals succeeded only in stifling their revolutionary ardor, while failing to provide them with any alternative faith. By alienating the workers from their own class, they had contributed to diverting a rich flow of socialist enthusiasm into a confused welter of divided loyalties and split personalities.[82]

The chief culprits, admitted Guieysse, were earnest humanitarians like himself and Halévy who had come to the Universités Populaires by way of Desjardin's Union pour l'Action Morale and who found in the Co-opération des Idées a congenial atmosphere for indulging their curiosity, and perhaps their vanity. For all their good intentions, these self-styled socialists were also seeking to immerse themselves

---

[81] Andreu, *loc. cit.*   [82] Cf. Anatole France, *op. cit.*, I, 26.

in the great purifying force of syndicalism. And by their didactic moralism, setting moral improvement above more immediate advantages, they had merely fostered their students' distrust of parliamentary democracy, undermining the recruiting efforts of the S.F.I.O. and the C.G.T. and crippling the Socialists' prospects of achieving a united front. Deherme's own astonishing assertion that "if the choice lay between the parliamentary Republic and traditional monarchy, we would all rally to the Orleanists," illustrates the paradoxical denouement of the whole movement.[83] It is no less paradoxical that Halévy's final verdict on the results of his endeavor should coincide with the anarchist's. "What had we finally achieved after so much pain and effort?" he asked himself much later. "We had stirred up, in this *faubourg* of La Chapelle, a new breed of Parisian litterati, of proletarian Orleanists, who were almost identical to those other Orleanists who had subscribed for a hundred years to the *Journal des Débats*." Reflecting on those persistent ambiguities, which were to beset the entire course of his career, he added significantly: "Always Orleanism, always the *Journal des Débats*; was this, then, to be my fate?" [84]

V

As might have been expected, Halévy's venture in popular education was not without its tragedies. In 1907, nine years after its foundation, the Enseignement Mutuel was dissolved, and the tale of its collapse was recounted by its founder in the form of a poignant novel, "Un Episode." [85]

[83] Cited in Michel Arnauld, "Georges Deherme et la crise sociale," *Nouvelle Revue française*, May 1, 1910, 585.

[84] Halévy, *Pays*, 200, cited in Andreu, *op. cit.*, 167, n. 1. See also Pierre Guiral in *Tendances politiques dans la vie française depuis 1789*, ed. Guy Michaud (Paris, 1960), 123.

[85] First published in *Cahiers de la Quinzaine* (6ème cahier de la 9ème série, Nov., 1907), reprinted in Halévy, *Luttes et problèmes* (Paris, 1911), it was dedicated to the students of the Enseignement Mutuel.

The futility of attempting to raise the intellectual level of the masses is told through the personal drama of the transformation of a pure anarchist into a bourgeois *lettré,* the whole tragedy of the Universités Populaires being epitomized in the proud despair of Julien Guinou, the novel's hero. This young apprenticed printer, burning with a zeal to emancipate his class, merely succeeds in raising himself above it with tragic results for himself and his companions. During the early months of the Dreyfus Affair—"in those beautiful days when the world was cracking, giving hope for justice"—Guinou joined the Foyer, the Université Populaire of his popular district in Mélimontant, where M. Dorsel, a Sorbonne instructor, transformed him into a budding man of letters, infatuated with the verses of Baudelaire and the Comtesse de Noailles. His literary vanity inevitably diverts him from his proletarian vocation; he abandons his girl friend, Adeline, shuns his family, and rejects the companionship of his working-class comrades, whose coarse manners and vulgarity now repel him. His anguish is aggravated by a deterioration in his health. Contracting tuberculosis, he is sent by the benevolent director of the Foyer for a cure to a provincial sanatorium. Nursed back to health, he finds himself cast adrift in a hostile world, and ultimately returns to Paris only to discover that he can no longer reconcile his new tastes and interests with what he now regards as a menial job in a printing shop. Despising himself, alienated from his class, increasingly at odds with family and friends, he is finally driven to suicide, justifying his act by the time-honored artist's apology: "I must kill myself since my life cannot be beautiful." [86]

To offset the ravages made on Guinou's mind by the altruistic M. Dorsel, Halévy introduces the character of Mégy, the uncompromising syndicalist who resists the en-

[86] Halévy, *Luttes,* 155.

croachments of bourgeois culture, and rebels against M. Dorsel's initiation to books and learning on the grounds that art and literature are incompatible with the true aspirations of his class. Rudoul, another inmate of the Foyer, represents the positivist *idéophagues*, typical of many simple-minded working-class students who, after an arduous day's work, are incapable of absorbing more than the bare rudiments of knowledge, easily falling a prey to empty generalizations.

Halévy's tale is, of course, deliberately, perhaps too deliberately, didactic, but the characters are imaginatively portrayed and the plot does not lack drama. It succeeded in stirring Péguy's enthusiasm, and Sorel, a constant admirer of Halévy's literary talents, regarded "Un Episode" as a most imaginative recreation of a significant aspect of proletarian morality. In a laudatory review, Sorel—perhaps with some nostalgia for the chambermaid he had married—stressed the love element in Halévy's novel.[87] It is Guinou's love for Adeline, he remarked, that epitomizes the novel's evocation of proletarian *moeurs*. The moment Guinou assumes the airs of an implacable romantic, he is lost not only to Adeline but also to his class, ceasing to serve as an exemplar of proletarian virtue. Mégy, on the other hand, stood for Sorel as the prototype of revolutionary intransigence. And he pointed out that the moral of Halévy's tale is that the death of his companion serves only to reinforce Mégy's resolution to avoid bourgeois contamination by preserving the exclusive *métaphysique des moeurs* of his own class. To underline the moral disintegration of his hero, Halévy made Guinou exclaim on the eve of his suicide that he pined for those days when he could share with his comrade Mégy, "a common wrath, a conviction, a purpose." Guinou's sinister end does not merely serve to illustrate the pitfalls of literary vanity.

---

[87] Sorel, "Trois Problèmes," *L'Indépendance*, Nov. 15, 1911, 238; cf. Edouard Berth's review in *Pages Libres*, Feb. 22, 1908, 217.

Halévy's novel also seems to bear out Bakunin's contention that the only way of establishing any sort of link between worker and bourgeois is for each to sever himself from his own class—with fatal results for both.[88]

Guinou's loss of identity, although deplored by Halévy, had not deterred him from persevering in seeking some middle ground between such a hazardous approach as M. Dorsel's, on the one hand, and a total repudiation of traditional humanism, on the other. Assuming the existence of an absolute cultural norm that could reconcile the varieties of class experience, aspiring to achieve a valid synthesis from the opposite poles of divergent cultures, Halévy had not entirely failed his students. By infusing into their drab existence some semblance of beauty and learning, he had sought at least to impress upon them a consciousness that their own destiny need not necessarily imply a rejection of the great achievements of the past.[89]

But if such an ambitious scheme proved impossible, this was not because of any flaw in Guinou's character, but rather because the real danger came from a different quarter. It was the irresistible appeal that clear-cut theories could have for simple minds that constituted the main threat to the Enseignement Mutuel and ultimately precipitated its disintegration. It gradually became clear to Halévy that the greater tragedy of his pioneering experiment lay not so much in the alienation of the uprooted Guinou, but rather in the transformation of such a decent but bewildered soul as Rudoul into a doctrinaire *idéophague.*

Of the principal characters of "Un Episode," each representing one of the three types of students drawn to Halévy's locale, Mégy stands out as the symbol of what became Halévy's socialist ideal. Harking back to the example of

[88] Halévy, *Luttes,* 166, 149; Sorel, *L'Indépendance,* Dec. 15, 1911, 264.

[89] Halévy, "Carnets," entries of June, 1902; Apr. and Dec., 1904; and May, 1906.

Proudhon—the prototype of a few elite workmen, the choice few whom Halévy befriended during these years—he alone emerged from the Universités Populaires with a renewed awareness of what Sorel called the "tragique des moeurs," of a genuine self-sufficient proletarian ethic. Rejecting the allurements of bourgeois culture, Mégy was stimulated by Halévy's efforts to cultivate his own class consciousness, creating from his own experience a purely proletarian moral philosophy. The self-reliance that he obstinately preserved was a fitting commentary on Proudhon's enduring boast— frequently cited by Halévy—"All that I am, I owe to proud despair. Deprived of everything, I dreamt of creating for myself from the shambles gathered from my brief studies, a science all my own which would serve my own class." [90]

In the following years, largely under Sorel's impact, but also as a result of his own maturing experience, Halévy's views on socialism underwent a radical change. Yet, although the Enseignement Mutuel had not lived up to expectations, he insisted that the experiment had not been a total loss since, after all, it had been created for the mutual edification of student and teacher alike. From Halévy's standpoint, it had been not only a purifying force, but also a personal revelation. By affording him an insight into the springs of working-class life, the venture had come to represent a transitional stage in his own socialist development, paving the way for a more sympathetic understanding of Sorel's vision of the epic quality of revolutionary syndicalism.

[90] Cited in Halévy, Essais, 157; cf. Halévy, Pays, 285.

CHAPTER V

The Socialist Writer

❧❦❧

THE first decade of the twentieth century witnessed another kind of endeavor to bring about the triumph of
socialism; and although a syndicalist magazine cannot be
exactly regarded as the counterpart of the Enseignement
Mutuel, a good deal of the moral intensity of Halévy's
nightly sessions at the Porte de la Chapelle can still be
recaptured in the flow of articles that he contributed to
Pages Libres. Serving as the unofficial organ of the Universités Populaires, this fortnightly review was launched in 1901
on the initiative of Charles Guieysse and with the active
support of Halévy who raised most of the necessary funds in
an effort to broadcast to a larger audience the implications of
the Dreyfusard victory. Highly regarded for its independent
stand, this pioneer experiment in social investigation survived the Universités Populaires movement itself by merging
in 1909 with *La Grande Revue,* where it preserved its
identity in the form of a separate rubric devoted to labor
questions. More self-consciously socialist than the *Cahiers de
la Quinzaine,* it outlived Péguy's review and illustrates even
more accurately the changing character of Halévy's socialist
aspirations.[1]

[1] Christian Sénéchal, *Les Grands Courants de la littérature française
contemporaine* (Paris, 1934), 26. Péguy endorsed Halévy's enterprise by

The first issue contained a moving manifesto in which its founders—Guieysse, Halévy, a provincial schoolteacher, and a typographer—proclaimed their resolve to continue the struggle for social justice. Declaring that their journal was conceived along the same lines as a cooperative, the editors invited their readers to participate in the joint ownership of the review by the simple process of purchasing a subscription, which would entitle them to a founding share in the enterprise. And they concluded with a stirring statement of purpose: "But we are all dedicating ourselves to one common aim: to supplant the old world with a new world, founded on the Solidarity of Labor, on Justice . . . on the Joy and Dignity of Work." [2]

Pages Libres belongs to that bewildering galaxy of publications that sprouted in the wake of the Affair in the Latin Quarter, around the Dreyfusard bastion of the Sorbonne. Unable to afford its own quarters, the review was at first welcomed by Péguy, who made way for Halévy and his associates in a corner of his *boutique* on the Rue de la Sorbonne, generously providing them with a desk, a bookcase and the one available stool. On the floor above was Mme Dick May's "School of Journalism," ambitiously called the Ecole des Hautes Etudes Sociales. Down the street, Jeanne Maritain published her *Jean Pierre*, an illustrated children's magazine with Dreyfusard overtones, while next door was Hubert Lagardelle's anarchist *Le Mouvement Socialiste*, where Sorel's "Reflections on Violence" were first published in 1906. In this already overcrowded editorial center, Péguy found room for a curious magazine called *Journaux pour Tous* edited by a Jewish emigree by the name of Vilbouche-

issuing a statement on their common aims. See *Pages Libres*, June 15, 1901, 333–336.

[2] "Courte Déclaration" in opening issue of *Pages Libres*, May 1, 1901, cover.

vitch who could pride himself on being the editor of the only journal in the world devoted to tropical agronomy. The aim of his new venture was to encourage popular education by circulating socialist material in the form of a reader's digest.[3]

All these people of good will, some eccentric, others with more solemn aspirations, rose above their different backgrounds to join in the spirit of a great collective undertaking. At first, many of them, mostly recent graduates from the Ecole Normale, found a suitable platform in *La Volonté*; but when its owner, the notorious Franklin-Bouillon, carried over what had originally been an anarchist paper into the Radical camp, his defection forced the Dreyfusards to fall back on the moribund *La Petite République*. This obscure daily with a limited circulation had become the semi-official organ of the Socialist party, counting among its contributors such intellectuals as Jaurès, Blum, and Péguy. But, once again, the Dreyfusards were robbed of a forum of their own when its business manager ruined its reputation by a financial scandal, so that by 1903 Lucien Herr resolved to start anew by launching a veritable socialist newspaper.[4]

Although abortive, this ambitious scheme was originally conceived as a major enterprise that would draw on all the best talent in the Dreyfusard camp. The projected paper was to be called *Le Journal Vrai*, a title meant as a tribute to Péguy, who in his student days had turned out with the help of his *Normale* roommate, Albert Mathiez, a weekly by the same name. Halévy, together with Blum, Lévy-Bruhl, and other wealthy Jews in Jaurès' circle, secured the necessary loans through their family connections with banking inter-

[3] Jules Isaac, *Expériences de ma vie*, Vol. I, *Péguy* (Paris, 1959), 140–143, 254; Henri Bergson to Daniel Halévy, "Lettre," reprinted in *Feuillets de l'amitié Charles Péguy*, no. 30, 13 ff.; Jérôme Tharaud, "Souvenirs," *Feuillets*, no. 43, 21 ff.

[4] Charles Andler, *Vie de Lucien Herr: 1864–1926* (Paris, 1936), 135–140; Daniel Ligou, *Histoire du socialisme en France: 1871–1961* (Paris, 1962), 165.

ests in Paris. Herr, however, squandered the capital entrusted to him by reckless speculation on the stock market. But the loyal fund raisers placed their trust in him yet a second time—and *L'Humanité* was born.[5]

Halévy's financial role in promoting the undertaking earned him the grudging gratitude of Herr. He had himself contributed a substantial sum to the original investment, and it was a thankful Jaurès who rewarded him with the choice post of news editor of the new daily.[6] Assuming his duties with enthusiasm, Halévy performed his task conscientiously, winning the respect of Jaurès, and for a while, even of Herr. The great socialist leader's resolution to make *L'Humanité* not merely the socialist counterpart of *Le Temps* but a forum representing all shades of progressive opinion, naturally appealed to Halévy. That his name should appear on its masthead is hardly surprising, and it is even less surprising that his association with *L'Humanité* in no way deterred him from remaining a regular contributor to *Le Temps*. Inevitably, however, his independent views drew him apart from Jaurès and Herr. As his opposition to the newspaper's editorial policy provoked increasing friction, he was flanked by two associates to check his actions; then, demoted to the post of roving correspondent covering syndicalist developments—abroad. Finally, three years later and with *L'Humanité* now a flourishing concern, Herr was able to repay his debt, thus releasing Halévy and himself from what had become an embarrassing commitment for both.[7]

Halévy's withdrawal from the staff of Jaurès' paper en-

[5] Andler, *Herr*, 140 ff.; Harvey Goldberg, *The Life of Jean Jaurès* (Madison, Wis., 1961), 320, 508, n. 67.

[6] Albert Thibaudet, "Du Vrai Socialisme," *Nouvelle Revue française*, July 1, 1931, 136; Goldberg, *op. cit.*, 320.

[7] Personal communication: Daniel Halévy. One of his most important foreign assignments was to cover Loubet's state visit to Rome. His series of articles which appeared in *L'Humanité*, Apr. 24–27, 1904, had important repercussions; see Goldberg, *op. cit.*, 320.

abled him to devote his best energies to *Pages Libres*, whose pragmatic approach he found more congenial than what was fast becoming a doctrinaire *L'Humanité*. *Pages Libres* seemed to him an even more exciting experiment than the *Cahiers de la Quinzaine*, for it displayed a refreshing "sense of working-class life," which Péguy, so instinctively "a man of the people," could not possibly give to his own review. By its very nature, the *Cahiers* were themselves a projection of its editor's *mystique*, and although Péguy did not neglect the important labor congresses in his first issues, he remained splendidly oblivious to strictly syndicalist affairs, failing to react to those pioneering working-class developments which were Halévy's principal concern.[8] To observe Péguy at his desk from his own corner of the same *boutique* was a rare treat for Halévy. To participate in the traditional *jeudis* when he could take delight in the affinities that he discerned between the visiting Sorel—holding forth from the only stool in the book shop—and his attentive listener, was a privilege that he always cherished.[9] But while Péguy always welcomed his contributions to the *Cahiers*, Halévy saved his choicest articles for his own journal. Here, he was virtually master of his own house.[10] As associate editor and roving correspondent, he was able to lend his review's support to a variety of proletarian efforts. For almost a decade, even after *Pages Libres* had merged with *La Grande Revue*, he remained at the helm, and he always looked back to this phase of his career as the most rewarding in his life.[11]

The magazine served as a clearinghouse for all shades of

---

[8] Halévy, *Péguy and "Les Cahiers de la Quinzaine*," trans. by Ruth Bethell, 61–62; cf. Georges Sorel, "Charles Péguy," *La Ronda*, Apr. 1, 1919, 59.

[9] Halévy, "Trois Maîtres: Proudhon, Sorel, Péguy," *L'Ordre français*, Aug., 1958, 31.

[10] Halévy, *Péguy*, 61–62.

[11] He also remained news editor of Desjardin's *Bulletin de l'Union pour la Verité* until 1939. See Frederic Lefèvre, *Une Heure avec . . .* (Paris, 1924), 162.

socialist ideas, as a springboard for bold cooperative experiments, as a channel of expression for the inquisitive reader who was always welcome to use its columns to voice his grievances or seek enlightenment. As editor, Halévy assumed a task which was admirably suited to his taste. Devoting himself to extensive investigations of labor activities, traveling incessantly to the provinces and abroad, he brought to bear all the resources of his talent in compiling what is virtually a chronicle of the growth of syndicalism in France during these years. The mass of data diligently gathered and set forth in a constant stream of articles, *enquêtes*, and editorials, constitutes an invaluable documentation for today's curious researcher. Moreover, the personal friendships that Halévy established with militants provided him with an opportunity for sharpening his powers of observation, and incidentally, of forging a forceful reporting style that served him well in all his subsequent writing.

With a dilettante's taste for the uncommon, he deliberately steered clear of the more prominent unions, concentrating on the obscure, yet for him more intriguing, aspects of working-class endeavor. In a broader sense, his achievement in *Pages Libres* is notable for the light that it sheds on a certain segment of syndicalist activity often neglected in the traditional socialist accounts of this period. Socialism at the turn of the century took the form of a staggering variety of ideologies frequently identified with a group of colorful individuals who broke new ground in socialist theory and practice. Rebelling against all organized authority, refusing to submit to any single party or doctrine, many of these resourceful militants were welcomed in *Pages Libres*, where their unorthodox ideas were also assured of a generous publicity. Albert Thibaudet, reminding us that "in France, the socialist flame is kept alive by isolated, learned individuals displaying a rare critical intelligence and constituting a kind of liberal *cléricature*," commended Halévy's part in bringing out this rich libertarian vein.[12] Halévy's own eccentricity drew him to such independent mavericks, and his record of their ephemeral experiments provides us with a useful corrective to the more conventional accounts of the course of syndicalist activity during these years.

II

One of Halévy's first contributions to *Pages Libres* was, appropriately enough, a vibrant plea for liberty inspired by a book on the Inquisition written by the American, Henry Charles Lea, which set the tone for a whole series of articles and reviews devoted to historical topics: man's progress through the ages, popular emancipation, freedom of thought.[13] These were accompanied by a spate of studies on the "revolutionary hope" of the nineteenth century: vignettes of Victor Hugo, Lamartine, and other romantics and their dedication to the revolutionary cause, followed by stirring accounts of the June Days and the Commune whose sentimental socialism Halévy invoked as the guiding spirit of *Pages Libres*. Such articles, admitted Halévy, were deliberately didactic. "History teaching by example," was meant to instruct, and his purpose was to awaken in his working-class readers a consciousness of their own destiny by reminding them of a glorious past. "We must make man conscious," he wrote at the time, "and when this has been achieved, the Revolution will be accomplished." [14]

Less didactic were his reports on trade-union congresses, strikes and lockouts, and new cooperative experiments, which he lovingly chronicled in his rubric on social developments. But it was undoubtedly in his thumbnail sketches of

[12] "Du Vrai Socialisme," 137; see also Jean-Richard Bloch, *Destin du siècle* (Paris, 1931), 20 ff.
[13] Halévy, "L'Inquisition au Moyen Age," *Pages Libres*, Apr. 15, 1902, 350; cf. *Le Mouvement Socialiste*, Apr., 1902, 759–766.
[14] Halévy, "Carnets," entry for Feb. 21, 1906.

the precursors of syndicalism—"this noble breed of men," as he called them—that he displayed his best narrative qualities and his real penchant for biography. Here we find the creative enthusiasm of Francis Place and George Holyoake, of Martin Nadaud and Gustave Lefrançais, the saga of the unsung heroes of an obscure Belgian cooperative who established the first European "Maison du Peuple" in Brussels.[15] Here too is the thrilling chronicle of the "Compagnons du Tour de France" some of whose diaries Halévy edited on the grounds that the forgotten lives of these *autodidactes*—Agricol Perdiguier, Louis Ménard, and his own contemporary, Abel Boyer—were "the most stirring example of the toiling *peuple*—of the potentialities of working-class organization"[16]

From these random articles scattered over a decade there emerges a fairly coherent socialist creed. The ideas that Halévy professed were frankly revolutionary and elitist, resolutely libertarian and anarchist, yet at the same time traditionalist. Like Sorel and Péguy, he was an avowed enthusiast for a libertarian form of socialism, but a socialism that he himself sought to unravel in his own manner. Péguy's libertarianism was implicit, his whole rebellious personality was dominated by it; Sorel, the moral philosopher, gave it a systematic form, raising it to the level of social theory. Halévy's libertarianism assumed a more explicit character and was gleaned from his personal investigations of working-class endeavor. He was neither a poet nor a social theorist, and even less a man of letters in the strict sense like Barrès, but merely a very alert observer with a particularly

[15] It was here that the last congress of the Second International was held. James Joll, *The Second International* (London, 1955), 162.

[16] Halévy, "Mémoires d'un ouvrier briquetier," *Pages Libres*, May 20, 1905, 424. Many of these articles subsequently inspired him to edit such books as *Agricol Perdiguier: Mémoires d'un compagnon* (Moulins, 1914), and others in the same vein. See Henri Peyre, *Louis Ménard: 1822–1901* (New Haven, Conn., 1932), 67, 568.

inquisitive turn of mind. Owing little to formal doctrine and rejecting any party allegiance, Halévy reached socialism by way of his own perception of the realities of syndicalist life. If his ideas possess little originality, they have at least a fresh, empirical quality, a certain buoyancy that stems directly from experience, reflecting the modesty of a man who could boast: "I went to school with my public," and who could fancifully compare his editorial desk with "a craftsman's bench in an open-air workshop, wide open on the busy street." [17]

Halévy's socialist beliefs were rooted in traditional liberalism, for he was at heart in line with Tocqueville no less than with Proudhon. Like Proudhon, he was also an "Alceste of democracy," calling himself a "démophile antidémocrate" —a cryptic label by which he meant to assert both his devotion to popular liberties and his hostility to all forms of mass democracy.[18] But he also resembled Tocqueville (with whom Albert Thibaudet has quite appropriately compared him), in that he too wished to preserve some semblance of human dignity and freedom from the menace of centralization and the perils of tyranny.[19] The drift of his own modest social theory is plainly a fluid synthesis of ideas that he derived from these two apparently incompatible thinkers, gathering from both, but especially from Proudhon, thought-provoking ideas that he believed could have great relevance for his times. From the historical standpoint, all of Halévy's studies on his country's past bear the distinct imprint of Tocqueville's emphasis on the value of "interme-

[17] Halévy, "Un Adieu," *Bulletin de l'Union pour la Verité*, Aug., 1912, 697, 698.
[18] Halévy, "Quatre Lettres inédites de Proudhon," *Le Mouvement Socialiste*, Jan., 1913, 13; cf. Pierre Guiral, "Mesure de Proudhon," *Revue d'Histoire moderne et contemporaine*, July-Sept., 1961, 162.
[19] Thibaudet, "D'Alexis de Tocqueville à Daniel Halévy," *Nouvelle Revue française*, Aug. 15, 1931, 317-326. See also Georges Guy-Grand, "M. Daniel Halévy et la démocratie," *La Grande Revue*, Oct., 1931, 679.

diate bodies." But as a *moraliste*, he added a further dimension to these liberal sympathies, and his disillusionment with the mediocrity of mass culture and the democratic abuses of the Third Republic had the effect of bringing him closer to the libertarian spirit of Proudhon.[20]

Proudhon's legacy, he discovered, could have a salutary effect on the regeneration of his country. Divorced from its historical context, pruned of some of its more extravagant trappings, Proudhon's scheme for a vast network of autonomous mutualist institutions seemed to offer the only sure foundation for a free society. Shaped by a fruitful anarchism and a strong liberal impulse it was the only system capable of providing that dynamic equilibrium which could reconcile order with freedom. Mutualism had the advantage of dispensing with the state and its monolithic encroachments; it steered clear of the deceptive allurements of the democratic process and of a system of parliamentary government that could only perpetuate the rule of authority; and it rejected the fraudulent fiction of the general will. Thus, mutualism alone could guarantee the real spirit of liberty, for its greatest virtue was that it could reunite all humanity in a great federation of voluntary associations of free men, in which the liberties of every individual, every region, every nation, and every collectivity, would be guaranteed by mutual accord.[21]

Proudhon's mutualist ideal, as Halévy interpreted it, had survived the suppression of the Commune and seemed capable of recovering from its setback at the hands of the Republic, one and indivisible, to inspire the dreams of a few scattered visionaries. It was in the syndicalist movement launched by such an elite that Halévy saw the encouraging

[20] E.g. Halévy, *Les Trois Epreuves* (Paris, 1941), 33 ff.; Halévy "La Bourgeoisie française," *Le Journal des Débats: Revue Hebdomadaire*, Apr. 6, 1934, 598.
[21] Halévy, *Le Mariage de Proudhon* (Paris, 1955), 215–216, 260.

possibility of its transformation into a practical social system of universal application. Here, he believed, was the only force in his time which rested on the assumption that the single greatest value was the freedom of the individual. This freedom could not be secured so long as the worker was subjected to an external discipline: it could emerge only from within the syndicates. Each class created for itself its own organs of emancipation by opposing its positive creations to traditional institutions. The syndicate was the peculiar institution of the working class, the spontaneous creation of the workman's maturing will, where the spirit of freedom, kept alive by a strong and dedicated elite, could usher in the revolutionary millennium.

The instrument of this transformation was direct action. Direct action would bring the proletariate closer to the final catastrophic struggle against the forces of tyranny, strengthening their heroic spirit and their drive for freedom. The emancipation of the workman would thus be the accomplishment of the workman himself, led by an ardent and self-conscious minority, imbued with a thirst for liberty, drawing the rest of the masses along with them in the struggle against capitalism. For Halévy, syndicalism was capable of a higher purpose than merely securing immediate gains through collective action. It had the unique advantage of elevating the individual by fostering his self-reliance, and by unfolding a heroic image of his destiny, the syndicate could constitute the framework of a superior society, free and elitist.[22]

Yet syndicalism was not only the unique expression of proletarian idealism. Its value reached out beyond the needs of the working class to embrace all of mankind. It was the only possible source of moral improvement, stimulating to the highest level the individual's faculties for sacrifice and

[22] Halévy, "L'Entre-Aide de Pierre Kropotkin," *Pages Libres*, May 26, 1906, 529–540; Halévy, "Georg Brandès et la démocratie," *La Revue Blanche*, Mar. 5, 1902, 192.

lifting all men to the sublime. If Halévy had an almost mystical faith in syndicalism, it was because he welcomed it as a purifying force, which could combine collective initiative and social grouping—an invigorating "morale de bande," as he called it—with individual liberty. In the midst of a decadent bourgeois society, syndicalism seemed to be the last refuge of liberty. Confronted by the growing tyranny of parliamentary democracy, increasingly the prey of an oppressive system that enslaved him to the machine or the electoral committee, the "uprooted and helpless" individual could find in the syndicalist faith a moral purpose and a new inspiration.[23]

Halévy was as staunch a supporter of syndicalism as he was a resolute opponent of Marxist socialism. He regarded syndicalism as the most valuable ingredient in the French labor movement precisely because it rejected the authoritarian elements that he associated with Marxism. "Marxism," he warned the French Socialists, "was a foreign accretion which, if grafted on a native socialist tradition, would lead to the most monstrous notion of the state." He deplored the growing power of the centralized state—for the state, whether capitalist or socialist, would always remain an instrument of coercion—at the expense of the healthy independence of a network of syndicates and other workers' associations in which he found a better safeguard for preserving the rights of individuals and collectivities. The syndicate, he predicted, stood for a libertarian pluralism that was far more likely to restore man to his liberties than the rigid collectivism implied in the Marxist doctrine.[24]

[23] Halévy, "Les Nouveaux Aspects du socialisme," *Pages Libres*, Oct. 2, 1909, 367–380. Cf. Sorel's estimate of Halévy's ideas in "Proudhon," *La Ronda*, Sept. 5, 1919, 765–778; and A. Cajumi, "Le preoccupazioni di Daniel Halévy," *La Cultura*, X (1934), 234.

[24] Halévy, *Essais*, 19; Pierre-Joseph Proudhon, *Confessions d'un révolutionnaire*, ed., Halévy (Paris, 1929), 5–11; and Halévy, *Proudhon d'après ses carnets inédits: 1834–1847* (Paris, 1944), 17 ff.

It is clear that in his appreciation of the value of revolutionary syndicalism Halévy displayed a characteristic preoccupation with moral improvement and character. But what is particularly significant is that his explorations into the labor movement provided him with a practical confirmation of elitist ideas derived from both Nietzsche and Sorel. Discovering in the leaders of syndicalism a living proof that the working class was capable of producing an elite in no way inferior to its predecessors, he attempted to relate his reflections on the emerging proletariate to a broader philosophical concept. His elitist views, for all their persuasiveness, were admittedly vague and rested on a rather sketchy theoretical basis. Yet, intuitively identifying his ideals of social progress with all elites—proletarian, intellectual, and even bourgeois—he found in the syndicalist militants the agents of a great transformation, the vanguard of a "superior humanity" which promised to create a new order which would supplant his own.

This conclusion led him to adopt a highly independent socialist standpoint. His unorthodox views were not always welcome in official Socialist circles, and it is small wonder that his collaboration with L'Humanité was as short-lived as Péguy's loyalty to its editor. Although he shared the general conviction in the inevitability of the class struggle he remained wedded to a position which was in every other respect resolutely anti-Marxist.[25] Deprecating the socialist principle of the conquest of state power as vain, or simply irrelevant to the real needs of the working class, he rejected Marxist doctrine in general as likely to perpetuate tyranny, and reinforce those very elements which stood in the way of any true progress. An American sociologist has recently expressed the view that Halévy's libertarianism strove to

[25] Halévy, "Sur L'Interprétation de Proudhon," Le Journal des Débats, Jan. 2, 1913, 3; see also Thibaudet, "Proudhon, Sainte-Beuve et nous," Nouvelle Revue française, Jan. 15, 1932, 92.

preserve a humanist content in socialism. Indeed, Halévy's originality lies in the fact that he was the first socialist to recognize that the real divide in socialist theory lay not in the artificial distinction between "utopian" and "scientific" ideas, but between authoritarian and libertarian beliefs.[26] Anticipating Sorel, and even Kropotkin, he discovered that syndicalism was the only force capable of reconciling social progress with individual dignity. His hostility to the Republic can be traced to the same sentiment. A republican in his own manner, he discovered in the syndicate an ideal blend of republicanism and elitism of the purest sort. The syndicates, he asserted, "are truly the most republican institutions, popular in character, yet rising above the masses, limited in membership [and] disciplined—that is to say, governed according to aristocratic principles." And he insisted on "the essential value" of such "an organic unit where the real elite of the people, molded by its daily experience, forged a genuine civic pride and stood as the champion of liberty." [27]

Halévy did not conceal his disdain for bourgeois values, for the abuses of parliamentary government and even the democratic process itself; nor is there any doubt that he viewed state socialism and capitalist exploitation with equal hostility. He rejected the egalitarian tenets of middle-class democracy and condemned the bourgeois order as leading, in his words, to "the levelling mediocrity of *les petites gens*." [28] Interested above all in moral progress, he favored a form of corporatism that, by regrouping all elites within a mutualist

[26] Irving Louis Horowitz, *Radicalism and the Revolt against Reason: The Social Theories of Georges Sorel* (London, 1961), 28–29. See also Jean Maitron, *Histoire du mouvement anarchiste en France: 1880–1914* (Paris, 1951), 13.

[27] Halévy, *Luttes et problèmes* (Paris, 1911), 93; Sorel, "Trois Problèmes," *L'Indépendance*, Dec. 15, 1911, 261.

[28] Halévy, *Décadence de la liberté* (Paris, 1931), 33; cf. Robert Brasillach, "Daniel Halévy et la liberté," *L'Action française*, Aug. 13, 1931; Georges Guy-Grand, *L'Avenir de la démocratie* (Paris, 1928), 194 ff.

society, would take into account the varieties, contradictions, and inequalities of human nature. Such a corporatism, he believed, would release the best popular instincts and serve as the basis from which higher forms of social life and political organization could ultimately evolve.[29]

Ideas of the same order were, of course, subsequently invoked by totalitarian regimes who associated similar theories with the corporative state. Yet the drift of Halévy's thoughts does not exactly conform to this pattern. Although certainly not unrelated to an ideological current that culminated in National Socialism, his haphazard observations were essentially those of a casual onlooker, of an amateur *moraliste* primarily concerned with elucidating the climate of opinion in which he lived and seeking to grasp the meaning of what he observed.[30] With his flair for the unusual he espoused ideas which were, if anything, more archaic than reactionary—and, to his mind at least, rooted in the past and still within the best traditions of liberalism. Perhaps his views were no more than the idle speculations of a curious observer reacting to one of the most intriguing phenomena of his times and trying to relate a nostalgia for a vanishing *mystique* of labor with a visionary ideal of his own. In short, what Halévy's social speculations amounted to was that he preferred the workshop to the factory, the artisan to the proletarian; with an affinity for character, he placed the dignity of the individual above any group or system, and sought above all to preserve the autonomy of the workman and the integrity of the craftsman and his labor.

In a more immediate sense, Halévy's random notes on the

[29] Robert de Traz, "Daniel Halévy," *La Revue de Paris*, May, 1933, 79.

[30] Cf. Jean Guéhenno, "La République des petites gens," *Europe*, XXXV (1934), 412–418; Georges Guy-Grand, "Libéralisme et révolution," *La Grande Revue*, Oct., 1934, 596 ff.; Guy-Grand, "Le Conflit des croyances et des moeurs littéraires dans la France d'avant-guerre," *Mercure de France*, Jan. 16, 1919, 193–222.

growth of the labor movement in the first decades of the twentieth century are an admirable summary of the shifting character of revolutionary syndicalism, constituting, as it were, a documentary addendum to Sorel's more systematic social theories. Independently and through a process of personal investigation, he reached conclusions which were virtually the same as those of the author of the *Reflections on Violence*. Sorel, who during these years was working out his own theory of the myth of the general strike, praised the younger man for having succeeded in detecting those elusive qualities that he had himself discovered in syndicalist endeavor. In a long review of his friend's *Luttes et problèmes*— a collection of Halévy's works tracing the growth of his ideas from Dreyfusism to revolutionary syndicalism—Sorel noted with satisfaction that they both shared an identical sympathy for the stirrings of a proletarian self-consciousness. Stressing the importance of Halévy's assertion that revolutionary syndicalism could become a source of heroic vitalism, Sorel went on to commend his judgment in identifying it with the wave of the future.[31]

Yet, if Halévy's views did indeed confirm Sorel's, they were only to mature under the greater man's impact. What is significant, however, is that before he himself contributed to launching the *Reflections on Violence*, he had already, quite independently, reached a position, which in a certain sense anticipated Sorel's. His own explorations into syndicalist life had revealed to him the importance of a "métaphysique des moeurs"—as Sorel later called it—which flowed spontaneously from a self-reliant proletarian morality. And he vaguely sensed that if syndicalism was the purest expression of the epic and sublime character of the class struggle, its ultimate triumph could be assured only if the

[31] Sorel, "Trois Problèmes," 261. See also extracts from Sorel MS letter to Halévy reprinted in *Fédération*, Nov., 1947, 2–4; and Sorel's letter to Croce, dated May 15, 1908, reprinted in *La Critica*, XXVI (1928), 106.

working class succeeded in preserving its essential heroic values.

III

These summary ideas, shaped by a moral pessimism that can be traced back ultimately to Renan, constituted the essence of Halévy's socialism. As befitted a man of letters, he set forth his views in his "Histoire de quatre ans: 1997–2001," a kind of fable, halfway between a moral tale and a utopia, which was published in the *Cahiers de la Quinzaine* in 1903.[32] This imaginative piece of work represents Halévy's attempt to illustrate his socialist philosophy in fictional form.

The gist of this extraordinary tale is a demonstration of the moral excellence of syndicalist leaders, who are represented as destined to become the ruling class of the future. The book was also meant to be both a critique of prevalent trends in socialist thinking and a program for action, containing a forceful disavowal of Marxist revolutionary dogma accompanied by a summons addressed to the elite of the proletariate to prove themselves worthy of preserving the essential values of humanism.

The fable carries us into the ideal democratic state of the future, similar to those traditionally conceived by a long line of utopian prophets, in which poverty has been banished and all social inequalities finally eradicated. Science has devised a process which assures the cheap production of albumen, an organic matter which possesses miraculous properties, since it not only serves to feed man at negligible cost but is also admirably suited to satisfy all his material needs. At first monopolized by the international trust of Simeon Kohnson, the production and distribution of this product is nationalized by the welfare state, which gradually gains control over

---

[32] 6ème cahier de la 5ème série, Nov., 1903, later reprinted in *Luttes et problèmes*.

all economic activities, ultimately succeeding in suppressing all vestiges of capitalism and providing abundance and a fair share for all.[33]

With society freed from servitude to the land and the machine, the age-old dream of man's complete emancipation is at last within his grasp. Working hours are drastically reduced, factories close down and the peasants desert their farms. As the growing metropolis supplants town and village, the laboring classes are swept by a wave of prosperity and can at last afford to devote their ample leisure to intellectual pursuits. Instead, they succumb to the pleasures of the flesh. After various hedonistic fads have been tried and discarded, a cult of felicitous death spreads across the country, and the wonder drug of the Russian, Novgorod, which assures its addicts fifty hours of uninterrupted eroticism, becomes as indispensable as albumen itself. Losing all conception of what Sorel was to call the "tragique des moeurs," a depraved humanity, debilitated by its own voluptuousness, easily falls a prey to a mass epidemic which mysteriously weeds out the weak and degenerate from the elite.

The latter were men and women of superior character who, at the height of the wave of national prosperity, had withdrawn to the abandoned provinces. There they preserved in their agrarian settlements an independent cooperative tradition that survived the encroachments of the centralized state, while their frugal mode of life protected them from the calamity which decimated society at large. It is they who formed what Halévy called "the indispensable elite," incarnating in their rules of conduct the true aspirations of a vanishing *mystique* of labor. Their moral and physical fitness sets them apart from the rest of humanity, and as everything else is swept away, their libertarian

---

[33] *Luttes*, 202.

institutions alone remain to constitute the nucleus of a superior social organization. These, we are told, will federate into a universal cooperative mutualism to supplant the perishing forms of parliamentary democracy and state socialism.[34]

This bizarre plot is marked by obvious analogies with prevailing ideas of heroic vitalism. Halévy's prophetic imagination predicted that a civilization that succumbed to naive theories of progress would dry up the springs of action, while at the same time his hostility to mere abstraction translated itself into an aversion for democracy and mass culture. But in a more immediate sense, Halévy's fable was really meant as a tract for his times. By giving vent to his skepticism about the final outcome of the revolution as conceived by some of his fellow socialists, he was attempting to define the limits of a common creed which he shared with many other Dreyfusard intellectuals. But by questioning the validity of prevailing socialist theory, he also meant to place some of the more earnest followers of Jaurès on their guard against the irrepressible enthusiasm generated by the great socialist leader.[35]

In retrospect, Halévy regarded this fable as representing a decisive transition in the character of his socialist beliefs.[36] Emerging from his first socialist phase, in which his ideas were shaped by the lingering optimism of the Dreyfusard struggle and his ephemeral collaboration with L'Humanité, Halévy moved closer to Sorel's more austere philosophy with the publication of his book. But the "Histoire de quatre ans" not only marked his first step in the direction of a deeper understanding of Sorel's moral pessimism, it also set the tone

[34] Ibid., 224, 229, 268.
[35] Halévy MS letter to Andreu, dated May 21, 1957, citing an earlier letter to Péguy, c. 1906.
[36] Ibid.

for an attitude that (maturing over the years but remaining virtually unchanged in its essentials) became an abiding article of faith in his own social philosophy and constituted the most permanent feature of all his subsequent writing.[37] It is significant that Sorel could scarcely conceal his admiration for the "Histoire de quatre ans," hailing it as "an authentic masterpiece, one of the most beautiful books that has appeared in the last few years." [38] It is no less significant that his review appeared neither in *Pages Libres* nor in Péguy's *Cahiers*, but in *L'Indépendance*, a reactionary journal founded by some of Sorel's Action Française admirers in an attempt to fuse his syndicalism with Maurras's nationalist principles.[39]

Henceforth, the chief difference between Halévy's ideas and orthodox socialism lay not in his social concern but in his views on matters of social order, where he differed from most Socialists. Interested above all in moral excellence, he rejected their egalitarian premises on the grounds that they distorted the true spirit of French socialism.[40] For him, the ultimate source of progress flowed from the forces released by an organic gradation within society. Only to the extent that it could be freed from its democratic and egalitarian trappings could socialism be adapted to meet the needs of the rising proletariate. Since authority does not reside in the anonymous masses but in a natural aristocracy of talent resting on a clearly established hierarchy of competence, it was only an elitist socialism that could foster the best

[37] Witness the consistently pessimistic tone of the prefaces to his first and last books, *Luttes* and his *Essai sur l'accélération de l'histoire* (Paris, 1961), or *La Fin des notables*, chap. II.

[38] Georges Sorel, "Trois Problèmes," 262; cf. Jean Variot, *Propos de Georges Sorel* (Paris, 1935), 166–167.

[39] Sorel called his endeavor "a new fertile synthesis," *L'Indépendance*, June 1, 1912, 336. See also Eugen Weber, *Action Française: Royalism and Reaction in Twentieth-Century France* (Stanford, Calif., 1962), 74.

[40] See especially, Halévy, *Les Trois Epreuves*, 61 ff.

energies of the working class, guaranteeing its emancipation while preserving its essential liberties.[41] The burden of the "Histoire de quatre ans" is that the working class can gain its freedom only after being sifted through a rigorous process. Put to the test by a severe trial such as the universal calamity evoked in the tale, humanity will spontaneously produce its own "indispensable elite." Halévy sought in effect to bring out the moral problem inherent in socialism, a problem which prevalent socialist theory tended to neglect. In his tale the consequences that result from the abundance of albumen demonstrate that once the social problem has been solved, the moral problem will remain in all its stark intensity to plague doctrinaire socialists. Rejecting as invalid the assumptions of a strictly economic theory which dismissed man's will as a negligible force, Halévy endorsed the opposite view that revolutionary syndicalism was exclusively a matter of *élan*, a vital impulse which would bring about the triumph of spirit over matter. The self-discipline emerging from the very nature of the syndicate would rescue the elite of the masses from the false hopes raised by its political leaders and the rigid fatalism inherent in Marxist dogma.[42]

Halévy's elite, however, although select and austere, was not a closed elite. It was open to all who are capable of heroic endeavor and excluded only the weak and the indolent. Clearly recognizable as Nietzschean in its overtones, his conception of an elite was also shaped by his still vivid memories of the Dreyfusard solidarity culminating in the "morale de bande" which had drawn him to Péguy's *Cahiers*.[43] In the light of his Dreyfusard experience and the

[41] Halévy, *Luttes*, 295; cf. de Traz, *op. cit.*, 82–83; Guy-Grand, *La Philosophie syndicaliste* (Paris, 1911), 125–132; Robert Dreyfus, "Bulletin bibliographique," *Pages Libres*, Jan. 9, 1904, 2–3.

[42] Halévy MS letter to Robert Dreyfus, dated May 13, 1911.

[43] *Ibid.*, cf. James H. Meisel, *The Genesis of Georges Sorel: An Account of His Formative Period followed by a Study of His Influence* (Ann Arbor, Mich., 1951), 120, 126.

teachings of Nietzsche, Halévy redefined the socialist ideal
in terms of cultivation of the will and the personality: his
proletarian elite being in fact a race of supermen sorted out
through a crisis leading to the survival of the fittest. By
demonstrating that syndicalist life could rebuild character
and breed heroic values, his fable suggested that revolutionary syndicalism would alone enable the working class to
rise to its destiny and accomplish its emancipation by its
own creative efforts.

But the "Histoire de quatre ans" also anticipated the
perils of irresponsible and precipitate action, drawing attention to the fact that the pusillanimity of the majority can
have the effect of undermining the resolution of the select
few—the "audacious minority." It also warned against a
more pressing danger. As material progress eliminates poverty, the class struggle will tend to lose its epic character, and
the workman, his sense of destiny. Seeking to check the
exuberance of the champions of direct action, Halévy
warned that the proletariate is vulnerable and, like its
predecessors, can also succumb to weakness and indecision.
If the workers can be induced by their leaders to join in a
general strike, lay down their tools and cross their arms, it
does not necessarily follow, predicted Halévy, that they will
do so in a great *élan* of heroism. His skepticism cautioned
him not to place too much faith in the regenerative process
of the general strike; and his tale pointed to the danger that
the old heroic instincts are likely to be submerged in a
general wave of material prosperity.[44] In a lyrical passage
where he recounted how the stirring example set by the elite
of the communal settlements failed to rouse others from
their lethargy, Halévy gave free rein to his pessimistic
imagination. Conjuring a grotesque image of the whole of

[44] Halévy, *Luttes*, 234 ff.; Halévy, "Les Nouveaux Aspects du socialisme,"
Pages Libres, Oct. 2, 1909, 367–380, a significant estimate and critique of
Sorel's ideas.

Europe debilitated by the evils of mass democracy, he evoked the plight of the degenerate West incapable of resisting a new barbarian invasion. "From Shanghai to Tangier," all the subject races of the crumbling Western empires immune from the European epidemic join with the Slavic hordes, finally awakened from their age-old torpor, to march on a decaying Europe, laying waste to its last surviving legacies. Even the oldest of instincts, military honor, can no longer be aroused to avert the impending disaster:

Alas, they were no longer Timoleon's Dorians or Scipio's legionnaires, the Gauls of Caesar or the Franks of Richard-the-Lion-Heart, Cromwell's Ironsides, Gustavus Adolphus's Swedes or Napoleon's *grognards*. . . . The West had lost its men.[45]

IV

We might perhaps hesitate to endorse Sorel's verdict when he hailed Halévy's "medical fable," as he called it, as "the severest criticism that has ever been levelled against democracy since Plato." [46] But it cannot be denied that the "Histoire de quatre ans" is a remarkably suggestive literary feat, which illustrates some of the most important problems raised by contemporary socialist theory. Péguy praised it as a brilliant commentary on the significance of revolutionary syndicalism.[47] Subsequently, Albert L. Guérard, ranking it with Samuel Butler's *Erewhon* and H. G. Wells' *Time Machine*, contended that Halévy's piece of science fiction revealed far greater insight than Anatole France's more celebrated *Sur la Pierre Blanche*.[48] In fact, the "Histoire de quatre ans" bears less resemblance to a moral tale or a *conte philosophique* than to a satirical prophecy, and its underlying pessimistic tone is in complete contrast with the

[45] Halévy, *Luttes*, 268.   [46] Sorel, "Trois Problèmes," 272.
[47] MS letter from Péguy to Halévy, dated May 12, 1905.
[48] Albert L. Guérard, *Five Masters of French Romance* (New York, 1916), 126.

buoyant sentiment which permeates *Sur la Pierre Blanche*. It is indeed significant that whereas Anatole France's tale was serialized in the first issues of *L'Humanité* when Halévy was still its news editor, the "Histoire de quatre ans" appeared simultaneously in the *Cahiers de la Quinzaine* at a time when Péguy's review was becoming more and more identified with an independent socialist stand, increasingly at odds with the orthodox doctrines of Jaurès' newspaper.

As might have been expected, the publication of Halévy's novel provoked a minor furor in socialist circles. Warmly greeted by a handful of subscribers to the *Cahiers* and *Pages Libres*, it was condemned by many others who could not conceal their resentment against the manner in which Halévy had maltreated democracy. Halévy's warning that progress does not grow out of a miracle but out of sheer effort, and that this effort can be achieved only by the "indispensable elite" ran counter to the strongest convictions of the enthusiasts of social progress. By its very timing the "Histoire de quatre ans" could not fail to stimulate comment, and Halévy himself later confided to Sorel that his purpose in writing the fable was to force some of his socialist comrades to re-examine their assumptions in the light of current developments.[49]

Appearing as it did at the height of Combism and as a wave of sporadic strikes was drawing attention to the strengths and weaknesses of the labor movement, his book was eagerly read not only by the intellectuals of the *Cahiers* but also by working-class organizers. But it was particularly among "Dreyfusards of the first hour" whose democratic illusions were beginning to crumble that the ideas set forth by Halévy found a ready audience.[50] It was published at a

[49] MS letter from Halévy to Sorel, dated Aug. 3, 1911.
[50] MS letter to Halévy from Robert Dreyfus, undated, but *c.* 1913, cf. MS letters from Louis Ganderax, Hubert Lagardelle, Claude Harmel, and others.

time when the *Cahiers* were torn by dissension on this very issue, and when its editor, who had loyally supported Halévy in his efforts, was himself giving vent to his resentment against those who were guilty of corrupting his Dreyfusard ideals. Yet socialist theory, even within the *Cahiers*, was still astonishingly flexible. Péguy was capable of printing his own articles (written with his customary verve and abounding in denunciations of what he called the "collectivisme normalien" of Herr and Jaurès) side by side with such trite Radical apologetics as Clemenceau's "Le Bloc" or his "Discours sur la liberté," which appeared in his review as part of the same series as Halévy's fable.[51] Published in the same issue of the *Cahiers* that also contained Romain Rolland's "L'Aube"—the first installment of *Jean-Christophe* suffused with a socialism in the best sentimental vein —Halévy's tale could not have made a more ironical contrast. It was also the most propitious moment for releasing his disturbing ideas on the most intense and perplexed, and also the largest reading audience that the *Cahiers* had ever mustered.

Péguy was quick to grasp the bracing novelty of Halévy's novel and published it with particular relish. Captivated by its fresh insights, he only regretted that Halévy never gave it a sequel; and much later, he was still reproaching him for not having pursued his theme by a bolder analysis of "the relationship between morals and politics." [52] Yet he took great pride in the fact that the "Histoire de quatre ans" had first appeared in his *Cahiers*. In his "Victor-Marie, Comte Hugo," carried away by his own conceit, he reminded Halévy that it was his editorial flair that had instantly made him realize the importance of this, his first major literary achievement:

[51] *Cahiers* (6ᵉᵐᵉ cahier de la 5ᵉᵐᵉ série, Dec., 1903).
[52] MS letter from Péguy to Halévy, dated Dec. 17, 1908.

Who better than I knew how to read, how to value from the very outset your marvelous "Histoire de quatre ans," who better than I proclaimed that it should be placed in the front rank, who better than I proclaimed at first sight its rare virtues, its singular novelty, its troubled and mysterious undercurrents, its breath-taking perspectives, its infinite and disturbing horizons, its distress and anguish—its unique grandeur? Who better than I is your faithful reader? And where would you find a more attentive, a more attentive and faithful reader than I? [53]

Less effusive in his praise, though somewhat more discerning in his judgment, was Sorel. Sharing Péguy's admiration for their friend's talents, Sorel regarded the "Histoire de quatre ans" as a more imaginative precursor of his own *Reflections on Violence*.[54] In his "Lettre à Daniel Halévy," which served as the preface to his book, Sorel stressed the "high moral value" of the pessimistic tone which pervades Halévy's earlier work.[55] He also acknowledged his gratitude for the insights he had derived from their innumerable discussions in the back room of Péguy's *boutique*, discussions which, he said, had the effect of persuading him that "we must place our trust in the workers." Remarking that he could not "often expect to find listeners as patient as you have been," he went on to tell Halévy:

In the course of our conversations, you have sometimes made remarks which fitted so well into the system of my own ideas that they often led me to investigate certain questions more thoroughly. I am sure that the reflections that I here submit to you, and which you have provoked, will be useful to those who wish to read this book with profit. . . . You have brilliantly shown in your "Histoire de Quatre Ans" that you despise the

[53] (Paris, 1934), 54–55.
[54] Sorel, "Lettre à Daniel Halévy," *Reflections on Violence* (Paris, 1906), 12, 39; Meisel, *op. cit.*, 43, 18; see also André Spire in *Feuillets*, no. 40, 3–4.
[55] Sorel, *Reflections*, 46.

deceptive hopes with which the weak solace themselves. We can
then talk pessimism freely to each other, and I am happy to have
a correspondent who does not revolt against a doctrine without
which nothing very great has been accomplished in this world.[56]

And in a subsequent letter, Sorel again reverted to the
underlying identity of their views on the regenerative process
of a revolutionary syndicalism which could alone raise the
individual to the loftiest ideal.

I saw with great pleasure to what extent we are in agreement on
the moral fundamentals with which the contemporary mind
concerns itself so little. . . . Not only does the world refuse to
descend to the depths, it busily spreads veils over the sacred well
from which the oracles originate. . . .[57]

In seeking to define the essence of moral greatness in their
time, Sorel found that the "Histoire de quatre ans" furnished him with a suggestive answer:

As you said [it is] to be found in man's self-confidence, which
foregoes any hope of instant realization; the confidence un-
tainted by utilitarian considerations. . . . The truly great man
reaches for the stars and does not care whether the end will bring
him happiness.[58]

Sorel's expression of confidence in Halévy's capacity to
understand his social philosophy sometimes bordered on
adulation for a man whom he singled out as the most gifted
of his disciples.[59] Indeed, it is not unlikely that the sympathy
that he expressed both here and elsewhere for the younger

[56] *Ibid.*, 26, 30 (trans. by T. E. Hulme and J. Roth from the Free Press, 1950 edition).
[57] MS letter from Sorel to Halévy, dated July 7, 1907, cited in Meisel, *op. cit.*, 43–44.
[58] *Ibid.*
[59] Variot, *Propos*, 13, 160, 163; Sorel to Lotte, MS letter reprinted in *Feuillets*, no. 34, 9; Fernand Rossignol, *La Pensée de Georges Sorel* (Paris, 1948), 39.

man was meant as a token of his esteem.[60] At the very least, these recurring professions of esteem bear out a remarkable affinity in their views on socialism and on moral questions in general. The "indispensable elite" of Halévy's communal settlements was a concrete prefiguration of "the audacious minority" summoned in the *Reflections on Violence*.[61] The somber yet simultaneously bracing prophecies of the "Histoire de quatre ans," its cataclysmic theme and the note of catastrophe on which the book ends coincided with Sorel's philosophy of moral pessimism. And there can be no doubt that Sorel's theories of heroic vitalism and the purifying effects of the myth of the general strike were worked out with Halévy's stirring evocations in mind.[62]

Vincent Tillier, for instance, the syndicalist-philosopher-hero of Halévy's tale, stands for the same principle of action that Sorel was to advocate later in his *Reflections*. It is Tillier who sought to inculcate in the comrades who had withdrawn with him to his provincial settlement a deepening awareness of the sublime quality of their "métaphysique des moeurs." It is Tillier also whom Halévy transformed into a heroic figure of truly Nietzschean proportions. In the seclusion of his community, this savant-anarchist, who bore a striking resemblance to the dead Pelloutier, declared war on mass democracy and all the creations of bourgeois culture, ranging vitality, intelligence, and imagination—those very things that had once sustained Western civilization—with the creative energies of the elite that he has gathered around him. And in Halévy's story, his isolated cooperative became the breeding ground of a superior cul-

[60] It was Halévy, of course, who professed a greater debt to the older man. See Halévy in *Bulletin de l'Union pour la Vérité*, Aug., 1912, 551. Cf. Horowitz, *op. cit.*, 29.

[61] De Traz, *op. cit.*, 82.

[62] Sorel, *Reflections*, 50–51; André Spire in *Feuillets*, no. 40, 3–4; MS letter from Robert Dreyfus to Halévy, undated, but *c.* 1912.

ture resting on the same principles of heroic endeavor that Sorel was to elaborate a few years later in his *Reflections*.[63]

Like Sorel, Halévy also regarded moral pessimism as indispensable for the ultimate triumph of socialism. The vivid account of his resolute elite who survive the disintegration and ultimate ruin of a European society which has lost all notion of "le tragique des moeurs," pointed to Sorel's belief in the value of the myth of the general strike as a catalyzing force which would release the energies of the working class and enable them to overcome the perils of universal decadence. The Sorelian thesis that only an austere and disciplined elite of the proletariate is capable of becoming the instrument of revolutionary change, was also anticipated by Halévy's imaginative evocations. The sublime and epic character of the architects of Halévy's socialist utopia clearly points to the myth of the general strike.

In short, by a remarkable affinity with Sorel, combined with a literary sensitivity all his own, Halévy foreshadowed to an astonishing degree the more systematic theories that Sorel set forth three years later. In the form of an intriguing tale, imaginatively conceived but without the intellectual scaffolding of the *Reflections on Violence*, his "Histoire de quatre ans" provided the more literary-minded readers of Péguy's *Cahiers* with a suggestive foretaste of Sorel's epoch-making book.

V

It was in the autumn of 1899, when Dreyfusism was transformed into a great moral crusade, that Halévy met Sorel for the first time in the library of the Ecole Normale. In the following year, swept by the same revolutionary current, the two men broke with Lucien Herr's circle and rallied to Péguy's *Cahiers de la Quinzaine*. During the

[63] Halévy, *Luttes*, 228, 267, 295; cf. Sorel, "Lettre à Daniel Halévy," *Reflections*, 56.

Combist aftermath, they protested against the decomposition of Dreyfusism, and although subsequently ostracized
from Péguy's *boutique*, they shared from a safe distance a
common admiration for the man who epitomized the
noblest spirit of their lost cause.[64] Their own friendship,
however, was never clouded by the petty feuds which raged
around the *Cahiers*, and until the end Halévy never failed to
acknowledge "our old Sorel" as his undisputed master.

Sorel, for his part, was also indebted to his young disciple
who, by publishing his *Reflections on Violence*, was largely
responsible for giving a wider currency to his unorthodox
ideas. The *Reflections*, the fruit of informal chats so gratifying to the discursive predilections of the two men, first
appeared in six monthly installments (from January through
June, 1906) in Hubert Lagardelle's obscure syndicalist review, *Le Mouvement Socialiste*. The publication of the
essays two years later by the printing press of *Pages Libres*
was entirely the result of Halévy's initiative and sound
judgment: although André Spire also participated in the
financial venture, Sorel's introduction—written in the form
of a long letter to Halévy and inserted in the first and all
subsequent editions of the book—clearly indicates the extent
of his special gratitude to the man whom he always called his
"*cher éditeur*." [65] The "Letter to Daniel Halévy," however, is
really not an introduction, but a summary of Sorel's conclusions on the myth of the general strike. It was first printed in
1907, once again in *Le Mouvement Socialiste*, in anticipa-
tion of the forthcoming publication which was virtually
identical both in form and content with the original articles.

---

[64] The first edition of Sorel's *La Révolution dreyfusienne*, appeared in
1908, two years before Halévy's "Apologie pour notre passé." There was a
second, revised edition in 1911. See Georges Goriely, *Le Pluralisme
dramatique de Georges Sorel* (Paris, 1962), 180–181; Meisel, *op. cit.*, 159;
Sorel, *Matériaux d'une théorie du prolétariat* (Paris, 1918), 247.

[65] André Spire, *Souvenirs à bâtons rompus* (Paris, 1962), 152–153.

Halévy's participation in editing the *Reflections on Violence* went no further than proofreading the original manuscript and polishing its style; but it was his "impertinent questions" that provoked Sorel to formulate his rambling thoughts in a more coherent fashion.[66] And also, by introducing Sorel to his own publisher, Marcel Rivière, Halévy deserves much of the credit for bringing the eccentric purveyor of ideas to the attention of a larger audience.

In the following years, Halévy spared no effort to champion Sorel's cause, but after 1918 the two men gradually drifted apart largely because of disagreement over the issue of the Russian Revolution, but also because the First World War had destroyed Halévy's socialist illusions and steered his curiosity in other directions. Too old to be called up for active duty, he served with the rank of captain as an interpreter with a British division in the Argonne, and after 1917, as a liaison officer with a unit of the U.S. Expeditionary Forces. *Avec les Boys américains* and a translation of an English short story—praised by Proust as the finest story on the war [67]—were the fruit of his military experience; it was in his capacity as one of General Pershing's press attachés that he gathered the material for his life of President Wilson, his first notable biography, published by Payot in 1918.

With the end of hostilities, Halévy resumed his profession as a man of letters. The "Cahiers Verts," which he edited for Bernard Grasset from 1921 to 1927, established him as one of the leading Parisian literary critics, and his authorship of a steady stream of books and articles earned him the reputation for being a gifted and versatile essayist. His publications, ranging from journalism to belles-lettres, testify to the remarkable scope of his interests. But it was undoubtedly in the art of biography that Halévy excelled, and his two major

[66] Meisel, *op. cit.*, 43.
[67] Marcel Proust, *A Un Ami* (Paris, 1948), 240.

historical works—*La Fin des notables* (1930), and its sequel *La République des ducs* (1937)—can be regarded as belonging to this literary genre.

Halévy's masterpiece is a splendid piece of historical evocation, reconstructed almost entirely from childhood memories of conversations around the family circle and the wealth of sources accumulated by his father. Drawn by the political personalities who presided over the destinies of the new France, Halévy illuminated the early years of the Republic by means of character sketches which give his narrative something of the grandeur of tragedy, raising it above mere polemics. Taken as a whole, the work is free from the bias which one might have expected from the author of *La République des comités*, a violent diatribe against the Radicals, hastily written in the summer of 1934 when Halévy was contemplating the second volume of *La Fin des notables*. In fact, *La République des ducs* (large fragments of which originally appeared in *La Revue des Deux Mondes*) shows even less trace of partisanship than its predecessor. And although his history illustrates the disintegration of the Republican *mystique* by tracing the mediocrity of *les petites gens* to the decline of the French political elites in the seventies, Halévy's account of the "halcyon age" [68] of parliamentary democracy is written with a certain serenity, less in anger and more with the detachment of a *moraliste* endowed with a rich historical imagination.

The publication of *La République des ducs* gave rise to a controversy over the precise role of the Council of State and the mayors in 1875. One result of the debate was the creation in 1937 of the Société d'Histoire de la Troisième République, an independent study group founded by Halévy, Emile Pillias and André Siegfried in an effort to investigate the history of their own times and raise the

[68] The expression is from Guy Chapman, *The Third Republic of France: The First Phase, 1871–1894* (London, 1962), 74.

Republic to the level of a respectable field of academic study. Halévy himself pointed the way in a statement of purpose, "Pour l'Etude de la Troisième République," in which he chided the Sorbonne for neglecting contemporary history and urged scholars to fill the gap by exploring new avenues of research.[69] His own edition of Gambetta's papers, published with the collaboration of a professional archivist, was an important contribution to historical study, and the Société itself, now under the guiding spirit of the Fondation Nationale des Sciences Politiques, has generally deserved well of its founder.

The Second World War was, of course, a sobering experience for all Frenchmen, but to Halévy who had predicted the coming catastrophe, it was also a personal tragedy. Estranged from his Gaullist son-in-law while at the same time harassed by the Gestapo, Halévy emerged from the Occupation a broken and disillusioned man. Yet he easily survived his past indiscretions and, although rejected by the Academy in 1952, was rewarded with a seat at the Institut. Shortly before his death, the City of Paris paid tribute to his achievement by awarding him its most distinguished literary prize.

Old age seemed scarcely to have impaired his critical faculties and he displayed until the end those qualities of heart and mind that had endeared him to so many of his contemporaries. From the Quai Conti where he faithfully attended the Monday sessions of the Institut, to the quaint, medieval hostel of the Compagnons du Tour de France which he had helped to restore in the shadow of the Church of Saint-Gervais, his bearded figure clad in simple corduroy and with his customary knapsack on his back was a bizarre but familiar sight to the neighbors of his *pays parisien*. But

---

[69] Cf. René Rémond, "Plaidoyer pour une histoire délaissée," *Revue française de Science politique*, July, 1957, 253–270; Robert Dreyfus, "Sous la Troisième," *La Revue de France*, Mar. 15, 1937, 330–354.

what gave him the greatest pleasure as he approached the end of his life was the delights of good conversation. His drawing room still attracted the most brilliant and the most eccentric people of Paris and the rest of Europe; as late as 1948 he could still entertain a gathering of learned historians with his impudent remarks.[70] Finally, on February 4, 1962, he died of a stroke in the ancestral home on the Quai de l'Horloge.

[70] Pieter Geyl, *Encounters in History* (New York, 1961), 140–141.

CHAPTER VI

The Biographer

AS a historian, Halévy's achievement has received the praise
that it deserves. All students of modern France agree that
such books as *La Fin des notables*, *La République des ducs*,
Le Courrier de M. Thiers, or the *Lettres de Gambetta*
remain solid works that have greatly contributed to our
knowledge of the Third Republic.[1] His position in French
letters is no less secure. A patron of the arts and a pioneering
publisher in his own right, he earned the reputation of being
Bernard Grasset's most valuable collaborator. As editor of
the "Cahiers Verts," one of the most notable literary
ventures of the inter-war years, his name was associated with
all the prominent writers of the time.[2] As a critic and essayist
his standing was firmly established, and in his capacity of
journalist, his accounts of the world at large were as highly
valued in Paris as his lively *chroniques* on his own country
were eagerly read abroad.[3]

[1] See, *inter alia*, Albert Thibaudet in *L'Encyclopédie française*, XVIII, sec.
17:18, 13.
[2] See, *inter alia*, Henri Clouard, *Histoire de la littérature française du
symbolisme à nos jours* (Paris, 1949), II, 133; Jean de Pierrefeu, "Daniel
Halévy et les *Cahiers Verts*," *Le Journal des Débats*, Aug. 31, 1921.
Bernanos was the only writer of note whose manuscript he rejected for his
"Cahiers Verts" series, but the early writings of Mauriac, Malraux,
Montherlant and others appeared under his auspices.
[3] Halévy was a regular contributor to *La Revue de Genève*. Some of
the more important pieces were reprinted in his *Courrier d'Europe* (Paris,
1933); and his *Courrier de Paris* (Paris, 1932). See also Jean Prévost in
Nouvelle Revue française, May 1, 1933, 845–846.

DANIEL HALÉVY AND HIS TIMES

I

Halévy's publications range from history and criticism to travel and biography, and among his works of a philosophical character, his *Essai sur l'accélération de l'histoire* stands in a class apart as a brief but suggestive speculative essay in the manner of Toynbee.[4] More controversial were his day-to-day polemical writings chiefly directed against the abuses of the Third Republic, upon which he heaped his disdain with relentless vigor. To be sure, such diatribes as *La République des comités* belong to a respectable French genre in which, like Albert Thibaudet and Robert de Jouvenel, Daniel Halévy also excelled.[5] Similarly, his *1938: Une Année d'histoire* (a spirited attack against the Popular Front), and its sequel, the more restrained *Décadence de la liberté*, or *Les Trois Epreuves*, are in the best tradition of French pamphleteering. Yet even the books that he wrote on the spur of the moment are not altogether devoid of merit; dictated by more urgent circumstances than his more serious endeavors, these tracts for the times, couched in his distinctively urbane style, also demonstrate the versatility of Halévy the publicist.

More important than their contents is the spirit in which they were conceived. Like the rest of his journalistic output, most of his ephemeral broadsides illustrate the extent to which Halévy reacted to the political and social malaise of his country and times. They also demonstrate the important fact that, like many otherwise well-meaning but increasingly disillusioned intellectuals, Halévy shared the prevailing senti-

[4] See also Halévy, "A. J. Toynbee et son étude de l'histoire," *La Revue des Deux Mondes*, Sept. 1, 1950, 38–42; "Histoire universelle," *La Table Ronde*, Nov., 1945, 101–130; and in the same vein his "Leibniz et l'Europe," *La Revue des Deux Mondes*, May 15, 1940, 258–277. Cf. Marcel Reinhard, *L'Enseignement de l'histoire* (Paris, 1957), 17, for a nodding approval of his ideas from the Sorbonne.

[5] Albert Thibaudet, *La République des professeurs* (Paris, 1927); Robert de Jouvenel, *La République des camarades* (Paris, 1914).

ment that his country and its institutions were out of joint, its leaders woefully inept, and its public spirit decadent. That a man of Halévy's stature should have joined in the general onslaught against the Republic is indeed a sad commentary on himself and the regime, and both have subsequently been roundly condemned for their blunders. Since its demise, the Republic has been charged by champions and detractors alike with moral bankruptcy, and it is now generally agreed that it somehow failed to preserve the allegiance of its own elites. For his part, Halévy has with equal justice been repoached for an irresponsible attitude that neglected to strengthen the viable elements in French government and society and concentrated instead on denouncing its shortcomings, thus further undermining the regime and contributing to its fall.[6]

Yet the fact remains that Halévy's past indiscretions, by and large, earned him only a mild reproof. Even his severest critics like Jean Guéhenno, while still rebuking him for collaboration—albeit a hesitant collaboration—with Vichy, now admit that this "Alceste of democracy" stands in a class apart from the other "gravediggers" of French parliamentary democracy.[7] Halévy's brand of dissent was certainly milder if not more dignified than the strictly negative incivisme of most of the followers of Maurras, or the cavalier vituperations of Henri Massis or Pierre Gaxotte, or the mere bravado of Maxence and Fabre-Luce, André Thérive, and Thierry Maulnier, and a host of lesser polemicists who ranged themselves among the opponents of the Third Republic. Although he made no secret of his personal admiration for Maurras, he never concealed his misgivings on the dogmatic

---

[6] See, inter alia, Edouard Dolléans, Histoire du travail (Paris, 1944), 249; Georges Guy-Grand, Au Seuil de la Quatrième République (Paris, 1946), passim.

[7] Guéhenno, La Foi difficile (Paris, 1958), 92 ff.; cf. Guéhenno, Journal des années noires: 1940–1944 (Paris, 1947), 19, 53.

spirit of his "integral nationalism." [8] As for the legend of Halévy's association with the Action Française, this was largely of his own creation. Halévy gained the unenviable distinction of being remembered to this day as a quasi-fascist because, as an incorrigible champion of lost causes, he spoke up for Maurras and Pétain at their trial.[9] By clinging to such scruples he also ruined his own chances of being rewarded with the one public honor that he felt he rightly deserved. It is indeed ironic that Henri Massis, representing one extreme, and Jean Guéhenno, the other, have both been subsequently elected to the French Academy, whereas Halévy's *faux pas* deprived him of his rightful place among his country's Immortals.[10]

If the object of Halévy's hatred was undoubtedly the same Republic which Maurras and—as we often tend to forget—many other less misguided critics so vigorously condemned, Halévy's aversion was shaped by considerations of an entirely different order. The target of his criticism was not so much the regime as such, but what had become, in his view, a distortion of a Republican ideal that he cherished in his own way. The note of despair that pervades all his writing sprang from a profound disillusionment with parliamentary democracy, with the mediocrity of what he called "les petites gens," with the electoral committees, the compromises and corruption that he identified with the Republic. But this

[8] Halévy, "Maurras et la tradition," *La Grande France*, Jan., 1902, 42–47; see also his remarks in *La Revue Universelle*, Jan. 1, 1937, 77–81; in *La Revue de Genève*, Sept., 1923, 343; and in his *Note concernant deux passages du "Journal des Années Noires" de Jean Guéhenno* (Paris, n.d.), 5.

[9] Cf. Henri Massis, *Hommage à Maurras* (Paris, 1959), 89; Ernst Nolte, *Three Faces of Fascism: Action Française, Italian Fascism, National Socialism*, trans. by Leila Vennewitz (New York, 1966), 87.

[10] Although he obtained the required majority for the seat left vacant by Jérôme Tharaud, Halévy was subsequently rejected by the Academy. This did not prevent him from publishing the traditional oration, *Eloge à Jérôme Tharaud: Pages écrites pour un discours qui ne sera pas prononcé* (Paris, 1954), dedicated to Tharaud's widow.

very despair was more than just negative despair, the normal disillusionment of a socialist Dreyfusard's hope deferred. Nor was it merely prompted by a spirit of destructive criticism or the common enough belief that what France needed was an honest government, which could really govern and free the country from the chaos of party strife and ministerial instability. Halévy's despair stemmed from a very genuine awareness of what the Republic—which, after all, he had himself defended as a "Dreyfusard of the first hour"—ought to be. It was for this reason that Maurras himself admitted that Halévy stood apart from the rest of his admirers, and most of his opponents agreed that he could not be hastily dismissed as yet another of the Republic's many talented detractors.[11] Indeed, Halévy's saving grace lies precisely in the positive contribution that he made in shedding light on a certain French ideal that few writers of his generation so persistently explored and so faithfully attempted to keep alive. With all the resources of his talent he preached the gospel that his country could regain its lost greatness only by the restoration of a genuine sense of civic virtue and pride of work. Yet by bringing to bear so much of his criticism on the moral rot that, rightly or wrongly, he identified with the Republic, he himself contributed to concealing the constructive side of the principles that he upheld. It is this positive aspect of his endeavor, his accomplishment as a *moraliste* rather than as a *politique*, which should receive the attention that it deserves.

[11] MS letter of Maurras to Halévy, dated June 7, 1931; see also Henri Massis, *Maurras et notre temps: Entretiens et souvenirs* (Paris, 1961), 366; André Gide, *Journal* (Paris, 1948), 648; Thibaudet, *Les Idées de Charles Maurras*, Vol. I of *Trente Ans de vie française* (Paris, 1920), 319; Thibaudet, "Lasserre et nous," *Nouvelle Revue française*, Jan. 1, 1931, 105; Regis Michaud, *Modern Thought and Literature in France* (London, 1933), 277; Robert Aron, *Précis de l'unité française* (Paris, 1933), 142; Raoul Girardet, "L'Héritage de l'Action Française," *Revue française de Science Politique*, Oct., 1957, 765.

DANIEL HALÉVY AND HIS TIMES
II

Halévy's curiosity ranged far and wide, but his sympathies drew him to fasten his loyalties on an ideal that he identified especially with three uncommon Frenchmen: Péguy, Sorel, and their common ancestor, Proudhon. It was by reacting to all three that Halévy evolved his own conception of an ethic of quality and of national energy. These three Frenchmen are themselves the subjects of his most endearing biographies, but their impact is also discernible in the bulk of his works, where the ideas that they inspired incessantly recur. In the course of an astonishingly long career as a writer, he tried his hand at no less than three biographies of Péguy and countless studies on Proudhon, while he repeatedly attempted to grapple with Sorel at different times and from different points of view.[12] All the subjects of Halévy's biographies displayed the stirrings of a creative enthusiasm which inspired them to rebel against their times.[13] Although it was especially in Péguy and Sorel, and their immediate precursor, Proudhon, that Halévy discovered the clearest examples of this spirit of dissent, all his other portraits are also of the stuff that rebels are made of.

Halévy's Proudhon was the precursor of a French *mystique* of socialism, deeply rooted in the national past, and which Sorel in turn tried to revive by broadening its relevance to his own times. Péguy was the poet who fought all his life for the same ideal, giving it a truly national dimension by incorporating it within two great historical

[12] Péguy was the central figure of his *Quelques Nouveaux Maîtres*, and of subsequent biographies in 1918 and 1941. His 1907 biography of Nietzsche was completely revised in 1944. His books on Proudhon range in time from *La Jeunesse de Proudhon* (Paris, 1913), to his last revised edition of Proudhon's life, *La Vie de Proudhon* (Paris, 1948).

[13] Georges Loisy in RTF broadcast delivered in May, 1960. Unpublished typescript, III, 3; Jacques Chevalier, *Entretiens avec Bergson* (Paris, 1959), 21.

forces, patriotism and Christianity. Halévy's Vauban, his favorite hero from the Old Regime, was not only the builder of border fortresses but also the Burgundian squire who pressed upon his king a scheme for a great social transformation that would stimulate a popular renaissance. Halévy's Michelet was a commoner of rare genius who conceived a national epic containing the seeds of a native socialism. Finally, it was Halévy's Nietzsche, source of the provoking query: "Can man be ennobled?" that gave Halévy the inspiration for a cult of moral excellence to which he responded with generous sympathy, a sympathy which often led him beyond exclusively national concerns.[14]

As we know, Halévy excelled in the art of conversation, and his writing also conformed to this particular pattern of discourse. Matching the precise idea with the right tone, he accurately noted the most elusive shades of his interlocutor's character by means of imaginative dialogue. His deliberate choice of biographical subjects gave him the opportunity of conveying the essence of his own liberal convictions by identifying them with his historical characters, using them as the vehicles for expressing his own sentiments. His portraits thus became to a large extent the living models of his own ideas, the prism through which he translated his thoughts. But, for all that, they lose none of their reality and under his adroit recreation they succeed in coming alive as credible human beings.[15] His life of Nietzsche, for instance, where the essence of the German philosopher's ideas is evoked by a perceptive account of his tormented life, is a good illustration of the peculiar quality of Halévy's method of ap-

[14] See especially his preface to Jean Czapski, *Terre inhumaine* (Paris, 1949); Halévy, "Vitalité de l'Europe," *Journal de Rouen*, Nov. 2, 1937.

[15] Cf. Halévy's preface to *Ecrits par André Chamson, André Malraux, Jean Grenier*, "Cahiers Verts," ed. Daniel Halévy, no. 70 (Paris, 1927), vii–viii; see also Henry Daniel-Rops, *Les Années tournantes* (Paris, 1932), 206.

proach.[16] In his *Michelet* and *Vauban*, but particularly in his numerous vignettes of Proudhon, he again revealed a talent for clarifying the ideas of others by a few deft strokes, bringing out to the full his rare gift for psychological penetration. Writing *con amore*, with a sparkling insight here or a revealing detail there, Halévy never failed to draw a wealth of insight from all that stimulated his curiosity.

But it was particularly with Péguy that he accomplished the feat of bringing to life a figure of almost heroic proportions. His devotion to the editor of the *Cahiers de la Quinzaine* kindled a flame of hero-worship that was not to be extinguished until his own death, nearly half a century after Péguy had fallen in battle. His feelings toward his friend were marked by a strong element of identification, which undoubtedly explains the excellence of his biography of his boon companion; but this very identification, standing in a class apart from his other attachments, also sheds some light on Halévy himself. Like Péguy, he too had been a "Dreyfusard of the first hour," a pure liberal and a true socialist. Together, they went through the same trials and suffered the same disillusionments—the Republic that they had championed, degenerated into an intolerant conformism; the university that had bred them, transformed into the dogmatic Sorbonne; the purity of their socialism, betrayed by opportunistic politicians. But the two friends also shared the same *mystique*, and the "Apologie pour notre passé," conceived in the same spirit as "Notre Jeunesse," gives the true measure of the identity of their sentiments below the surface differences which drew them apart.[17]

[16] Sorel to Croce, letter dated Jan. 25, 1911, reprinted in *La Critica*, XXVI (1939), 343–345; Romain Rolland, *Choix de lettres à Malwida von Meyensburg* (Paris, n.d.), 306; Geneviève Bianquis, *Nietzsche en France* (Paris, 1929), 32; Hubert Lagardelle in *Le Mouvement Socialiste*, Mar., 1913, 260.

[17] Charles Péguy, *Situations* (Paris, 1940), 219, 250; Romain Rolland, *Péguy* (Paris, 1944), I, 160.

A superior polemicist but also a greater visionary, Péguy
the poet undoubtedly expressed more eloquently the
mystique that the two men shared. Asserting his genius
through his overbearing personality, he seemed destined to
become the *chef de file* of all those who rallied to his modest
boutique on the Rue de la Sorbonne to carry on the
Dreyfusard crusade on the morrow of the Affair. Like all the
others who joined his plucky band, Halévy was inevitably
overshadowed by the more assertive editor of the *Cahiers*.
But if he too subordinated his personality to that of his
friend, he stood out from the rest by the intensity of his
devotion to their leader, and Péguy picked him out from
among all his other followers as his most congenial collaborator. Halévy remained for Péguy a constant source of
encouragement, fulfilling the function of critic and mentor
—"the most precious and invaluable of my readers," as
Péguy declared.[18]

Naturally inclined to be a foil to others, Halévy took
delight in acting as a spur to his friend's genius. It was his own
"Apologie" which provoked "Notre Jeunesse," perhaps the
most stirring expression of the impact made by the Dreyfus
Affair on their generation and certainly the greatest of
Péguy's *cahiers* in this genre, and "Victor-Marie, Comte
Hugo," Péguy's lyrical reassertion of their Dreyfusard ideals,
was also written in the form of a dialogue with his repentant
friend.[19] Eclipsed by Péguy, Halévy was cast in the humbler
role of the chronicler of his *Cahiers*. Yet in a sense, the
innumerable studies that he devoted to his companion are
also autobiographical, for it was only through the medium of
Péguy that Halévy the critic could most suitably mirror the
ideals that he shared with his Dreyfusard generation. More

[18] MS letter from Péguy to Halévy, undated but *c.* 1905, to thank him for
his review of "Chad Gaya" in *Pages Libres*.
[19] Rolland, *Péguy*, II, 17; Marjorie Villiers, *Charles Péguy: A Study in
Integrity* (London, 1965), 261–266.

than any other member of the *Cahiers*, Halévy bore the indelible mark of Péguy's influence, an influence that shaped his form and attitude, and to some extent, even his character. Valuing Halévy as his most trustworthy associate, Péguy singled him out as the one most worthy to succeed him as editor. At the time of "A Nos Amis, à nos abonnés," despondent and on the verge of bankruptcy, Péguy actually offered to turn over the *Cahiers* to his reluctant associate. To his subsequent dismay, Halévy refused the opportunity that might well have been the turning point in his life.[20] But his own "Cahiers Verts," which he edited with such success after his friend's death, were directly inspired by the earlier, more celebrated, review and demonstrate beyond doubt that he would not have been unworthy of Péguy's trust.[21]

Deliberately keeping his distance from the *Cahiers* so as to be better able to live up to his resolve to write its history, Halévy succeeded at the same time in remaining a full-fledged member of that fraternity, sharing in its life perhaps more fully than any of the other members of the group. It is generally agreed that the *équipe* of the *Cahiers* differed in a very special sense from other contemporary coteries, for it represented to the loftiest degree the aspirations of an entire generation, of all those "men of forty," as Péguy called them, who had come to manhood with the Dreyfus Affair. In Péguy's words, his book shop was literally the last meeting place of all men of good will, "le dernier rendezvous des hommes de bonne compagnie." [22] All those who gathered

[20] Yvonne Servais, *Charles Péguy: The Pursuit of Salvation* (Oxford, 1953), 321 ff.; Rolland, *Péguy*, I, 160, 224 ff.; Jean and Jérôme Tharaud, *Notre Cher Péguy* (Paris, 1926), II, 151. See also Halévy, *Charles Péguy et "Les Cahiers de la Quinzaine"* (Paris, 1941), 145.

[21] Albert Thibaudet, *Les Princes lorrains* (Paris, 1924), x; but see also Halévy's preface to Emile Clermont, *Le Passage de l'Aisne*, "Cahiers Verts," ed. Daniel Halévy, no. 5 (Paris, 1921), xii.

[22] Péguy, *A Nos Amis, à nos abonnés*, reprinted in *Péguy et les Cahiers*, ed. Mme Charles Péguy (Paris, 1947), 279–280.

around him were unanimous only in their devotion to his endeavor, but they were never bound to conform to any single doctrine. They formed "neither a sect nor a cabale," but—again in Péguy's words—"a kind of natural family, a family of kindred souls, literally, the most beautiful thing that has ever existed in the world—a friendship; and a cité.[23]

Proust fancifully referred to the *Cahiers* as resembling the rose window of a cathedral, "en rosace." But although he resisted Halévy's attempts to draw him into this charmed circle, preferring to admire it from afar, he secretly envied his former schoolmate for being in the center of what he called "the melting pot of all the great French debates."[24] Albert Thibaudet, the most penetrating observer of his generation, described the *Cahiers* as "a group of congenial minds . . . , the center of a dialogue" where such diverse and incongruous temperaments as Péguy and Halévy, Sorel and Benda, revived all the traditional French controversies and gave them a fresh dimension. It was like a stage where the whole drama of the national past was performed by new actors and a utopian vision proclaimed by new prophets.[25]

Halévy's role in this process was that of a catalyst. During Péguy's lifetime, observed Thibaudet, Halévy stood out as his sturdiest "bodyguard," more deeply marked than Benda or Romain Rolland by the contagious genius of this remarkable champion of lost causes. Although himself a "mild man," but with an incorrigible predilection for dialogue, Halévy emerged as the principal protagonist in all the

[23] *Ibid.*, 281; cf. Thibaudet, *Histoire de la littérature française de 1789 à nos jours* (Paris, 1936), 476–478.

[24] MS letter from Proust to Halévy, dated Apr. 12, 1911; but see Laurent Lesage, *Marcel Proust and His Literary Friends* (Urbana, Illinois, 1958), 45.

[25] Thibaudet, "L'Ecole des *Cahiers*," *L'Encyclopédie française*, XVIII, sec. 17:18, 13; see also Lucas de Peslouan in *Le Journal des Débats*, Feb. 1, 1910; Halévy in *Le Temps*, Dec. 12, 1909; Romain Rolland, *Choix de lettres à Malwida von Meyensburg*, 306.

dissensions which raged within the *Cahiers*. His impertinent questions provoked the great debates which contributed to raising the *Cahiers'* reputation as the most exciting journal in Paris, while the high purpose of Péguy's endeavor is epitomized in all of his own works. Both before and after the publication of the "Apologie," Halévy's preoccupations reveal the inner tension of the *Cahiers*, in Thibaudet's words, an underlying dialogue between "a *mystique* of labor and a nationalist *mystique*," the groping for a valid synthesis "between the spirit of Jaurès (the "Histoire de quatre ans") and the spirit of Maurras (*La République des comités*)." [26] After his companion's death and the collapse of his review, Halévy remained its lone survivor, representing in his own inconspicuous but engaging manner the contradictions that Péguy had sought to uphold. By a peculiar twist of fate it was the same Halévy whom Péguy had ostracized from his *boutique* who remained, as Thibaudet wrote, "the greatest living witness" of his friend's accomplishments and dilemmas.[27]

André Gide's *Nouvelle Revue française*, the only other significant literary venture to be launched during this decade, was too strictly literary to make the same kind of impact as did the *Cahiers*. Broadening the scope of literature beyond the conventional limits, Péguy gave to his journal a special flavor of its own, while his own inbred populism awakened among his collaborators and readers alike a renewed awareness of France's past and a fresh dedication to its future greatness.[28] Yet, for all that, even in the domain of criticism, the *Cahiers* holds a high rank among other publications. Many notable men of letters served their apprenticeship in the *boutique*: Thibaudet, whose "new criticism" set the tone for literary taste in the twenties, was himself a by-

[26] Thibaudet, "L'Ecole des *Cahiers*," 13.   [27] *Ibid.*

[28] Fernand Baldensperger, *L'Avant-Guerre dans la littérature française: 1900–1914* (Paris, 1919), 39.

product of the *Cahiers*, while Romain Rolland and André
Spire, Benda, the Tharauds and others, show in all their
works the trace of this formative schooling.[29] The *Cahiers'*
contribution to enlarging literary sensibility was entirely
Péguy's personal achievement. Péguy's originality lay in the
fact that, having gone through the Ecole Normale without
sacrificing an iota of his peasant origins, he was able to
inspire all the university men in his circle with the desire to
explore for themselves the popular culture which he so self-
consciously incarnated. Rebelling against Barrès' dictum
that "nothing noble was ever conceived save in an armchair," he forged in its place a brand new criticism all his
own, steeped in a sense of realities and reacting against the
official curriculum of the Sorbonne ("that house across the
street," as he would call it), against academic criticism and
the professorial chair.[30]

Halévy's training with the *Cahiers*, however, had a greater
effect than merely to enlarge his critical judgment, for in his
eyes, Péguy's review stood for something much more significant than the republic of letters.[31] What he treasured above
all from his association with the *Cahiers* was what he called
its *"morale de bande,"* while Péguy's personality, teeming
with a spontaneous earthiness, stimulated his own quest for

[29] G. Turquet-Milnes, *From Pascal to Proust: Studies in the Genealogy of a Philosophy* (London, 1926), 121–123; Alfred Glauser, *Albert Thibaudet et la critique créatrice* (Paris, 1951), 177–180.
[30] Thibaudet, *Histoire de la littérature française*, 467; Jules Isaac, *Expériences de ma vie*, Vol. I, *Péguy* (Paris, 1959), 242, 284 ff.; Thibaudet, "Péguy et Bergson," *Nouvelle Revue française*, Apr. 1, 1931, 580–592; Pierre Moreau, "L'Obsession de la vie dans la littérature contemporaine," *Revue Bimensuelle des Cours et des Conférences*, Apr.–June, 1939, 256 ff., 673 ff.; Pierre Nora, "Ernest Lavisse: Son rôle dans la formation du sentiment national," *Revue Historique*, July–Sept., 1962, 84–88. For Barrès' comments see his "Péguy," *L'Echo de Paris*, Sept. 17, 1914.
[31] Halévy, "Chad Gaya," *Pages Libres*, Apr. 15, 1905, 482–484, where in a review of Péguy's first major work he wrote: "Je m'institue Voltaire de ce nouveau Pascal."

French values. All those who came in contact with the
Cahiers could not fail to be impregnated with this spirit.[32]
Noting that the cast of Halévy's mind had certainly been
molded by Péguy's example, Henri Bergson reminded
Halévy in 1939 that the mere sight of Péguy sitting at his
desk like a craftsman at his bench revealed to all those who
beheld him the simple truth that the toilers of the soil and
the artisans in their workshops possessed a distinction all
their own. Such a sentiment, wrote Bergson, should at all
costs be kept alive, and he stressed the enduring value of a
mystique of labor "identified with a rural and artisanal
France, where a preoccupation with a job well done
broadens into a general craving for excellence, and where
also an attachment to the land bestows on all those who
cultivate it a certain nobility, an aristocratic distinction." [33]
Recalling that he too had shared Halévy's fascination for
that admirable commoner, Bergson contrasted Péguy's
modest *boutique* in the Latin Quarter scarcely able to
accommodate more than a single visitor with "the lofty ideals
which emerged from it to spread far and wide, settling here
and there, often very far away, in every place where there are
men who want to live according to truth and justice." [34]

If Bergson welcomed Halévy's yeoman service in keeping
the memory of the *Cahiers* alive, it was not only because he
shared the younger man's dedication to Péguy. He was also
flattered by Halévy's loyalty because it confirmed the impact
that his own ideas had made in shaping the character of
Péguy and his review.[35] Bergson was in a very special sense

[32] Halévy, *Quelques Nouveaux Maîtres* (Moulins, 1914), 127; Jean
Delaporte, *Connaissance de Péguy* (Paris, 1944), II, 39.

[33] Bergson MS letter to Halévy, reprinted in part in *Feuillets de l'Amitié
Charles Péguy*, no. 30, 13; cf. Guéhenno, *La Foi difficile*, 91.

[34] Bergson, in *Feuillets*, 14.

[35] Cf. Robert J. Niess, *Julien Benda* (Ann Arbor, Mich., 1956), 12;
Jacques Chevalier, *Entretiens avec Bergson*, 26.

the presiding spirit of the generation of the *Cahiers*, and Halévy himself has recounted how his teaching, after first casting its spell on his students at the Ecole Normale, had later taken by storm all those who like Sorel and himself had flocked to his lectures at the Collège de France.[36] The Bergsonian philosophy of time as continuous flow and his theories on the continuity of consciousness had, indeed, a decisive effect on Péguy and all his collaborators.[37] But the impact of these ideas on Halévy, though no less profound than on some of the others, was more elusive, for it took the form of shaping his attitude rather than the hard core of his beliefs. What Bergson accomplished in Halévy's case was to foster in him a private sense of the significant qualities in life. It was essentially the manner in which Bergson's philosophy impregnated the *Cahiers* with a sense of common purpose that was to win over Halévy's sympathies.

The value of Bergson's ideas was that they served Halévy as a key which unlocked the inner depths of the life of the *Cahiers*, arousing his awareness of the bond that united him with Péguy and Sorel, whose qualities he would otherwise never have appreciated as fully as he did. While even his more serious works show little trace of the direct influence of Bergson, they clearly reflect a lively sense of the more tangible aspects—of the form rather than the content—of the philosopher's ideas. What remained ingrained in Halévy's memory, for instance, was not so much the way in which Bergson affected Péguy's thinking but rather the more salient features of the celebrated Collège de France lectures. Each Friday, following the traditional meetings inevitably resumed from the night before, he would meet Péguy at the

[36] Halévy, *Péguy*, 29, 71.
[37] Thibaudet, "Péguy et Bergson," 588; Henri Brugmans, "La Notion du peuple chez Michelet et Péguy," *Feuillets*, no. 20, 9; Delaporte, *op. cit.*, I, 71–73.

boutique. Accompanied by Sorel, they would make their way across the Rue Saint-Jacques to the Collège de France to watch the performance which began promptly at five.

We were all ears . . . and all eyes too, for Bergson's teaching was a sight to be seen. He worked at his philosophy under the public gaze like a craftsman alone at his work. . . . What marvelous lectures they were! [38]

There was, however, an even stronger reason which drew Halévy (his mind constantly seeking to ferret out affinities) to Bergson. For he found in the *élan vital* a remarkable analogy with the heroic vitalism of his first and lifelong love, Nietzsche. In his discovery of Bergson's ideas, he encountered the same enchantment that had first led him to the German philosopher. Like many other Nietzschean converts delving into the Dionysian depths which lay below the Apollonian surface, Halévy found that the horizons revealed by Bergson's intuitive philosophy provided him with an equally bracing tonic against the intellectual malaise of the time. Yet the attraction of Bergson, personal no less than intellectual, was not strictly philosophical, nor was it purely literary, for to Halévy his real appeal lay in the fact that he was more of a *moraliste* than a philosopher. And, in a peculiar way for a man who was the principal opponent of a decaying positivism, he seemed to possess some of the same qualities that Halévy had admired in Renan.

In a more immediate sense, it was the general drift of Halévy's own thinking that was in tune with Bergson's ideas. His revolt against the dry scientism of the Establishment, his revulsion against the facile optimism of a centralized state curriculum that, reaching down from the Sorbonne to the primary school, disseminated a crude moral rationalism, his growing hostility against bourgeois mediocrity in general—in

[38] Halévy, *Péguy*, 65; Halévy, "Sur Un Nouveau Péguyisme," *La France Catholique*, June, 1952, 14.

short, all his antipathies and some of his sympathies found an echo in a philosophy that confirmed his frankly elitist and antidemocratic speculations. And although he never made any pretense to have mastered more than the broad outlines of Bergson's metaphysical system, he found that the intuitive process of Bergson's moral philosophy could liberate his mind from the confining ideas which still hampered his intellectual curiosity.

Yet the fact remains that Halévy reacted to Bergson only in a roundabout manner. If he was a Bergsonian at all, it was only in a derivative sense, for it was essentially through the medium of Péguy and Sorel—both of them disciples of Bergson in their own way—that he came to grips with the master's philosophy. Here again he displayed his talent as a critic, being one of the first to detect a perceptible link uniting these three uncommon thinkers in the first decade of the twentieth century.[39]

His fascination with both Sorel and Péguy, however, dates from before the vogue for Bergson. Although the process of intuitive perception unfolded by Bergson undoubtedly contributed to deepening his appreciation, enabling him to reap greater rewards from his association with his two friends, the roots of this appreciation can be traced to an earlier period, to the intense intellectual ferment precipitated by the Dreyfus Affair. It was in the wake of what Halévy has aptly called "the exchange and reshuffling of ideas" provoked by the Affair that he was first captivated by his two heroes, for it was then that he discovered that their concerns coincided with his own deeper preoccupations.[40] The very first issues of Péguy's *Cahiers*, devoted to the great promise of the socialist

[39] Cf. Maurice Merleau-Ponty, "Hommage . . . à Bergson," *Bulletin de la Societé française de Philosophie*, Jan.–Mar., 1960, 35. Cf. André Rousseaux, "Péguy, Bergson et Proust," *Fontaine*, June 22, 1960, 136.

[40] Halévy, "Trois Maîtres: Proudhon, Sorel, Péguy," *L'Ordre français*, Aug., 1958, 28.

movement, the implications of Dreyfusism, the limitations of reason, and the nature of historical objectivity—all dealt with subjects which aroused Halévy's interests. At the same time his own sympathy for Renan, which had hardly been shaken by the Affair, found an echo in Sorel's early studies on the character of Renan's historical system.[41]

If, as Péguy asserted, Bergson's great achievement was to liberate his generation from the fetters that bound it to the tottering positivism of the dying nineteenth century, Halévy as a critic maintained sufficient detachment from this decisive phenomenon to situate the celebrated Collège de France lectures in their proper perspective.[42] For if Bergson's ideas were a watershed, they were also a transition. By stressing the continuity underlying the maturing ideas of Sorel and Péguy, Halévy succeeded in bringing out the real significance of Bergsonism in shaping the development of his generation. With unfailing judgment, Halévy observed that whereas Bergson's influence on his two companions had certainly deepened their perception, it had also enriched a latent genius which flowed from a deeper source. While the *Reflections on Violence*, published in 1908, and the *Mystère de la charité de Jeanne d'Arc*, which appeared in 1909, expressed, in Halévy's words, "a new lyrical morality" for which Bergson had paved the way, both have their origins in earlier and perhaps more significant efforts. Sorel's lectures, first delivered in 1897 and later collected under the title of *L'Avenir socialiste des syndicats*, and the first draft of *Jeanne*

---

[41] Cf. Pierre Andreu, *Notre Maître, M. Sorel* (Paris, 1953), 212, 294; Dolléans, *Histoire du travail*, 26–27; James H. Meisel, *The Genesis of Georges Sorel: An Account of His Formative Period followed by a Study of His Influence* (Ann Arbor, Mich., 1951), 16, 39; E. H. Carr, *Studies in Revolution* (London, 1950), 153–154.

[42] Halévy, *Péguy*, 29, 65; Alain Guy in "Bergson et nous," *Bulletin de la Société française de Philosophie*, numéro spécial, 1959, 139.

THE BIOGRAPHER

d'Arc which Péguy had written as early as 1898 while still a
student at the Ecole Normale, already contain the germ of
their subsequent books.[43] Bergson once remarked that philosophers can keep on writing all their life because they
always say the same thing: Sorel's "social poetry" and
Péguy's *mystique* of heroism were abiding themes around
which they wove all their life's work.

III

The most striking feature of Halévy's career as a writer is
the extent to which his works reflect the persistent influence
of Péguy and Sorel, and their common ancestor, Proudhon.
These three Frenchmen who earned the constant admiration
of a Parisian *notable* were themselves provincials with deep
roots in the French past, out of their element in the capital
and always at odds with the Establishment. To the *grand
bourgeois* of mixed ancestry, steeped in Orleanism, moving
in the most select circles, possessing an entree to the Institut
and the *Débats*, all three men represented a tradition that
was the very antithesis of his own.[44] Yet such was the force of
their attraction that Halévy was to become not only the
most stalwart champion of what they stood for, but also,
paradoxically, one of its most representative types. Albert
Thibaudet was not far from the truth when, seeking to
define that vanishing *mystique* of labor which from
Proudhon to Péguy animated the best in French working-
class endeavor, he could do no better than to associate it
with the living figure of Daniel Halévy. Evoking the image
of that earnest gentleman-commoner, clad in his corduroy
suit, wandering through the Paris *faubourgs* or visiting on
foot the villages of the Bourbonnais, he presented Halévy as

[43] Halévy, "Péguy et Bergson," *Feuillets*, no. 30, 7.
[44] Cf. Péguy, *Victor-Marie, Comte Hugo* (Gallimard ed.; Paris, 1934), 12,
17–18; see also "Fidus," in *La Revue des Deux Mondes*, Dec. 15, 1936, 901.

the last vestige of a perishing ideal of labor, anachronistic and archaic, but still remarkably resilient.[45]

Halévy's devotion to this popular tradition can be explained, in the first place, by his predilection for opposites, and in the second, by complex sympathies which were at bottom moral and humane. His predilection for opposites, although an integral element of his calling as a critic, can be traced to a singular trait in his personality. His stubborn attachment to an ethic that was so clearly the reverse of his own betrays a deep craving to complement his status both as a *notable* and as a man of letters by reaching out beyond the limitations imposed by his own class and profession. Yet the determination with which he adopted his chosen calling as a gentleman-commoner, the sedulous application with which he set about exploring the popular *mystique*, above all the dogged tenacity of his devotion to Péguy—all these are also symptoms of a psychological order. Taken together they point to an underlying sense of inadequacy, which took the form of yearning for an external force that would fill what he regarded as a personal gap in his experience.

It has often been suggested that Halévy's social instability can be attributed to his Jewish ancestry. Not unlike his school friend Proust, he never felt that he had succeeded in being totally assimilated, and it would not be too farfetched to venture the guess that the kind of compensation that he sought was the emotional equivalent of what Proust had found in the Faubourg Saint-Germain. In Halévy's case the Orleanist element in his complex heredity, aggravated by the awareness that his father had himself been a parvenu, was a further source of instability. His excessive filial piety and the veritable cult that he professed through both his father and his uncle for the Orleanist legacy seems to

[45] Thibaudet, "Péguy et Bergson," 583; see also Maurice Martin du Gard, *Les Mémorables* (Paris, 1960), II, 117; and Halévy, *Visites aux paysans du Centre* (Paris, 1934), 327.

confirm the extent of his own insecurity. The exaggerated weight that he placed on his rank as an Orleanist reveals the disturbing fact that he could never legitimately stake a claim to such an exalted rank.[46]

But this basic ambiguity—the dominant trait in Halévy's character—however intriguing in terms of his own personality, is of far greater relevance when translated into the realm of criticism. For it was precisely this ambivalence, largely hereditary and psychological, which fostered his love of opposites, lending to his writing that fresh, almost eccentric quality that sets him apart from others.[47] Moreover, in the best tradition of his first master, Renan, he faithfully sought to live up to the dictum that truth lies in nuances, and, as a disciple of Bergson, that only by immediate communication could he really come to grips with reality.

The task which Halévy set himself was a most exacting one by any standards. If, indeed, he succeeded—as Henri Clouard and other admirers contend—in integrating not only in his works but even in his person the manifold strands of the national heritage, this was achieved only at the price of considerable emotional and intellectual strain.[48] For what he attempted to do was nothing less than to elucidate that

---

[46] Halévy, *Pays parisiens* (Paris, 1929), chap. II; de Traz, *op. cit.*, 76, 87; Clouard, *op. cit.*, II, 133; Hector Talvart and Joseph Place, *Bibliographie des auteurs modernes de la langue française* (Paris, 1938), VIII, 19. On Proust, see Richard H. Baker, *Marcel Proust: A Biography* (New York, 1958), 130–137.

[47] Romain Rolland, *op. cit.*, I, 222; Julien Benda, *Les Cahiers d'un clerc: 1936–1949* (Paris, 1950), 274–275; Marcel Wiriath, *Silhouettes* (Paris, 1949), 37.

[48] Clouard, *op. cit.*, II, 131; Guéhenno, *La Foi difficile*, 90; Charles Maurras, *Le Chemin de paradis* (Paris, 1921), 262; Martin du Gard, *op. cit.*, II, 116; Jean Grenier, "Daniel Halévy," *Nouvelle Revue française*, May 1, 1933, 845–846; Eugène de Montfort, *Vingt-cinq Ans de littérature française* (Paris, 1922), I, 257; see especially Emmanuel Berl, *Mort de la pensée bourgeoise* (2d ed.; Paris, 1929), 130.

vast heritage in all its diversity, to reconcile the different impulses that made up the national ethic, and to sort this tangled skein into a coherent whole. An effort of this magnitude entailed obvious stresses. By bringing to bear all his critical powers on such an ambitious endeavor, he was in fact conforming to the ideal function of a critic. But by stretching his energies to the utmost, he inevitably dissipated his own creative talents and wrecked his own chances of self-fulfillment.

Halévy was also drawn to what he called, not without solemn piety, "the mystical trinity of Proudhon-Sorel-Péguy" by affinities of a moral nature. It is these affinities which enabled him to seize the essence of their ideas and to translate it with such consummate skill. That their heritage was elusive, he was the first to admit. They were, he tells us, "des chercheurs irréductibles, indomitable pathfinders, so pioneering that their legacy, which can never be quite fully grasped," took Halévy a lifetime to unravel. Yet the printer artisan of Besançon, son of a cooper and a barmaid, the provincial bourgeois of obscure Norman parentage, and the only child of the widowed chairmender of Orléans were bound together by some mysterious link. And at the end of a lifetime devoted to probing "these three masters whom I have known best and studied most" Halévy believed that he had at last unravelled the riddle: "I see this link," he wrote shortly before his death at ninety:

All three were self-taught, they shaped their own minds by an energetic effort carried out against the currents of a passionate century. These currents could well have swept them away, but all three were masters of a great art. . . . They excelled in a kind of sport where superior athletes are rare: the art of swimming against the tide.[49]

[49] "Trois Maîtres," 28.

THE BIOGRAPHER

In short, all three were dissenters and the source of their attraction lay in the fact that Halévy was himself a dissenter who also stood against the spirit of his times. Being at heart, as Sorel once described him, "a philosopher of social life," the drift of his thinking was in complete accord with their deeper preoccupations.[50]

That their brand of dissent stemmed from a profound moral conviction has been endorsed by all those who also have attempted to understand their ideas. All three were socialists not because of any party allegiance, but because they found in socialism a redeeming force which would raise man to a superior dignity.[51] In a suggestive essay on Proudhon, a veteran British student of French history noted:

He was not a philosopher; he was not an economist; he was a moralist. . . . For Proudhon, socialism was primarily a solution to a moral problem, the deliverance of the individual from the fetters imposed on him by the industrial system.

This judgment was unanimously confirmed by all his other biographers.[52] As for Sorel, he himself insisted that the sum and substance of his random notes on revolutionary syndicalism was a philosophy designed to provide his readers with "lessons in moral life." His obsession with what he called a "métaphysique des moeurs" bore out his firm belief that socialism was first and foremost a rule of conduct which could guide men in achieving moral perfection.[53] Similarly,

---

[50] Jean Variot, *Propos de Georges Sorel* (Paris, 1935), 166.

[51] Dolléans, *Proudhon* (Paris, 1948), 497; Meisel, *op. cit.*, 181; Andreu, *op. cit.*, 286; Jean Onimus, "La Genèse de *Clio*," *Feuillets*, no. 47, 5, 8–10.

[52] D. W. Brogan, *Proudhon* (London, 1934), 38, 43; cf. Elie Halévy, *Histoire du socialisme européen* (Paris, 1948), 294; and more recently, Abbé Pierre Haubtmann, *Proudhon: Sa vie et sa pensée* (Paris, 1961), 10 ff. See also Henri de Lubac, *Proudhon et le Christianisme* (Paris, 1945), 316.

[53] Andreu, *op. cit.*, 185.

Péguy's famous assertion that "the socialist revolution will be moral or will not be at all" was analogous to the conviction that Sorel shared with Proudhon—that chastity, socialism, social justice, and moral progress were indissolubly linked.[54]

To admirers and detractors alike, Proudhon, Sorel, and Péguy have come to be regarded as the principal exponents of a native form of socialism, which they interpreted in terms of moral purpose and personal sacrifice. "For Péguy and Sorel," Pierre Andreu wrote, "socialism has as its object not to alleviate man's work, but to endow it with a higher significance, to ennoble and exalt his soul." [55] Speaking for the other side, Edouard Dolléans, a true-blood Republican, conceded that they were the patron saints of a French *mystique* that from mutualism to syndicalism has always pointed the way to the loftiest of proletarian aspirations.[56]

It was this underlying identity which has been aptly brought out by Halévy, for what he stressed in all his socialist essays was the importance of a cult of labor that would set men free from the constraints of an alien morality. But he rendered an even greater service by communicating to others the enduring value of a form of socialism that embraced the best in French popular experience. Much of what Dolléans and Goguel, Louis Chevalier and others have sought to convey in their own writings testifies to Halévy's success in propagating the ideas of his heroes. It was also largely as a result of his endeavors to keep this sentiment alive among the younger generation that such activist groups as Fédération or L'Ordre Français adopted the same ideas as part of their platform.[57]

The uniqueness of Halévy's interpretation of this

[54] *Ibid.*, 286.   [55] *Loc. cit.*   [56] *Histoire du travail*, 10.
[57] Cf. Henry Daniel-Rops, *Péguy et la vraie France* (Montréal, 1944), *passim*; Jean Sauvenay, *Bilan du Péguyisme*, "Hier et Demain," no. 9 (Paris, n.d.), 148–156.

mystique flows from the rare intimacy that he succeeded in establishing with all three of its exponents. No one else can compare with him in this respect, for no other single biographer managed to achieve that sympathetic communion that comes from such an exceptional familiarity with the "sources." It is precisely this intimacy which invests his dissection of their ideal with the authentic quality of a *témoignage.* But as a biographer whose main object was to delineate character, perhaps his greatest feat was to illuminate ideas by recapturing the individual personalities of these socialist innovators. Witness this extract from his preface to a recent biography of Sorel where, more than half a century after their first encounters in Péguy's book shop, he defined the soul of the *Cahiers* in terms of the harmony that bound the older man—"this bizarre Socrates who had fallen from the skies, plump into the Latin Quarter"—with his junior.

The two men were linked by a bond, which was entirely personal and which our turbulent youth made us incapable of fully grasping at the time. It has taken me many years to discern that one of the most interesting features of our gatherings at Péguy's lay precisely in this accord, which bound the older man to the younger—and all its secret *raisons d'être!* I once wrote Péguy's life, I tackled it again and then once more, and I have only barely touched upon what I am trying to say more accurately today. The intimacy between these two men flowed to a large extent from their common destiny. . . .[58]

Or consider how he seized the essence of their philosophy by sketching a portrait of Sorel and Péguy sitting at Bergson's feet in the plain lecture hall of the Collège de France.

Each Friday, at five o'clock, they walked together to hear Bergson at the Collège de France. Sitting side by side, like docile schoolboys, the fifty year old man and the younger, still in his

[58] Preface to Andreu, *op. cit.,* 13.

twenties, listened in silence, motionless, as the master exposed the weak spots in the traditional and highly-regarded dogmatics of rationalist idealism and scientism. . . . Bergson succeeded in destroying the positivist scholasticism of the nineteenth century and in elucidating what Sorel had attempted to unravel during thirty years of solitary study. . . . For Sorel no less than for Péguy the way was cleared for a new historical sensibility and a new lyrical morality.[59]

The narrative charm of such passages betrays an almost musical sensitivity, which is one of the most engaging features of Halévy's critical approach.[60] Steering clear of mere rhetorical flourish (a common weakness among certain French biographers), he wove together the various strands of his heroes' personalities into a harmonious whole, bringing out their underlying unity by the very concreteness of his style. Thus the interplay of ideas in all his books often takes the form of dialogue: opinions emerge naturally from the juxtaposition of character and personality, and recorded conversations serve as the vehicle for setting forth shades of meaning. Moreover it is by evoking such tangible realities as Courbet's painting of Proudhon or a leisurely chat with Sorel along the Rue de Rennes or a walk with Péguy across the plain of Saclay that Halévy succeeded in coming to grips with their ideas.

These ideas are themselves reduced to their most palpable expression. Placing Proudhon at the apex of his trinity, Halévy sought to demonstrate that both Sorel and Péguy conformed to the archetype of what he labelled *homo proudhonianus*, the prototype of "the man of old France."[61] Their ideas are defined in terms of temperament, as a function of their character. Such ideas can only be detected through living persons, for Halévy insisted that "Proudhonism is not a doctrine, it is a rare breed of men, or, to be

[59] Halévy, *Péguy*, 65.   [60] Meisel, *op. cit.*, 18.
[61] Halévy in *Le Journal des Débats*, June 2–3, 1913.

more precise, it is, if you will, a doctrine, but a doctrine which can be grasped only through the medium of a human being—in the flesh." [62]

Halévy's treatment of Péguy (clearly the most endearing of his portraits and the central figure of his trilogy) traces his originality to his parochialism, to the solid realities of a personal experience that was rooted in that small part of France that he knew so intimately—an area confined within the limits of Orléans his birthplace, of Paris and its intellectual attractions, and of the plain of the Beauce lying in between. Péguy loved the simple folk of the Ile-de-France and of the valley of the Loire, and the stones with which their ancestors had erected the great medieval cathedrals. Like Proudhon, he was a man of the people, and his simple manners and coarse appearance, his crude Rabelaisian humor, reflected a taste for realities—"realities of men, realities of God." [63] Even Péguy's Christianity, contends Halévy in his Quelques Nouveaux Maîtres (a significant starting point for any study of Péguy's thought), was itself a condition of his humanism, for his religious fervor was of the same order as Proudhon's or Sorel's moral conviction and bore not the slightest sign of sorrow. All three were men of faith, embedded in life. [64]

Halévy stretches his interpretation to the point where he suggests that the greatest achievement of Péguy and Proudhon—and only to a lesser extent of Sorel—lay more in the example which they set by their lives than in any creation of their pen. By resisting the currents of their time, they demonstrated the same kind of intransigence; but what stood out more than the intransigence of their thinking was

[62] Halévy, "Proudhon, Sorel, Péguy," Fédération, Nov., 1947, 13.

[63] Halévy, Péguy, 14.

[64] Halévy, Nouveaux Maîtres, 127; Halévy, "Péguy," Le Divan, Feb., 1916, 6. See also W. B. Gallie, "Péguy the Moralist," French Studies, Jan., 1948, 68–82; and Delaporte, Connaissance de Péguy, II, 313–321.

the rugged individualism that gave their revolt an identical flavor. Between Sorel and Péguy, Halévy could, as he fancifully put it, "ferret out affinities" to his heart's delight, but equally significant are the parallels that he draws between Proudhon and Péguy.[65] These parallels are reduced to striking resemblances in their lives. Both were born near provincial capitals, Proudhon in the Petit-Batant outside Besançon, Péguy in the *faubourg* de Bourgogne, on the outskirts of Orléans. Their mothers, widowed early and forced to rely on their own initiative, were ordinary peasants, but also artisans in their own right and commoners of rare distinction. As children, neither Péguy nor Proudhon showed any signs of rebelliousness; exemplary students noted for their diligence at school, they advanced to the *lycée* where they dutifully studied Homer, Virgil and the French classics. At their parish church they were taught the sacred texts of the Catholic liturgy. Proudhon started his stormy career by becoming a typographer, and Péguy, after feeling fenced in "like a wolf" in the cloister on the Rue d'Ulm, also resolved to take up a trade, and until his death, personally attended to the printing of his own *Cahiers*.[66]

Adopting the same life-and-character method, Halévy derives Sorel's ideas from similar significant aspects in his life. Thus the bond which united Sorel to the younger editor of the *Cahiers* is traced to their identical reaction to the rigors of an education that demanded strict conformity with the positivist principles of the Sorbonne. Both gained in stature by breaking free from the rigid curriculum of their respective *grandes écoles*. Just as Péguy escaped from the confinement of the Ecole Normale, defying his teachers by deliberately turning down a career for which he had been

---

[65] Halévy, *Péguy*, 65.

[66] Halévy, "Proudhon-Péguy," *Terre des Hommes*, Feb. 2, 1946, 17; see also Celestin Bouglé, *Socialismes français: Du socialisme utopique à la démocratie industrielle* (Paris, 1933), 146 ff.

trained by the state, Sorel also seized his opportunity—
belatedly, no doubt—to repudiate all that he had been
taught at Polytechnique by resigning from the Department
of Roads and Bridges after more than twenty years of
obscure service as a civil servant.[67] Molded by the State but
scorning its authority, they both refused to comply with the
requirements of their profession and their time.

In the same way, Halévy traces the analogies between
Sorel and Proudhon to a similar event in their past, for he
reminds us that both these self-taught intellectuals had
married almost illiterate commoners. Sorel's common-law
wife was a maidservant from a Lyon hotel who had nursed
him back to health during his tour of the provinces.
Proudhon's wife was a Parisian seamstress whom he had
courted from his prison cell at Sainte-Pélagie after the June
Days. Both these women were simple in their tastes, devout
and docile, and exemplified in their modest way the finest
traits of their class; the popular virtues which they exemplified helped to shape the character of their husbands'
social theories.[68]

Péguy's intimacy with Sorel was quite clearly to their
mutual advantage, while Sorel's debt to Proudhon was of
capital importance in inspiring his "social poetry." [69] Yet
Péguy was never really aware of his "secret brother"
Proudhon, who is scarcely mentioned in all his scattered
writings. This is all the more astonishing in that the affinities
between these two sons of provincial artisans, these rebels of
genius, are strikingly obvious. Once more Halévy attributes
this anomaly to the defects of a centralized system of

[67] Halévy, "Trois Maîtres," 32.
[68] Cf. Halévy, Le Mariage de Proudhon (Paris, 1955), passim; Andreu, op.
cit., 15, 112. Both of them married women bearing the most uncommon
Christian name of Euphrasie.
[69] Sorel, Matériaux d'une théorie du prolétariat (Paris, 1918), 2. See also
Sorel in L'Action française, Apr. 14, 1910.

education. Neither at the *lycée* nor at Sainte-Barbe, let alone at the Ecole Normale, did the young Péguy have occasion to encounter Proudhon's name, for the powers that be stood in fear of Proudhon's subversive socialism and deliberately banned his unorthodox ideas from university teaching.

Yet there is a "secret bond" linking these two heretics, a common sentiment which Halévy calls "a consubstantiality of their most profound being." [70] Although Péguy was only dimly aware of it, Proudhon was in fact his direct precursor. The connection between these two perpetual renegades, claims Halévy, lies at the root of a French tradition of dissent to which they both belonged, and their underlying identity is so striking that Halévy reduces their personalities to that of a single figurative person, "the Proudhon-Péguy tandem" (as he calls it in a suggestive essay), a constant factor in the history of France since the Revolution.[71]

Both these rebels directed their attack against the same opponents, repudiating with identical force all that smacked of dogmatism and coercion. Scorning the anonymity of the masses, Proudhon and Péguy placed their trust in the people. All of Proudhon's mutualist schemes were designed to preserve the integrity of the common man, while Péguy, less given to devising utopian nostrums, instinctively shared the same faith in an archaic ideal that would combine social justice with individual freedom. As a peasant from the plain of the Beauce his sentiments flowed from the same source as did those of the shepherd from the hills of the Jura. Like Proudhon, he also stood for a lyrical populism which was the natural product of his native *pays*.

In a more immediate sense, their voices pitched to the same key, were raised against those politicians who from Ledru-Rollin to Combes had distorted the principles they professed to champion. Péguy's outbursts against the Repub-

---

[70] Halévy, "Proudhon-Péguy," 5.   [71] *Ibid.*, 3.

lic with its university degrees and bourgeois *rentes* coincided with Proudhon's bold challenge: "We deny the validity of the state, any state, because we proclaim the sacred individuality and the autonomy of the people." [72] The "Proudhon-Péguy tandem," a recurring theme in French dissent, hurled a defiant protest against the parliamentary trimmers of the Bourgeois Monarchy, the Ralliés of Méline, the *Blocards* of Combes, against all those doctrinaire philosophers who from Victor Cousin to Lavisse and Seignobos have perpetuated a state philosophy of positivism. Twice defeated by Caesarism and Radical demagoguery—after 1848 by Bonapartist despotism, and after the Dreyfus Affair by Combism—the "Proudhon-Péguy tandem" survived as the noblest expression of a sturdy libertarianism. It is this kind of sentiment, springing from a wholesome tradition of dissent, that Halévy presents as the truest expression of a genuine French socialism. [73]

Sorel's ideas also fitted into this dissenting tradition, for he too shouted defiance at bourgeois conventions and political deceit. His vision of an epic class struggle corresponded with the heroic vitalism that Péguy shared with Proudhon, and his advocacy of direct action and collective endeavor formulated in his myth of the general strike and the "métaphysique du groupe" was analogous to Péguy's "morale de bande" or Proudhon's federal mutualism. Sorel hailed Proudhon as the real prophet of French socialism. "There is nothing more vital for the future of the proletariate," he insisted in his final work, "than to initiate it into the teachings of Proudhon." [74] What he denounced as "le parti politico-scolastique" was identical to Péguy's bête noire, "le parti intellectuel moderne." When Péguy rebelled against

[72] Cited in Bouglé, *op. cit.*, 146.
[73] Halévy, "Proudhon-Péguy," 12. See also Sorel, *La Révolution dreyfusienne* (Paris, 1909), 72.
[74] Sorel, *Matériaux*, 394; cf. Dolléans, *Proudhon*, 499.

habit and stagnation, against the decomposition of Dreyfusism or the deterioration of the socialist *mystique,* he was
in fact displaying the influence of Sorel, and, only less
directly, of the author of the *Confessions d'un révolutionnaire.*[75]

All three, however, left a very positive impression on
Daniel Halévy's mind. The originality of his own endeavors
as a critic and biographer was to demonstrate that the
individual efforts of these saints and rebels were in fact
variations on the same theme—a theme that is one of the
most permanent but intractable threads running through the
modern history of his country. Virtually all that Halévy
wrote bears the unmistakable imprint of this persistent
influence. Some of his most controversial books, like *La
République des comités,* were written in the same vein as
Péguy's most belligerent *Cahiers,* while his *Décadence de la
liberté,* directed against the Radicals and Socialists of his
day, takes after Proudhon's daring sallies against their nineteenth-century precursors. At the same time, his "Apologie
pour notre passé" shows the same merits as "Notre Jeunesse"
or Proudhon's *Confessions d'un révolutionnaire,* and his
socialist essays, almost lyrical in their tone, are clearly
impregnated with Sorel's "social poetry." Perhaps only his
more notable historical evocations, *La Fin des notables* and
La République des ducs, stand in a class apart as creative
achievements in their own right, although even here his
concern with elitist principles betrays more than a trace of
his constant preoccupation with an ethic of quality.

During his lifetime it was Halévy the publicist who alone
caught the public eye. By his diatribes and polemics he
incurred the enmity of many of his countrymen and won a
certain notoriety as an opponent of democracy and an

[75] The title of Proudhon's version of *Notre Jeunesse* and which Halévy
edited in 1931. See George Woodcock, *Pierre-Joseph Proudhon* (London,
1956), 155.

apologist of fascism. Yet this judgment, only partly accurate, fails to do justice to the less ephemeral aspects of his work, for Halévy's greatest achievement was to act as a prism through which the common features that bound Proudhon with Sorel and Péguy were revealed as one of the most valuable elements in the national culture. With characteristic diffidence, Halévy preferred to subordinate what was undoubtedly a strong craving to emulate his masters to the more modest pursuit of disseminating their greater accomplishments to a wider audience. By choosing this less conspicuous vocation he made perhaps a wiser decision. For if he refrained from setting out on an independent course, he did not so much stifle the stirrings of his creative talents as steer them to the higher purpose of interpreting at one remove an ideal that was also his own. As a guide and interpreter Halévy had few equals. As the interpreter par excellence of this ideal he was unsurpassed. An American historian has recently drawn attention to Halévy's indispensable role as "a clarifier and a go-between." [76] Nowhere is this role better illustrated than in the way he grasped the affinities that linked Sorel and Péguy with Proudhon, a grasp which he also demonstrated by drawing analogies of the same order between Sorel and Nietzsche.[77] It was by translating the varieties of this great dissenting tradition that Halévy displayed his real gifts as a writer and earned his rightful place among French critics.

But if this exegesis was, after all, his proper function as a critic, on which his reputation in French letters will ulti-

[76] H. Stuart Hughes, *Consciousness and Society: The Reorientation of European Social Thought, 1890–1930* (New York, 1958), 55.

[77] Cf. Georges Guy-Grand, *La Philosophie syndicaliste* (Paris, 1911), 81 ff.; Irving Louis Horowitz, *Radicalism and the Revolt against Reason* (London, 1961), 151–153. Halévy published his *Nietzsche* in the same year that he published Sorel's *Reflections*, and Sorel recommended the biography to his friend Croce. See Letter of Sorel to Croce, dated Nov. 23, 1908, reprinted in *La Critica*, XXVI (1928), 191.

mately rest, his personal virtues surpassed by far his accomplishments as a writer. As a critic and essayist, Daniel Halévy belongs to the hinterland of competent and worthy authors whose books are written to be read for sheer pleasure rather than to be studied and dissected. As a man of letters whose life spanned two centuries and who was himself a protagonist in some of their events he has gained the respect of his profession and the gratitude of many who can still find in his works a valuable commentary on his times. But he also stood out as an endearing person in his own right, and for all his errors of judgment and eccentricities of character he succeeded in winning the esteem of a small but select band of admirers, and of all those who have been privileged to know him.

Index

INDEX

INDEX

INDEX

INDEX

France, Anatole (*cont.*)
Mme Straus's salon, 91; and Dreyfus Affair, 96; signs revisionist petition, 96; and Universités Populaires, 154
Sur la Pierre Blanche, 191-192
Franco-Prussian War, 26
Franco-Russian Entente, 85
Franklin-Bouillon, Henry, 171
French Revolution: and emancipation of Jews, 1; legacy of, 61-62, 67-69, 111-114, 134, 232

Gambetta, Léon, 84, 86; acquaintance with Ludovic Halévy, 14; and *nouvelles couches*, 18, 50
Ganderax, Louis, 44, 78
Garric, Robert, 39, 130
Gauguin, Paul, 37
Gaxotte, Pierre, 205
General Staff, French, 97-98; and Dreyfus Affair, 89, 95, 98; Statistical Section of, 93; *see also* French Army
General Strike, Myth of the, 184, 190, 196; *see also* Direct Action, "Myth," *and* Sorel
Gide, André, 44, 103, 214; and Symbolism, 57; see also *Nouvelle Revue française*
Goblet, René, 85
Goguel, François, 226; and *le parti du mouvement*, 87
Goncourt, Edmond and Jules de, and Second Empire, 23
Gonse, General Charles-Arthur, 93
Gounod, Charles, 3, 33
Grand Prix de la Ville de Paris, 26, 201
Grand Prix de Rome, 4
La Grande Revue, 169, 173
Granville, Lord, 17
Grasset, Bernard, 48, 199, 203; *see also* "Cahiers Verts"
Grave, Jean, 56
Gregh, Fernand, 158; studies at Lycée Condorcet, 42-45; and Symbolism, 57; and Dreyfus Affair, 94; on labor movement,

Gregh, Fernand (*cont.*)
138; on Barrès, 140; and Universités Populaires, 156
Grévin, Alfred, 23
Grévy, Jules, 50
Griffuelhes, Victor, 149
Guéhenno, Jean, 39, 130; on Halévy, 53-55, 205; elected to French Academy, 206
Guérard, Albert L., on Halévy, 191
Guermantes, Duchesse de, 47
Guesde, Jules, and French labor movement, 135, 148-149
Guesdists, see Jules Guesde
Guieysse, Charles: and Universités Populaires, 156, 158, 163; and *Pages Libres*, 169-170
Guillaumin, Ernest, 157
Guinou, Julien (*Un Episode*), 165, 166, 167
Guizot, François, 20; greets Prévost-Paradol to French Academy, 13

Haas, Charles, 46, 47
Hachettes, the, 29
Halévy, Daniel: family background, 1, 13, 32-35, 41; resemblances with grandfather, 8-10, 64; upbringing, 12, 32-35, 41, 52; and his father, 18-22, 26-31, 64, 79-80; need for roots, 30, 145-147; personality, 30, 32-35, 37-40, 47, 53-54, 58, 64-67, 90, 108-109, 118-121, 130-132, 158-159, 221-225, 235-236; birth, 32; family acquaintances, 34-36; and brother, 41, 42n, 58; studies at Lycée Condorcet, 41-45; career, 42-50, 55, 77-80, 139-140, 142-144; and his home on Quai de l'Horloge, 54, 79-80; and Third Republic, 54-56, 61, 68-71, 73-74, 82-83, 87-89, 136-138, 148-149, 178-179, 200-201, 204-207; and Dreyfus Affair, 57, 66, 70, 76-80, 82-84, 89-132, 210-212, 219-220; as a critic, 59, 203,

241

INDEX

INDEX

INDEX

Halévy, Ludovic (*cont.*)
  general secretary of the Corps
  Législatif, 16-17; and Duc de
  Morny, 16, 17, 18; affinity
  with Orleanism, 16-20; Sorel
  on, 21-23; André Siegfried on,
  26; and Franco-Prussian War,
  26; relation with son Daniel,
  26-30, 222; and Degas, 36
  L'Abbé Constantin, 14-15
  La Belle Hélène, 22
  Carnets, 20-21, 24-26
  Criquette, 14-15
  La Famille Cardinal, 14, 22-23
  La Vie parisienne, 29
Halévy, Marianne (Mme Daniel),
  80, 156
Halévy, Valentine, 10
Hamp, Pierre, 130
  La Peine des hommes, 157
  Le Rail, 138
D'Haussonville, Comte Othenin, 46
Haute société protestante, 32
Henry, Major Hubert, 93
Herminie, 4
Heroic vitalism, 141, 184-185, 187,
  196, 218, 235; *see also* Elitism
Herr, Lucien, 78, 125, 197; and
  Dreyfus Affair, 105-106; and
  foundation of *L'Humanité*,
  171-172; and Péguy, 193
Hervé, Gustave, 98
Hervieu, Paul, 46
Holyoake, George, 176
Homer, 230
Horace, 5
Horowitz, Irving Louis, on Halévy,
  181-182
Howland, Mrs., 35
Hughes, H. Stuart, on Halévy, 235
Hugo, Victor, 175
L'Humanité, 136-137, 181, 187,
  192; foundation of, 171-172

Ibsen, Henrik, 44
Idéophagues, 166, 167
Ile-de-France, 126, 229
Ile de la Cité, 54, 80; *see also* Quai
  de l'Horloge
Impressionism, 36

L'Indépendance, 103; and Action
  Française, 188
Ingres, Jean-Auguste-Dominique, 35,
  36
Inquisition, Spanish, 175
Institut, 6, 29, 32, 201, 221
Intellectuals, French, 145; and
  Dreyfus Affair, 82, 87-89; and
  socialism, 134, 137-139, 161-
  162, 163-164; and Third Re-
  public, 137-138
Inter Sollicitudiness, 86; *see also*
  Ralliement
L'Israélite français, 2

"J'Accuse" (Zola), 94, 97-98
Jacobinism, 67, 112, 117, 125; and
  Radicals, 115
James, Henry, 35
Jaurès, Jean, 125, 187, 192, 214;
  and Halévy, 96-97, 105, 135-
  137, 171-172, 187; and Opportunists, 99; and Dreyfus Affair,
  105-106, 134-137; Halévy on,
  137; Péguy on, 137, 193; and
  Universités Populaires, 154;
  and *L'Humanité*, 171-172
Les Preuves, 106
Jesuits, and Dreyfus Affair, 114
Jews, French, 2-3, 111-112, 127-
  128; Sephardi, 3; and Saint-Si-
  mon, 6-7; and Dreyfus Affair,
  90-93, 102; and *Cahiers de la
  Quinzaine*, 127-128; and Universités Populaires, 155; and
  foundation of *L'Humanité*,
  171-172; *see also* Anti-Semitism
Jockey Club, 46
Johannet, René: on Halévy, 53,
  142; on *Cahiers de la Quin-
  zaine*, 127
Le Journal, 96
Le Journal des Débats, 11, 13, 33,
  38, 101, 164, 221
Le Journal Vrai, 171; *see also*
  L'Humanité
Journaux pour Tous, 170-171
Jouvenel, Robert de, 204
Jouy-en-Josase, 126

INDEX

INDEX

INDEX

Pages Libres (*cont.*)
ism, 169-170, 172-176; Halévy's contributions to, 175-176

Palais de Justice, 97

Palais-Royal, 7

Panama Affair, 85, 99

Paris, 21, 24-25, 29-30, 79-80, 145, 147, 149, 201-202, 203, 214, 229

Parnasse, 55; *see also* Symbolism

Pasteur Institute, 35

Pater, Walter, 35

Payot, 199

Péguy, Charles, 39, 43, 66, 74-75, 107-108, 116-117, 120-132, 135, 140, 173, 188, 189, 191, 193, 208-236; and Third Republic, 13, 56; and *mystique*, 73; and La Librairie Georges Bellais, 78; and Dreyfus Affair, 82, 88, 97, 98, 120-127, 209-215, 219-220; and Orleanism, 118; reconversion of, 122; views on history, 122-123; on time as duration, 122-123; theory of *époque* and *période* in thought of, 123-125; and Action Française, 124-125; and Jews, 127-128; and Catholics, 127-128; provincialism of, 146-147; death in battle, 147; on Universités Populaires, 155-156; on socialism, 162, 226; and socialism, 208-236; and *Pages Libres*, 169-170; and *La Petite République*, 171; publishes *Le Journal Vrai*, 171; libertarianism of, 176; offers to turn over *Cahiers de la Quinzaine* to Halévy, 212; and Christianity, 229;
and Barrès, 146, 215; and Bergson, 122, 216-221; on Bergson, 216; and Halévy, 10, 30-31, 118, 122-132, 208-236; on Jaurès, 137; and Bernard Lazare, 91, 95, 127; attitude toward Renan, 63; Romain Rolland on, 130; quarrel with

Péguy, Charles (*cont.*)
Sorel, 128-129; Sorel on, 130; on Sorel, 139
"Clio," 122
"Dialogue de l'histoire et de l'âme charnelle," 122
Jeanne d'Arc, 127, 220-221
Mystère de la Charité de Jeanne d'Arc, 220
"A Nos Amis, à nos abonnés," 126-127, 212
"Notre Jeunesse," 100, 102-103, 116, 120-128, 210-211, 234
Notre Patrie, 107-108
"Victor-Marie, Comte Hugo," 100-101, 129, 131, 132, 193-194, 211

Péguy, Marcel, 126

Pelletan, Camille, 85

Pelloutier, Fernand, 150-153, 196; quoted, 152; *see also* Bourses du Travail

Perdiguier, Agricol, 176

Pereires, the, 7

Pershing, General John, 199

Pétain, Marshal Henri-Philippe, 206

Petit-Batant (Franche-Comté), 230

Petit bleu, 93

La Petite République, 171; revisionist petition in, 96-97

Philippe, Charles-Louis, 138

Picquart, Colonel Marie-Georges, 93-94

Pillias, Emile, 200

Piou, Jacques, 86

Place, Francis, 176

Place Dauphine, 97, 141

Place de la Nation, 134

Place Pigalle, 32

Plato, 191

Ponts et Chaussées, 231

Popular Front, 105, 204

Populism, 118, 130, 138, 142-146, 149-153, 159-164, 174-196, 214-216, 221-222, 223-224, 232-234; *see also* Socialism *and* Syndicalism

Porto-Riche, Georges de, 46

INDEX

INDEX

La Revue Lilas, 43
La Revue Verte, 43
Ribot, Alexandre, 85
Rivière, Marcel, 130, 199
Robinson, Mary, *see* Duclaux, Mary Robinson
Rochefort, Henri, 25
Rodrigues, Benjamin Olinde, 7
Rodrigues, Olinde, 3
Rodrigues-Henriques, Isaac, 4
Rolland, Romain: and Universités Populaires, 56, 57, 155; attitude to Renan, 64; on Dreyfus Affair, 90; and Combism, 101; on Halévy, 109; and Péguy, 130; and *Cahiers de la Quinzaine,* 213, 215; *Jean-Christophe,* 129, 193
"L'Aube," 193
Romains, Jules, 71-72
Rome, 86
Roquès, Mario, 97
Rosny, J. H., 138; *Sous le Fardeau,* 138
Rothschilds, the, 18, 45
Rue de Douai, 32-33
Rue de la Sorbonne, 170-171, 211; see also *Cahiers de la Quinzaine*
Rue de la Victoire, 1
Rue de Rennes, 228
Rue d'Ulm, *see* Ecole Normale Supérieure
Rue Montholon, 3
Rue Mouffetard, 153-154
Rue Paul Bert, 154
Rue Saint-Jacques, 218
Rue Saint-Martin, 156
Russian Revolution, 199

Saclay, 126, 228
Saint-Gervais, Church of, 201
Saint-Simon, Claude-Henri, Comte de, 4, 6-9, 159; *Opinions littéraires, philosophiques et industrielles,* 7
Saint-Sulpice, Seminary of, 68
Sainte-Beuve, Charles-Augustin: on J. F. Fromental Halévy, 4-5;

Sainte-Beuve *(cont.)*
and Second Empire, 23; and Proudhon, 159
Nouveaux Lundis, 4-5
Sainte-Pélagie, 231
Salle, Louis de la, 42
Sandherr, Colonel Jean-Conrad, 93
Sarcey, Francisque, 12
Scheurer-Kestner, Senator Auguste, 99
Schlumberger, Jean, on Halévy, 103
Schneider, Hortense, 23
Scientism, *see* Positivism
Seailles, Gabriel, 155
Second Empire, 15-16, 19, 23-24; and Sephardi Jewish bankers, 4; Parisian salons and, 14, 24-25; frivolity of, 18; class structure of, 22-23; shortcomings of, 25-26; collapse of, 50-51
Section Française de l'Internationale Ouvrière (S.F.I.O.), 155, 164
Sedan, Battle of, 50, 60
Seignobos, Charles, 233
Seine, 80
Seize Mai, 51, 86
Shanghai, 191
Siegfried, André, 200; on Ludovic Halévy, 26
Sils-Maria, 71, 79
Slavs, 191
Social Darwinism, *see* Darwinism, Social
Socialism, 6-9, 20-21, 74, 142-146, 148-154, 157-159, 163-164, 168, 176-196, 181-185, 188-190, 207 ff, 232-233; before Dreyfus Affair, 84-86; and Dreyfus Affair, 133-138; and Universités Populaires, 157-159; intellectuals and, 161-162; in 1900's, 174-175; *see also* Syndicalism *and* Populism
Socialists, French, 164, 171-172, 180, 188-190, 233-234; and Dreyfus Affair, 82-83, 87, 104-106; and Radicals, 85-86; antimilitarism of, 105-107; in 1900's, 133-138; and Déléga-

249

INDEX

Socialists (*cont.*)
   tion des Gauches, 135; and *La Petite République*, 171; and *L'Humanité*, 171-172
Société d'Histoire de la Troisième République, 200-201
Socrates, 227
Sorbonne, 122, 201, 210; and Radicals, 155; and Universités Populaires, 155; and Dreyfus Affair, 170; and Péguy, 215; moral rationalism of, 218; and Positivism, 230
Sorel, Georges, 39, 53, 74-75, 141, 156, 168, 182, 186, 194-199, 208-236; syndicalist myth of, 73; on Dreyfus Affair, 81, 88; and Combism, 101; on Orleanism, 118; anti-Semitism of, 128; and *Cahiers de la Quinzaine*, 130, 139, 173; "social poetry" of, 141, 161, 221, 231, 234; and Universités Populaires, 162-163; and "métaphysique des moeurs," 166, 168, 184, 186, 196-197, 225; and libertarianism, 176; and elites, 181; moral pessimism of, 187-188;
   and Barrès, 146, 147; and Bergson, 217-219; resemblances with Degas, 37; and Daniel Halévy, 10, 22, 103-104, 108, 166-167, 184, 191, 194-195, 197, 198, 225; on Daniel Halévy, 22, 103-104, 108, 166-167, 184, 188, 191, 225; on Ludovic Halévy, 21-23; and Nietzsche, 235; on quarrel between Péguy and Halévy, 126; and Péguy, 128; quarrel with Péguy, 128-129; on Péguy, 130; and Pelloutier, 150; on Proudhon, 233; and Renan, 59, 70, 220; and André Spire, 198
L'Avenir socialiste des syndicats, 220
"Lettre à Daniel Halévy," 194-195, 198

Sorel, Georges (*cont.*)
   Matériaux d'une théorie du prolétariat, 231
   Reflections on Violence, 170, 184, 194-199, 220
   La Révolution dreyfusienne, 104, 126
Spencer, Herbert, 60
Spire, André, 58, 129; Jewish origins of, 90; and Combism, 101; *quoted,* 134; and Universités Populaires, 156; and Sorel, 198; and *Cahiers de la Quinzaine,* 215
Spuller, Eugène, 86
Staël, Germaine de, 46, 52, 104, 117
Straus, Émile, 45
Straus, Geneviève, 4, 29, 33, 45-48, 91, 99; *quoted,* 91
Sucy-en-Brie, 79
Swann, Charles, *see* Charles Haas
Symbolism, 42-43, 55-56, 57
Syndicalism, 27-28, 66, 76, 130, 168, 176-195, 226; and Pelloutier, 150-153; and Universités Populaires, 153, 157; growth of, 160, 173-185; and intellectuals, 163-164; precursors of, 176; as a purifying force, 179-180; and Marxism, 180-181, 185, 189; and elites, 188-191; and revolutionary *élan,* 189; moral value of, 194-195; *see also* Socialism and Populism

Taine, Hippolyte, 23, 24, 139; and Ecole Normale Supérieure, 12; and Prévost-Paradol, 12, 13; and Halévys, 33; and Mary Duclaux, 36; and Renan, 59, 60, 61; and positivism, 59-61; and legacy of the French Revolution, 61, 67-69, 113-114; and Barrès, 143
   Les Origines de la France contemporaine, 61
Tangier, 191
Le Temps, 132, 172

INDEX